Penguin Books

OUT AFTER DARK

Hugh Leonard was born in Dublin in 1926, was educated at Presentation College, Dun Laoghaire, and then spent fourteen years as a clerk in the Land Commission. He was able to give up this job when he began to have some success as a playwright. He was Literary Editor of the Abbey Theatre from 1976 until 1977 and has been Programme Director of the Dublin Theatre Festival since 1978. His plays include *A Leap in the Dark* (1957), *A Walk on the Water* (1960), *The Saints Go Cycling In* (1965), *The Au Pair Man* (1968), *The Patrick Pearse Motel* (1971), *Thieves* (1973), *Summer* (1974), *Irishmen* (1975), *Time Was* (1976), *Moving Days* (1981), *Kill* (1982), *Scorpions* (1983) and *The Mask of Moriarty* (1985). His real breakthrough came with *Da*, which in the United States won a Tony Award for the Best Play of 1978, the Drama Desk Award and the New York Critics' Circle Award. He also won the Harvey Award for the best play of 1979/80 with *A Life*.

Hugh Leonard has also written a number of plays for television, including *Silent Song*, which won the Italia Award for 1967, and his adaptations for television include works by Emily Brontë, Dickens, Flaubert, Maugham and Saki. His four-part drama series *Parnell* will be shown on BBC Television in 1991, and he is at present working on a novel, *Parnell and Katherine*, to be published by Penguin. *Home Before Night*, his autobiography, was published in 1979. Hugh Leonard lives in Dublin, where he writes a weekly satirical column for the *Sunday Independent*.

Out After Dark

Hugh Leonard

PENGUIN BOOKS

For the Big Three –
Ray, Gerry and (again) Zorro

PENGUIN BOOKS

Published by the Penguin Group
27 Wrights Lane, London W8 5TZ, England
Viking Penguin Inc., 40 West 23rd Street, New York, New York 10010, USA
Penguin Books Australia Ltd, Ringwood, Victoria, Australia
Penguin Books Canada Ltd, 2801 John Street, Markham, Ontario, Canada L3R 1B4
Penguin Books (NZ) Ltd, 182–190 Wairau Road, Auckland 10, New Zealand

Penguin Books Ltd, Registered Offices: Harmondsworth, Middlesex, England

First published by André Deutsch 1989
Published in Penguin Books 1990
1 3 5 7 9 10 8 6 4 2

Copyright © Hugh Leonard, 1989
All rights reserved

Made and printed in Great Britain by
Cox and Wyman Ltd, Reading, Berks.

A confessional passage has probably never been written that didn't stink a little of the writer's pride in having given up pride.

- J.D. Salinger

Ambrose Flood had a model railway, but none of us ever saw it, for it was under the floorboards of his bedroom. It was a Tube train, and Ambrose, who was literal-minded, believed that it should accordingly be kept underground or at least out of sight. Once, when I expressed doubt that the thing existed, he hustled me down to his house on Carysfort Road and brought me upstairs. He pressed a switch, and at once I could hear a humming and a rattling from under the linoleum. The noise travelled in a circle beneath the bed and the wardrobe and past the window and wash-hand stand and was accompanied by a faint, intermittent 'beep-beep'.

'Do Tube trains have whistles?' I asked him.

'Poetic licence,' Ambrose said.

He and I nodded whenever we met, but for the most part that was all. His cronies were Cloggy Lacey and Holy God Furlong. Cloggy was so called because when young he had had adenoids and spoke as through an obstruction; Holy God derived his nickname from his favourite expletive, employed promiscuously either to express amazement or simply to fill a void in conversation. The three were bachelors. They drank, played golf, swam, fished, strolled on the hill or Vico Road and went to plays and concerts at the town hall. Nothing like marriage or parenthood had ever scarred their lives with milestones. Their faces had a kind of priest-like serenity: unruffled, clear, unbothered with time. The town was theirs; they may not have ruled it, but in a sense they owned it. They took part in nothing, sat on no committees, knocked on no doors. What they did do

1

was observe and, to use their own expression, argufy, and if I tell a little of their story here it is because to know them is to know our town. Strangely, considering the tranquillity of their lives, none of them made old bones, and with the death of the last – Cloggy – two months ago as I write this, it was as if the street lamps in Castle Street had blinked out.

They were all three of them reasonably well-read, although Cloggy could not hold a candle to his elder brother, Jimmy, who read the *Iliad* in Greek, hidden behind a copy of *Ireland's Own* lest he be suspected of affectation. Cloggy himself was a railway clerk; Holy God was a maker of gloves; and Ambrose stayed at home – living on what means, I have no idea. They had little regard for the trappings of progress. None of them, for example, ever learned to drive a car: such a departure might have implied that in their lives there was room for improvement, that they did not already inhabit their private, perfect, self-made Fiddler's Green. They disdained to be at the world's beck and call: only illness, an accident or a funeral could dent the immutable pattern of their days, which so gracefully slipped into weeks, months and seasons. Some years ago, I wrote a television play about them and called it *The Virgins*. In Dalkey, to keep a secret is to be guilty of a crime against nature, and one evening when all three were drinking in the Queen's an acquaintance broke the news to them with a muttered: 'I hear tell that the queer fella' (myself) 'has writ a play about yous.'

He might more effectively have tried to elicit casual chatter from a bishop during a canonisation. The pint tumblers did not waver on their slow odyssey from bar-top to lips, and there was little or no small change left out of a minute before the three pairs of eyes turned towards him.

Ambrose said: 'About us?'

Cloggy said: 'You're coddin'.'

Holy God said: 'Holy God.'

Their informant went on to tell them – basing the gist of it on the theorem that no one in our town ever said anything good about anyone who was not yet dead – that the play would parade their lives for the world to make mock of, and if they had a tittle of sense they would watch it, then camp on their solicitors' doorstep and sue the author for slander, libel and God knew what else. What I have encompassed in a single sentence took two John Jamesons to say in fits and starts, but what it amounted to was that the injured parties would make a mint.

'Begod, we might look at it, so,' Cloggy said at length. 'When is it on the goggle box?'

'Sunda' evenin'.'

Holy God said *'When?'* in some disbelief.

Cloggy said: 'Shag that for a lark.'

Ambrose said: 'Can't be did. Sure on Sundays we drink in Finnegan's.'

This last was uttered with the amused incredulity of a pope replying to a suggestion that he had a lie-in on Good Friday morning. Not even the lure of infinite riches could keep them out of Finnegan's on Sundays any more than it could deflect them from the Druid's Chair on Mondays, the Club on Wednesdays, or where they were now, the front bar of the Queen's, on Fridays. They were not the world's messenger boys, to go here and there at its bidding. In the upshot, they missed the play and, as far as I know, could not even find time to inquire from friends who saw it as to the full iniquity of the libel.

My title, *The Virgins*, may have been inaccurate, for it was said that in his youth Ambrose had been 'implicated' with an American woman. It had ended badly; one story went that she had refused him, another that she had turned out to be already married. Whatever the reason, he was thereafter done with women and carried the hurt around with him, as he did a small box that had most of its blue velvet lining rubbed off from fondling and contained a ring with a modest diamond which he had purchased in the Happy Ring House in O'Connell Street. On evenings when the drink took him in a certain way, he would stare broken-heartedly into the box for minutes on end. No one knew why he had not returned the ring for a refund, and if you attempted to ask others about his blighted romance, the only answer you got was a deep sigh and a cryptic 'Ah, sure poor Ambrose.'

On the first evening I returned home after an exile in

London, I saw him, Cloggy and Holy God in their Friday hidey-hole, the Queen's. They gave me the kind of wink coupled with a 'Howyah' and a nod which suggested that it had been two days instead of nine years since they had clapped eyes on me. Ambrose had put on weight and was pasty-faced. At school, he had been handsome in a sullen way, with limp blond hair and stork's legs that seemed all the longer because he wore the shortest short trousers in the town. He was an only child, and his parents indulged him; he had the most pristine football boots, the pearliest-handled six-gun and – what we all envied – a bushranger side-of-the-head hat with a chinstrap. He was the kind of superior boy I craved to be; now he seemed broody and dull. Holy God, in contrast, wore the confident smile a company director might bestow on a nervous stockholder. He was big, pink-faced and barrel-chested, with a full head of corrugated white hair; he walked his dog with the air of a country gentleman. I liked Cloggy best of the three, for he had never been known to say a defamatory word about another being. He was small and brown-haired; he wore spectacles, and with age his face took on the worried, wrinkled appearance of a walnut. With them in the Queen's was a girl named Jo Ann, who came over to where I was sitting and asked if it was true that I had come home for good. After we had talked for a while, she looked back at Ambrose, Holy God and Cloggy. 'Aren't they a hoot?' she said. 'They invite me out for a jar so's people will think they're terrible men for the women.' Then, fondly: 'God help me, I'm in shocking danger!'

The trio had in the beginning been a quartet, and the fourth member was named Rory Cafferky. It took me some time to find out what had happened to him. It was Rory who provided the adventure they preferred to enjoy at second-hand, if at all. As young lads, they robbed orchards and, with even greater daring, hooted after girls in the street. Very occasionally, the girls would call their bluff by hooting back at them, whereupon Ambrose, Holy God and Cloggy would go red and hurry around the nearest corner, each blaming the others for making a show of him, while Rory would brazenly stroll over to the girls whose turn it now was to scurry away.

His daring scandalised and fascinated the three. He acquired an invisible wheelbarrow which he trundled around Dun Laoghaire, asking ladies to hold shop doors open for him and it as he wheeled it through. Often, caught off-guard, they did so and stared at him as, half-stooped over and with fingers clasped around shafts that were not there, he would say 'Thank you' and go past them at a half run. Once, in the Carnegie Library, an assistant paid him the ultimate compliment of saying: 'You can't bring that thing in here.' When he became tired of the invisible wheelbarrow, he abandoned it for a more elaborate toy. He would get off a bus with the others and, as they were about to start down Marine Road either for a walk on the pier or to see the picture at the Pavilion, he would say 'Excuse me a minute, lads,' dip into his pocket and take out a key. With half of Dun Laoghaire looking on, he would jab it into midair and turn it. He then proceeded to open a door that only he could see. It was a heavy door; he grunted, strained and went red with the effort. By now a crowd had gathered. He reached in, took hold of a bellrope that was no more visible than the wheelbarrow had been, and gave it a single almighty tug. The great vibration of the bell caused him to reel for a moment, then he recovered, pitted his shoulder against the door, heaved it shut and used the key to lock it again. Ambrose, Holy God and Cloggy had watched the performance from the asylum of the porch of St Michael's Church, with Holy God intoning over and over, lest the other two forget, which was unlikely: 'We're not with him, we're not with him.'

Adolescence marked a watershed: Rory went after girls; the others steered clear. They were Irish bachelors. They treated their homes as comfortable inns; their mothers – or, in Cloggy's case, a doting sister – cooked for them, darned, washed and ironed their shirts, made the beds, scrubbed, polished and even wallpapered, asking for no more in return than the housekeeping on Friday. The three stayed single because they were sensible men who saw no reason why they should hobble themselves for life to creatures to whom a contented smile on a man's face was a foe to be routed. When Ambrose was crossed in love Cloggy and Holy God saw it as a blessed escape. 'He had somebody's good prayers,' one told the other.

Rory had gone his own way; they saw him infrequently. Once, while they were out walking on the Vico Road, he drove past them with a bit of stuff beside him, the car bonnet pointed towards Bray five miles away.

'Going to a hop at the Arcadia,' Ambrose said.

'Will you go 'long out of that,' Holy God said. 'Is it coals to Newcastle? He's taking her up the mountains.'

He paused for a moment, allowing a picture to form in his brain, then did a little dance of lust at the image of Rory and the bit of stuff flattening the crab-grass above Glencree, and the pair of them in their skins or next door to it.

Cloggy was silent. He did not go in for scandal. He looked patiently at the calm sea below, thinking of later on and the few pints he would enjoy as a reward for all the exercise and the fresh air.

For a time, no one knew for certain how Rory made his living except that he had a gift for robbing Peter on the pretence of paying Paul. A pretence was all it was, for he kept no promises, paid no debts. One might as well expect an egg to go back the way it had come. He liked to think of himself as a lovable rogue, a gleam of romance in a drab world; those who had done business with him called him a chancer or, less charitably, a hook. One of his sidelines was smuggling anything from butter to Durex across the six-counties border. In the beginning, he travelled cautiously, at night and by unapproved roads. Later, he bought himself a second-hand Rolls Royce that had been vandalised into a station wagon. Thereafter, he used the main roads and in full day, crossing the border with a cigar clenched between his teeth and a lordly wave that told the customs men that God was passing.

There are people who are born unlucky and remain so for life, who in moments of despair may be heard informing the heavens that if they owned a duck it would surely drown. Rory was the opposite. For him, thin ice never broke, and policemen were always looking the other way. Like the hero in the weekly follower-upper at the Picture House, he unfailingly broke free from his bonds an instant before the blazing roof crashed in.

Others, less favoured, muttered peevishly that there was no justice, that hookery paid, and honesty was an also-ran. Rory seemed invulnerable, and so the shock was all the more profound one day in 1961 when Cloggy, on the train home from work, unfurled his *Evening Herald* and saw on the front page the headline: DALKEY MAN DROWNED ON HOLIDAY. A blurry photograph of Rory, taken at a dress dance, grinned up at him.

Rory had no claims to fame, or even infamy, but in Ireland there is an unwritten code of journalism which holds that when an Irishman dies abroad and from unnatural causes it is the equivalent of a hundred Asians perishing when a ferry boat overturns. (If the demise occurs in Britain, the news receives even greater prominence – there are those who claim to have seen a headline in the *Irish Times* that said: IRISH GIRL KILLED BY ENGLISH TRAIN.) Thus a place on the front page was, quite simply, Rory's by birthright. He had died while swimming in Sardinia, of all places. A friend, one Sharon Drexel (23), had sat on a rock overlooking the sea, preferring to sunbathe than swim. She heard shouts, saw him struggling, but even as she looked on he was gone.

The lads were devastated, Cloggy most of all, for he and Rory had shared a passion for swimming. They had competed every year in the race from Coliemore Harbour to Dalkey Island and back, fighting a four-knot current. If Rory had drowned, Cloggy thought, such a fate could be his, too. The lads met that evening and exchanged astonishments. What the hell had brought Rory to foreign parts, they asked, and, come to that, where was Sardinia when it was at home? They went back to Ambrose's house and looked it up in his school atlas, but it yielded no clue. Was Brittas Bay not good enough for Rory, Holy God wanted to know. And if he was all that mad keen to globe-trot, Cloggy said, why else did the Isle of Man exist? As for her nibs, Sharon Drexel, they had never heard of her. The name, Ambrose said, sounded English. Probably, Holy God said, she was a right good thing.

This gave them a new topic: the state of Rory's soul and its present whereabouts. They pulled at what-ifs and buts like three bored dogs tugging at a piece of rag, then Ambrose said gloomily: 'There's no jar in the house, lads.'

'We ought to drink to him that's gone,' Holy God said.

Ambrose nodded and put the atlas back on the shelf, tucked in between Knight's geometry and Hall's algebra. They walked up to the Club (it was a Wednesday) and gave Rory a two-minute silence while their pints went from grey to black under the tap. Next morning, Ambrose went to the parish priest and asked that a novena of masses be said for the repose of the deceased's soul. The offering was ten pounds and each of the lads chipped in three pounds six and eightpence.

That was in 1962. By sheer chance, I was a witness to the end of the story eight years later, or at least to the beginning of the end of it. There was in our town a restaurant where the food was middling when the owner was sober and vile when he was not. It was a last-ditch haunt of Cloggy, Ambrose and Holy God whenever a long-suffering publican asked them if they had no homes to go to and refused their pleas for 'a bang of the latch' – a last quick pint that would fuel them down the road. They were drinking red wine at the table by the window. My wife was abroad, visiting relatives, and I was alone, as was a bearded man across the room. As the waitress, a blonde girl named Pat Moran, passed, he attempted to grasp her arm, but missed.

He called out after her, his accent English, the tone grandiose with drink: 'I requested the favour of a brandy. Might I now be served?'

Pat veered in mid-course. She was an easygoing sort who did not mind a drunk, but had no patience with messers unless they happened to be Dalkey messers. She took a bill from a spike, put it on a saucer, brought it to the man's table and slapped it down.

'I did not ask for "*l'addition*",' he said. 'I ordered a brandy.' He saw another opportunity to speak French and added, '*Un cognac.*'

She said: 'You were told, and you're being told again. We can't sell spirits, we haven't a licence.'

'Brandy is not a—' he said, but she was already gone from

him. He addressed the air: 'Then might one be permitted a glass of port?'

He sat, scowling. Ambrose, Cloggy and Holy God had been looking on, interrupted in whatever topic they were pulling and hauling at, and now Ambrose kicked the ball back into play. 'Where was I?' he asked, but before he could remember Cloggy said: 'Wouldn't your man there put you in mind of Rory Cafferky?'

'Who?' Ambrose said.

Holy God said: 'Not at all.'

'That fellow?' Ambrose said. 'He's pissed.'

'I know he's pissed,' Cloggy said, becoming testy. 'What's that got to do with whether he looks like Rory? For Jasus' sake, will you be germane?'

(It was at this point that I began to take notes.)

'Rory got drowned,' Holy God said.

Cloggy said wearily: 'I know he got drowned. We had the mass said, hadn't we? That's proof he was drowned. What I'm saying is that Jembo there looks like him. Rory could have had a cousin, couldn't he? Family resemblance. What's wrong with that?'

'The Prisoner of Zenda,' Ambrose said.

'Exactly.'

Holy God seemed unconvinced. He picked up their empty wine bottle and waved it at Pat, signalling for more. She made a face. Wait, she was saying, until the drunk is gone. Without warning, Cloggy lurched to his feet, said 'I'm going to ask him', and started across the room.

'Cloggy, no.'

'Aw, holy God.'

We saw Cloggy talking to the man, who seemed slow on the uptake. He stared at Cloggy and said: 'Hafferty?'

'Cafferky.'

The drunk caught hold of Cloggy's jacket and, using it as a climbing net, pulled himself erect. He stood swaying, blinking at the new perspective as if from a mountain top.

'The name is Leeds,' he said. 'As in Yorkshire. J. G. Leeds.'

He pulled three bunched-up pound notes from his pocket,

tossed them any-old-which way on the table, and went out. He seemed in a hurry. Cloggy returned to the others.

'It wasn't him.'

'You wouldn't be told, would you?' Holy God said.

'I wonder where he is,' Ambrose said.

'Gone,' Cloggy said. 'You just saw him.'

'Not him,' Ambrose said. 'I mean Rory.'

'Ah, Jasus,' Holy God moaned. 'Not religion.'

Of a sudden, it came to me that I must seem friendless and miserable sitting there alone and eavesdropping on others. I got up to leave just as Ambrose, a sentimentalist, was declaring that God would not have permitted Rory to drown without allowing him time for an act of contrition. Even a quick ejaculation, he said, would have done the needful. Holy God pooh-poohed the theory. The Almighty, he said, did not intervene. In fact, there was a school of thought that held that God was a mass of ions.

'Of what?' Cloggy asked.

'Ions, Cloggy. Energy. Vapour. Steam.'

'God is steam?' Cloggy said, getting worked up.

'It is a matter,' Holy God said, 'of astrophysics. You would want to ask a Jesuit.'

I paid my bill, nodded to the three and left. There was no sign of J. G. Leeds. The time was a few minutes past midnight, and the street lamps went out with a suddenness that was almost a sound. It was an April night, the sky mad with stars.

Had I remained in the restaurant, I would have seen for myself what all Dalkey was told about within days. Cloggy continued to take umbrage at the assertion that the deity was a mass of steam. Holy God went on acting the know-it-all, his face and voice magisterial. Finally, Cloggy snarled: 'If God is gas, what's the Blessed Virgin, then? Drizzle?' Before the others, appalled by such coarseness, could answer, he said: 'I'm going to the jacks,' and went out in a temper. A moment later, there was a cry of 'Jasus' from the hall followed by the world's end of a crash.

'Struck dead!' Holy God said and led the rush into the hall.

Cloggy, who had slithered backwards down the stairs on

his face, was trying to stand up. The light bulb in the hall was missing or had gone out, and it was only when Pat brought out one of the candles from the dining room and Cloggy recovered the power of narrative speech as an alternative to effing and blinding that anyone understood what had happened.

J. G. Leeds had not, after all, left the building. He had gone upstairs in search of the lavatory and had either fallen down or lain down on the top landing. Cloggy, in a temper and taking the stairs two at a time, had stepped on him in the dark and slid back the way he had come, banging his knee and bending the frame of his glasses. It was not until he had been examined and removed from the danger list that J. G. Leeds was attended to. Ambrose and Holy God sat him up and shook him until he began to groan.

'Where do you live?' Holy God asked.

'Wha'?'

'Tell us where you live, and we'll get you home.'

'He can't stay here,' Pat said.

'*Will* you *tell* us *where* you *live*?' Holy God said in a sing-song, shaking him in rhythm with the words.

J. G. Leeds began to stutter until at last the truth hiccupped out, and his accent was no longer English: 'Rory Cafferky, 10 Infant of Prague Terrace, Dalkey.'

A bed was found in Ambrose's house, and next morning when Cloggy and Holy God called around the born-again Rory Cafferky had the greenish look of a copper dome, but was otherwise his unabashed old self. He was shaving as they stood behind him, like angels come to deliver a soul to judgment. He had faked his death, he said, because there was a warrant out for his arrest on a charge of smuggling. The girl mentioned in the newspaper had been his accomplice. 'I got on the soft side of her,' he said. 'Old Sharon was a decent skin.'

'I'm sure,' Holy God all but sneered. 'What happened to her?'

Rory gave a shrug that told them don't-care as much as don't-know. He said: 'She gave a sworn statement to the police, so she could hardly go back on it and do the dirty on me.' The tone of his voice suggested that somewhere, somehow he had given her good cause to do the dirty on him.

He had stopped off in the town, he said, on his way to Connemara for a break. It was the long way around, but a tender heart had drawn him back to the scenes of his youth, even if the likelihood that the police were still on the look-out for him meant that he was already on the wing. Nowadays, he told them, he lived in Northern Ireland as J. (for Jeremy) G. Leeds and called himself an entrepreneur.

'You pronounce the word well, mind,' Cloggy said with a stone face on him. 'Very French.'

Rory either missed the coolness or chose to ignore it. 'So what's new with the three of you?' he asked.

'What is new,' Holy God said, 'is the matter of the expenditure of ten pounds for a mass for the repose of your soul.'

When Rory realised that they had indeed had a mass said for him, he was obliged to put the razor down lest he cut himself from laughing. Cloggy, Holy God and Ambrose, who had had a council of war over his lying-in-state the night before, waited, expressionless, until he was done. 'Still, lads,' he said, 'it was damn nice of yous.' He tried to pull his lips into a tight straight line, but it failed to hold. 'Damn nice.'

'We want our ten quid back,' Cloggy said.

'Yous what?'

'You rooked us,' Ambrose said mildly, 'so it's a matter of principle.'

'Yous rooked yourselves,' Rory said.

'We want it back,' Holy God said.

Rory tried to make light of it. 'Are yous sure that Ambrose wouldn't like to charge me for bed and breakfast as well?'

When he saw the set of their faces, he shrugged and went to where his trousers were hanging on a chair. He was wearing the boxer shorts he had slept in, and his thing peered through the front. Cloggy, Ambrose and Holy God looked away demurely. Naked at the Men's Bathing Place or the Forty Foot was permissible; in a house it was another matter.

Rory went through the pockets and found a pound note and some change. 'Don't worry,' he said. 'I'm not broke. I'm staying at the Royal Marine, and I left my travellers' cheques in the hotel safe.' He began to pull his trousers on. 'Tell yous what. Why don't I get the money. Then we can have a jar for old time's sake at the Queen's, and yous can see me off to Galway.'

'Proper order,' Holy God said as the three watched Ambrose's garden gate squeal shut behind him. 'It may be only a tenner, but it's one bit of hookery he won't be let get away with, not if we have to follow a crow for it.'

It would have been better for Holy God if he had taken flying lessons, for of course that was the last they saw of Rory Cafferky – at least for a couple of years. In the matter of the ten pounds, there was, as Ambrose had said, a principle at stake: he had made fools of them, if only in their own eyes; and, quite apart from paying a priest to say a dud mass, there was the waste of wit, argument and conjecture over where his soul had gone. Rory, however, had at least one principle of his own, and it was never to pay a debt – its smallness in this case made it all the more vital that the ideal be preserved.

When he next came south on a flying visit – and he appears fleetingly every year or so – he espied his three old friends in some pub or other. He hailed them with the amnesia of roguery. They turned their backs on him, drank up and went elsewhere. He was not forgiven or again spoken to.

Ambrose, Holy God and Cloggy all died in their late fifties and in that order. Ambrose had been in indifferent health for years, but his passing was the envy of all who knew him. He got up early one winter morning, found that the *Irish Independent* had arrived, made tea in the kitchen and took it and the newspaper back to the warmth of bed. And there, glasses on the tip of his nose, he went out like a tiptoe.

Holy God died of a heart attack, Cloggy more painfully. We miss all three.

13

1

When I was twenty-two and a rebellious teenager (we mature late in Ireland), I wrote the first and only chapter of a novel to be called, devastatingly, *Sex on Thursdays*.

It was not as sensational in intent as the title might suggest: quite simply, when the annual mission – the Retreat, we called it – came to our town, the preachers invariably chose Thursdays for the homily on immodest and immoral behaviour, for it was then that domestic servants had their evening off and could attend church. In those well-ordered days when feminism had still to cut its milk teeth, no one questioned the bland assumption that girls up from the country and in service were so much ripe fruit, helpless on the bough and palpitating for damnation.

Everyone enjoyed the Thursday sermon. On that one evening in the year the parishioners could hear sex being talked about without worrying that it might be a sin to listen. Plain speaking was *de rigueur*. The Jesuits, when they came to Dalkey, were too effete for a town that liked its religion to be the spiritual equivalent of a bowl of stirabout or lashings of bacon and spuds. 'Too much old codology,' my mother once daringly said under her breath – and the Franciscans extolled charity and compassion, neither of which virtue has ever commended itself to the Irish ethos. The star performers were the Redemptorists, who promised the impure of heart an eternity on the hottest hob of hell. 'And, as for those who touch their *bodies* . . .!' a missionary would hiss, his own eyes like burning coals, and the entire congregation crooned in an ecstasy of terror.

The idea for the book was the imaginary collision of two

14

quite unconnected events. One of these was the birth of twins to a girl whose name, Honor, was in the circumstances inappropriate, given that the father was unknown, unhonoured (except in the punning sense) and conspicuously unsung. She was not, by the way, a domestic servant, and so the title, *Sex on Thursdays*, was a rank imposture. She was an attractive girl, with shapely legs superb in stockings that had come out of a bottle, with only slightly askew pencil-drawn seams – this was in 1949, when clothes were still rationed. Whenever I passed her on Hyde Road as she trundled a rickety pram with a small bald head protruding from either end, I pictured myself pencilling her stockings on for her, and my lower abdomen tied itself in such tumescent knots that I was obliged to hang on for modesty's sake to the Fannings' pebble-dashed wall. What was worse, her seeming unconcern at the world's opinion suggested that she might actually have enjoyed her misfortune and spiced my fantasies with images of such unbridled abandon that I went on clinging to the wall, until old Fanning appeared at his front window and made feck-off gestures of great savagery.

Our town is only nine miles from O'Connell Bridge, and so, even in those backward times, we considered ourselves not unworldly. Sex, as we all knew, was the worst sin of all, but a single biological mishap could be borne stoically. Twins, however, were not to be glossed over. Quality is commonly deemed to be more important than quantity, but our then parish priest did not apply this criterion to illegitimate births. Contrary to both good taste and theology, he got it into his head that, in Honor's case, the sin was doubled.

Not only was Father Kearney a man of the cloth, but that cloth was of a deep-dyed, if metaphoric, green. Just as Napoleon declared that every French soldier carried in his cartridge case the baton of a Marshal of France, so the good Father believed that every young Irishman went through life with a Miraculous Medal in one hand and a hurling stick in the other. For a godly man who thought the best of his fellow creatures, especially if they happened to be Irish, it was the bitterest of pills to reflect that probably the twins' father was, like their mother, one of his parishioners. (Honor, when interrogated on the subject, merely smiled and hummed a bar or two of an old come-all-ye.) He ended up by not swallowing the pill at all, for, within a week of the double christening – done discreetly at St Joseph's, Glasthule, a mile away – he had devised what we would nowadays call a scenario. A post-war tourist boom had set in, and, counting on his fingers, Father Kearney reasoned that the twins had been conceived early the previous August: therefore the father could not have been other than an English visitor.

He even managed, on no evidence at all, to pinpoint the scene of the crime. Early in 1939, work had begun on a new scenic road between Dalkey and Killiney Hills; then, a year and five hundred yards later, the war brought the project and the road to a dead end. Because it wound sharply uphill, it was nicknamed the Burma Road, and, then as now, it stopped on the edge of a meadow with woods beckoning darkly beyond. Honor Prendergast's virginity had ended, Father Kearney confided in an apocalyptic whisper, on or fornenst the Burma Road.

Within days, he convened an emergency meeting of the prefects of the Men's Confraternity and revealed how he intended that no other young girl would share the fate that had befallen the happily unhappy Honor. A pair of iron gates would be erected where the Burma Road began, and these would be padlocked every day at sunset. The ways of the Almighty, Father Kearney told the Confraternity, were mysterious, and if the Prendergast twins had been permitted to come into the world, it was for the good and sufficient reason that others of their kind might thereby be kept out of it. God, he said, almost rubbing his hands with excitement, was a queer harp.

Mr Mundow, who collected offerings at the fourpenny door on Sundays and was to Dalkey what the captain of the Swiss Guards was to the Vatican, could and did outdo Father Kearney when he came to aphorisms. Iron gates, he said, pithily, did not grow on trees.

'We will raise funds,' Father Kearney said calmly. 'A concert.'

A committee was promptly formed, with one of the curates as its chairman. The town hall was booked and posters were printed announcing an All Star Concert. Artistes were engaged, including Mrs Quinn's Irish Dancers, a spoons player, a gipsy

16

harpist named Silvio, Miss McGuinness the soprano, and a housepainter who called himself Sallynoggin's Al Jolson. The main items would be a one-act comedy entitled *The Young Man from Rathmines* and an actual opera singer out from Dublin.

The play, so the curate told his committee, was a howl: all about this flibbertigibbet of a young one who throws over the man she is engaged to, a good Catholic, and titivates herself in hopes that the new lodger, when he arrives, will go wild out over her. Maybe he will even marry her. At the end, he comes in, and when she sees that he is only a black she screams and faints. The committee laughed, and Scurty White, who had built White's Villas, said 'The divil's cure to her, Father', while carefully tearing bits of cigarette paper from his lower lip. The curate told them that the play not only had a strong moral but would also end the first half of the evening on a cheerful note.

The second half would consist of the opera singer and no one else. This was partly in deference to his renown – he was described on the posters as '(Star of Stage and Radio)' – but also because, alone of all the artistes, he had insisted on being paid. 'If he wants blood money,' the curate said with a small forgiving but unforgetting smile, 'we'll make sure he earns it.'

Such is the contrariness of Dalkey that no matter how worthy a cause is it will have its detractors. If a golden chariot with an angel in it were to descend, however briefly, from heaven into Castle Street, it would set off again with 'M. O'B. = J. F.' written on the side in purple pencil and tin cans tied to the back bumper. And so it was a matter for sadness, but not surprise, that a small group of dissidents existed in the matter of the iron gates. It was in vain that Father Kearney preached from the altar that the gates would be a bulwark, not only against the tide of English summer visitors, all of them only after the One Thing, but also the one or two local youths, if they existed, in whom by some freak of nature an alien lust had taken root and festered. Actually, as far as the second category went, he had erred on the side of understatement, for there were at least a dozen of us.

Outwardly, we insisted that the gates would be a violation of basic human rights (we paraphrased bits from Hollywood films in which James Stewart and the like made stumbling speeches ending with 'Well, I guess that's kinda what ya call democracy'). The truth was not nearly so idealistic. We each nursed the frail and private hope that somehow the Burma Road might prove to have erotic properties conducive to the loss of a virginity that persisted in clinging to us like stickybacks. In entertaining so implausible a theory, we were not simple-minded, merely desperate.

We met nightly as conspirators in the Roman Cafe in Dun Laoghaire, monopolising three tables for an entire evening, so that now and again the son of the *padrona* would appear with an unconvincing snarl to say: 'Two hours . . . glass-a hot-a milk . . . fourpence . . . smart-a fellas.'

Probably, the matter would have dribbled away in empty talk had it not been for Mikie Nixon, a pale little whisper of a fellow in whom, for some reason, any attempt at standing still would bring about a fit of staggering. He had grown up brotherless, but with six sisters, and in consequence hated all females on sight. He was the only one in our group who, with utter sincerity, saw Father Kearney's grand design as an infringement of what in years to come would be called civil liberties. Mikie, not to put too fine a point on it, frightened us. He was by our lights unnatural. Not only had a dirty thought never entered his head, but mere talk was not in itself good enough for him: the zealot wanted action as well. Were we, he wished to know, men or mice? If the former, we should make our anger known by a protest outside the town hall on the night of the concert. His idea was that we would carry placards.

The first image to enter my own head was of my mother and my mad aunt Mary crossing the street to pay their one-and-threepence admission and catching sight of me walking up and down, publicly defending the Burma Road's status as a fornicating amenity. In my mind's eye, I saw my mother's face and a wave of faintness washed over me. Other foreheads gleamed besides mine. 'We'll be read off the altar,' someone said.

Mikie Nixon's pale eyes became spears of sleet. He was

18

on the point of telling us that we were cowards and good for damn all else but talk, which of course was true, when a fellow named Looby said with a show of smooth reason that Mikie's plan was masterly, ingenious and a credit to him. Then, with the diffidence of a man in hobnails walking on a brand-new Navan carpet, he put it to the meeting that no strategy devised by mortal man was so flawless that it could not be improved upon. He was sure that Mike would not take it amiss if a modification or two were added.

We all mumbled gravely at the fairness of this: all of us, that is, except Mikie, whose sixth sense whispered that the same Navan carpet was about to be pulled from under him. We talked, streamlining his master-plan here, beautifying it there, until the Roman Cafe's electric sign flickered out. By then, the plan had been refined to the point where, instead of carrying placards, we would bang loudly on the windows of the town hall while the concert was on and then run for our lives. Mikie was outraged. He attempted to make a speech from among the cafe's dustbins, but we all suddenly said 'Look at the time' or 'It's all hours, I'm destroyed' or 'The last shaggin' bus is gone, I'll have to hoof it', and fanned out in all directions, compounding betrayal with desertion.

The Irish have always fatally combined a passion for conspiracy with an inability to keep a secret. That, in tandem with a natural apathy, has put paid to an assortment of rebellions down the centuries, and our own modest endeavour was not fated to break the mould. To begin with, on the night of the concert no more than half of our number turned up at the bandstand in Dillon's Park. One of these, to our surprise, was an unsmiling Mikie Nixon, who, it was agreed by all, was a decent skin, whatever else.

We straggled up Coliemore Road and into Castle Street. A distant grumble of laughter confirmed that *The Young Man from Rathmines* was, as the curate had predicted, a howl. We paused, six or seven of us, at the gate of the old tramyard. 'We'll wait for the opera singer,' Mikie said.

'No,' Tony Dowd said (everyone in Dalkey had, and still has, a nickname, and his, for reasons lost in time, was Doodah).

'It's too cold to hang around. We'll do it now and have it over with.'

Without waiting for argument, Doodah went swiftly past the Queen's public house and vanished into the laneway that ran alongside the town hall. We had hardly begun to follow him when he reappeared, his walk now eating its heart out to become a run. 'Polis,' he said out of the corner of his mouth as he went past, and sure enough two smiling policemen emerged from the lane.

Some of us, without breaking step, executed an instantaneous about-wheel, while the others crossed the street wearing the kind of determined look that betokened urgent business in a far place. Later, by the long way round, we found our way back to Dillon's Park and crowded into the little sweetshop at the entrance where, such was her girth, there was hardly room enough for Miss Dillon on her own. There we reflected that our rebellion, like all that had gone before, had been blighted by loose tongues at best and informers at worst. Mikie Nixon did not appear, and we assumed that he had gone home in disgust. We were mistaken: what we had all along failed to realise was that through his veins flowed not merely the blood of a fanatic but of a martyr.

While the rest of us were in retreat, he had somehow slipped past the policemen and entered the town hall by the door at the rear. Still unnoticed, he ducked into the backstage lavatory and bolted the door. There he remained throughout the interval, making no sound when the knob was rattled. He heard someone curse, then another voice told someone to use the laneway or the gentlemen's in the Queen's. A few minutes later, the second half of the concert began. The curate introduced the opera singer, saying that he needed no introduction; there was a chord on the piano; the audience applauded, and Mikie heard a tenor voice starting in on 'She moved through the fair'.

Mikie waited a minute and then pulled the lavatory chain.

Some water closets are well-mannered and flush demurely; this was not one of them. The arm with the iron ball attached fetched the roof of the cistern an appalling clout, whereupon water gushed out with the noise of ten simultaneous cases of asthma and five of whooping cough. Mikie had no idea as to whether the sound travelled out as far as the audience, but that the tenor heard it was evident from a kind of soprano wobble that entered his voice on the last word of 'As the swan in the evening moves over the lake'.

Mikie sat on the rim of the bowl and waited for the cistern to refill, but be became impatient after a minute or two and once again pulled the chain. The iron ball rose and dropped repeatedly with a sound like falling kettles. Through the door a voice hissed at him to be quiet, saying 'There's a man out here trying to sing a song.' For answer, Mikie redoubled his efforts, yanking on the chain like a pocket-sized Quasimodo.

Within the lavatory, the noise was so deafening that the cause of it did not realise that the tenor had by now fallen silent. As we learned from eye-witnesses, he signalled to the pianist to rest from her labours, then himself leant on the piano, favoured the audience with a smile of suave forbearance and waited for the bedlam to cease.

Instead, it worsened, for people backstage began to hammer on the door of the lavatory. Shouting was heard. The climax came when Mikie's frenzy reached a pitch where the cistern itself shattered and slabs of vitreous china crashed to the floor, one of them hitting him on the head. Bloody, but unbothered, he now found himself holding the chain, to which were attached sundry bits of rusty metal, the ballcock and the iron ball. He began to swing the chain, using the ball to attack the door as if it were Sports Day in medieval times and he were a knight of old pulverizing an opponent's shield. By now, the audience had become restive. Four hundred eyes looked at the tenor, and he, still leaning on the piano, looked back at them. A voice from the back of the hall asked him if his mother knew he was out. Another wanted to know if he would work for a farmer. Slow hand-clapping began, and this was accompanied by a chant of 'Sing the song . . . sing the song.'

The impoverished nature of the lyrics did not inhibit their popularity, and the volume grew as new voices joined in. Respectable people in the front seats attempted to quell the noise, but in doing so only provided an accompaniment. For some minutes, the tenor's smile had become thinner than of yore, and now he and it decided to depart together. He bowed with elaborate irony and was answered by a storm of whistling and catcalls. In the wings, he confronted the curate, who was looking helplessly at the lavatory door.

'They told me about Dalkey,' he said cryptically. 'And now I know.'

He took his overcoat and silk scarf down from the dressing-room nail and went out into the dark. He was not seen again, any more than he himself ever saw his fee.

As for Mikie, he held out for a few minutes longer until a walking silo of a man known as the Horse Heenan was brought backstage. He bade everyone stand clear, then turned away from the W.C. door as if disowning it, only to knock it clear off its hinges with a terrible backward kick that explained how he had earned his nickname. A groan, not of fury but of revulsion, went up as Mikie stood revealed. Water from the broken cistern had escorted the blood from his scalp wound down his face and over his shirt front. In places, the mixture had combined with dirt from the cistern lid to create a flan of brown mud, deepening to a runny black. He resembled an earthquake victim who had been dug out after a week. The gruesomeness was only embellished by the entrails of the cistern which now hung limply from his hand. People looked away. Even the Horse Heenan blenched.

To any sensible being it was obvious that Mikie was not, after all, a saboteur, but an unfortunate who had been horribly injured in some way, and the noise was his delirious attempt to attract assistance. At any rate, and to his astonishment, no one attempted to lay hands on him. Rather, the onlookers backed fastidiously away, stamping on each other's feet as he scuttled bloodily past them and was swallowed up by the Dalkey night, ballcock and all.

As for the concert, after urgent consultation with Father Kearney, the curate came out to still the uproar and announced that, in response to public demand, those performers on whom the audience had doted in Part One and had not already gone for their buses home, would reappear and endear themselves still further. This was the signal for sullen mutterings and an hour of encores, rounded off with a raffle and a community sing-song. There was, of course, no question of reprising *The Young Man from Rathmines*, a howl though it had been. 'Sure they'll all know the surprise at the end when the golliwog comes on,' Father Kearney said, thereby displaying a grasp of dramaturgy such as lay at the very heart of Aristotle's *Poetics*.

In spite of the noise from the lavatory and the defection of the tenor, the concert was accounted a great success. Which is to say that, as far as the parish priest was concerned, its artistic merits or lack of them were not at issue. There was nothing that Father Kearney liked better than a bar of a song, and he could gaze as if mesmerised for tens of minutes on end at Irish dancers, the maniacal thudding of whose silver-buckled, patent-leather shoes more than compensated for their corpselike rigidity from the knees up. What gave him matter for concern was an awareness that the human mind was the seat of both art and religion, and in that confined space there was the danger that the one might become mistaken for the other. It was safest all around to smile and say that what the know-it-alls affected to look upon as art was known by plump and plain everyday people to be no more than old codology. In short, there was no such thing. The success of the concert resided wholly in its having been a Good Cause, and to enquire if the audience had had their money's worth was as impudent as daring to ask if the ten o'clock short Mass on Sunday had been prettily done.

At the end of the tale, the gates were never erected on the Burma Road. Father Kearney was an unworldly man, and the last thought to enter his head was that the county council might not fall over itself to permit a holy priest to block off a quiet road here and a bosky avenue there in the name of purity. An official letter arrived at the presbytery containing extracts from various by-laws. These – and fair was fair, Father Kearney conceded – upheld the right of couples, mixed or unmixed, to walk abroad after dark. It was, regrettably or not, a free country. To his bafflement, however, the thooleramawns who had drafted the by-laws had omitted to insert a clause making it an offence for

23

strollers in public places at night-time to slow down to a stand-still except in certain designated areas, such as under lighted street lamps. It was only thanks to God's all-loving mercy, the priest was heard to say, that such crass ham-handedness had not resulted in Honor Prendergast having had triplets.

None of us believed for an instant that the Council would prove a match for Father Kearney. We expected him to continue blithely on his way, scattering his critics from him as a dog shakes away water after a swim. In our part of the world it was held to be incontrovertible proof of divine intervention in human affairs that court actions against members of the clergy usually came to grief. Unfortunately, another snag arose, and this one was insoluble. No one could be found who, in return for a 'God bless you and sure you'll have your reward in heaven', would agree to padlock the gates every evening, winter and summer, and open them again at dawn. Father Kearney asked for volunteers, jovially saying that he expected to be knocked down in the rush. Weeks passed, and he remained vertical.

As for the profits from the concert, they quickly burned a hole in his soutane. First, the youngest Fagan girl whose father was in the fever ward at Loughlinstown was crying her eyes out for a First Communion dress. Next, after a week as a part-time postman, Liamy Cleary had fecked a postal order, and it was either nine months' gaol or find the mailboat fare to Holyhead. Then there was the very real emergency of the younger curate's bicycle falling to pieces on his way to a sick call. Every day, new hungers came like mice to nibble away at the money, until finally, tormented by seeing his dream vanishing – not in one decent, brutal awakening, but piecemeal – Father Kearney splurged what was left on an old folks' outing to Glendalough and, for those who could hoist themselves into it, St Kevin's Bed. Thereafter, the Burma Road gates assumed the roseate and unsubstantial glow of the Heavenly Gates themselves.

As for Mikie Nixon, when he arrived home two of his sisters fainted, and the other four washed him down lovingly, cleansed the blood from his clothes and put him to bed before his father could come home from a whist drive in Sallynoggin and take a strap to him. I met a lady at a party last Christmas who told me that Mikie had died some months previously in Australia. 'He wasn't the marrying kind,' she said, then blushed and added 'He was a bachelor gay.' She had never, I am sure, heard 'gay' used in a sexual sense; but the blush told me that she might just as well have done.

When, as a twenty-two year old, I began to write my book that never was, I took the story of the gates and added to it an entirely separate event. I had just learned that my father knew the whereabouts of an arms cache from the time of the Civil War.

One evening on Railway Road, I saw him walking just ahead of me. We were both on our way home: I from eight hours of daydreaming at the Land Commission where, over fourteen years, I was to set a kind of record as the world's longest-serving temporary clerical assistant; he from his work tending the gardens of a house that had once been called 'Enderley' and was now 'Santa Maria'. As I caught up with him, I saw that his face was dark. His gait was stiff-legged, as much from anger as rheumatics. I saw his clenched fists, the knuckles visible at the sleeve-ends of someone's hand-me-down overcoat that was too big for him. He was moving so fast that as I caught up I said: 'Run, why don't you?'

He said, without malice, 'Run me arse,' and walked faster.

His new employers were making the last of his working days a misery. From boyhood until old age he had worked in 'Enderley' for a Quaker family named Jacob, who manufactured biscuits. They were The Quality. Personal honour was to them not a luxury or even a virtue, but as innate a part of their lives as lavender in a pillow, or the genuflection of flowers as they passed. They took honesty and service for granted for no other reason than an inability to imagine their absence, and so they left the cook, the maidservants and the two gardeners to go about their duties in peace and unmolested. When the Jacobs died and the house became 'Santa Maria', the new owners kept my father on. They were Catholics and self-made. Being themselves part of an evolution from peasantry to a new and native middle class, they, the grandchildren of servants, looked at my father and their housekeeper from Claregalway and saw a reflection of themselves. They interfered, they bullied; in their own eyes they were islands of probity in an ocean of petty theft and a day's work for a week's pay. The new owner, a schoolmaster who had married a successful *couturière*, would stand over my father and, with a smile as thin as a penny ruler, say: 'Mr Keyes, aren't you the great man for finding work to do that keeps you out of the sun?'

At home afterwards, he treated my mother and me and, incidentally, my mad aunt Mary, to a recital. 'The Master, God rest him, always called me "Keyes". But the whoor's ghost that's in it now has to stick a "Mister" in front of it. And do yous know why? I'll tell yous why. Because he knows he hasn't the shaggin' right to call me "Keyes" without the "Mister". And why hasn't he the shaggin' right? Because he hasn't the shaggin' breedin'!' He struck the table with his fist; a cup jumped and Mary said 'Jesus'.

When the Jacobs died they had taken not only their own world with them, but also his. Bog-trotters like the school-master were the new Quality, and, as we walked towards home, I needed not ask him how the day had gone. Our way home brought us past Foley's pub at the corner of the Barrack Road, where several cornerboys – my mother's brother Sonny among them – habitually decorated the window sill. Sonny would give my father a distant, dark-eyed nod suggestive (quite falsely) of old injustices, while the others would defer to him with a respectful growl of 'Ha'sh oul' day' or 'That's not a bad one.' My father, holding a poor opinion of idlers, would reply, if he deigned to do so at all, with a grunted ''Tis, so,' or ''Tisn't.' Today, however, one of the group seemed to have drink taken, for he staggered both my father and myself by calling out: 'Eh, Keyes, where did you bury them guns?'

My father was wiry and had red hair that even in old age turned grey only at the edges. His temper, whenever he was called out of his name, would flare up like a match and splutter out as quickly, but today it was the shattering of an oil lamp. The jeer had hardly been uttered when he was across the road and took the cornerboy (who was all of forty) by the throat. The others were too taken aback to move, except for my uncle, Sonny, who had a nose for danger that was acknowledged to be second to none and went hopping off around the corner on his short leg.

A verbal barracking began, with my father shouting several times over, as if it were an incantation, 'Are you blackguardin' me, you whoor you?' This was accompanied by a shake which, if it did not snap the other's head off at the neck, threatened not only to put him through Foley's window but the Tullamore Dew looking-glass behind it. The cornerboy's comrades began to gather round, saying 'Aisy, aisy,' and 'Sure all the man said was'. They plucked at my father's sleeve, but not with such force as might impede what, given the passion he was in, bade fair to bring sunshine to the greyness of their day.

The man in my father's grip was one of the kind who loitered on the outside of a public house solely because indigence prevented them from doing so on its inside. I knew him to be a crony of my uncle Sonny's. He habitually wore an askew smile of disgust as if, no fool he, he had the world's measure. Like Sonny, he had put it to the test and it had failed. His face was usually suffused with a kind of porter flush, but now, with hands around his throat – calloused hands, with the clay of a day's planting still under the nails – it was turning purple, and his smile was far away.

My own role in all this was the passive one of standing across the road in the lee of the Bank of Ireland and saying 'Da . . . Da . . .' in a low voice audible, I hoped, to my father, but not to passers-by who might associate me, the wearer of a collar and tie, with a street brawl. Of a sudden, I saw him release his victim and heard him say: 'There's still a few of us left. From here on in, wherever you go to at night, keep lookin' behind you.'

He set off again, as fast as before, ignoring a frightened shout of 'You bloody oul' madman' from his rear. I was too shocked to follow him at once: not merely because of the attack on the cornerboy, although I had seen no reason for it other than the bad temper he was bringing home with him from 'Santa Maria'. I had often heard him make threats, usually incoherent and always empty; this time, he had used the language of a gunman.

He had been 'out' in the War of Independence and remained 'out' during the Civil War that followed. He was given a rifle, but never saw a bullet. He did arms drill at weekends, wearing an empty bandolier, but the nearest he came to engaging the enemy was on the day he saw a news picture in the *Irish Independent* purporting to show a squad of Black and Tans capturing armed I.R.A. men in County Kerry. The caption was 'Hands Up!'

A gateway in the background seemed oddly familiar, and it came to him that the photograph had been taken at the entrance to Killiney Hill, or Victoria Park, as the Protestants called it, up the road from Dalkey. It was a fake, a piece of trumped-up propaganda. Incensed, he took a tram into Dublin, laid siege to the public office of the *Independent* and demanded to see the 'man in charge'.

'Do you mean the editor?' he was asked.

My father had never heard of such a being as an editor and assumed that he was being fobbed off. He replied that he did not want to see any gobshite of an editor; he wanted the boss man. Matters deteriorated at this point, and he was asked bluntly to state his business. He flung his newspaper upon the counter with a flourish, then took two steps back and all but folded his arms like Tom Mix in the pictures. 'What kind of gobdaws are yous,' he said, 'to be made eeejits of be the English? Do yous not know Killiney-shaggin'-Hill when it's there in black and white in front of yous? Are yous blind or what?'

He was shouting. The few people who were in the office put their own business aside and looked on. One of them was an R.I.C. man who, as yet unnoticed by my father, was there on duty in case the Republicans should attempt to gain control of Independent House. My father leaped forward and struck the newspaper a blow of his fist.

'Them and their "Captured in County Kerry",' he said. Then, his face livid, he emitted a roar of 'County Kerry me arse!'

A tremor ran through the R.I.C. man like a ripple over a lake. It may have been that he took exception to what in 1921 was strong language or, perhaps, like many of his kind, he happened to be a Kerryman.

'Oh, them's the Black and Tans for you,' my father said. 'The dirt and the leavin's of English gaols.' Then, moving off down one of his own favourite by-roads, he declared: 'Aren't they in me own town at this minute, shootin' innocent women and childer in their beds?' As he spoke, he knew that no Dalkey person of any sex or age had ever been shot dead in bed or out of it, but he had never been so disloyal as to remain silent and see his own town made little of by the failure of the English to put it to the sword. 'Aye,' he went on, 'an' they lifted babbies in the air on their bayonets.'

'Is that a fact now?' a voice said into his ear.

'It is,' he said and saw that he was addressing the R.I.C. man.

He was led twice from the office and twice returned, each time to describe a new and more colourful atrocity. Finally, thrown out bodily into Middle Abbey Street, he informed the receding back of the R.I.C. man that it belonged to no true Irishman but a paid hireling of the Crown.

'The coward wouldn't stand his ground,' he said to my mother that evening. 'But he heard me right enough, bad scran to him.' 'Aye,' she said drily, 'and you got the worth of the half-day's pay you lost and the return tramfare to the Pillar.'

Where the growing of flowers was concerned, my father had genius, but as a gunman he could be relied upon always to grasp the wrong end of the revolver. Nor could he have won an argument, never mind a war, for, once vehemence took possession of his tongue, sense went from it, evicted like nestlings by a cuckoo. When I heard the chill in his voice as he warned the cornerboy to keep looking behind him, it was as if I were listening to a stranger.

When I caught up with him a minute later I asked: 'What was all that about?'

'Nothin'.'

'What ailed you? I thought you'd have to be dug out of him.'

29

Silence.

'Anyway, what was all that about burying guns?'

'Hold your tongue.' He fetched me a look. 'You have too much old talk out of you.'

At this point, the Dublin bus drew up, the driver's door opened and our dog, Blackie, alighted. Travelling by bus into town and out again was his hobby: he did it all day every day until tea time. He had begun three years before by accompanying a neighbour of ours, Mr Keogh, who was a tram-driver. The dog would sit happily on the front platform, his makeshift leash tied loosely to the driver's handle that was like an outsized coffee grinder. Last year, when the trams gave way to buses, he adapted more easily than most of the crews, including Mr Keogh, who opted for retirement. I never met the busman who was not glad of the black dog's company. More than once, the melancholy thought occurred to me that he was more widely travelled than I.

We walked home together, the three of us. As the garden gate screeched open, my father said: 'C'm'ere to me.' He looked towards the house. 'You're to say nothin' to herself, do you mind me?'

I nodded, then thought to put a price on my silence.

'What about burying guns?'

'Will you shut it!' For a moment it was as if he would make to throttle me as he had done the cornerboy. Beyond the front window I could make out the inquisitive silhouette of my mother; probably she was wondering why, instead of coming in for our tea like Christians, we were in the garden colloguing. My father said something indistinctly.

'What?'

Snapping. 'I said I hid things.'

'What things? Do you mean *guns*?'

'Uhh.'

'What's the big secret? Look, if every waster in the town knows about it, then —'

Fiercely, hating them: 'They know shag all!' He looked across the dark roofs of St Begnet's Villas towards the granite cliffs of Dalkey Hill, as if he were their equal for silence.

Wresting the truth from him – or, rather, his version of the truth – was as wearying as tweezing splinters from a finger, and so let me put in one sentence what took the beginnings of a hundred. When the Civil War was dribbling to a standstill, my father was summoned to a dawn meeting with his Commandant and informed that he had been chosen to hide a residue of arms, ammunition and explosives until the day came when, to use the phrase beloved of the diehards, 'We shall rise again!'

Once his story was at last out, a familiar sob arose in his throat and a dampness came into his eyes. 'An' I done it,' he said. 'I stripped the guns an' I iled them, and then I wrapped up the shaggin' lot, Mills bombs an' all, in ile-cloth. An' they'll be waitin', ready an' willin' when the call comes, even if I'm dead an' gone itself.'

It was past believing. For a trust as sacred as it was secretive, the Commandant had chosen a man who was reputedly the most garrulous in all of the Old Dublin Brigade. What was even more remarkable was that, against the odds, my father kept his mouth shut. All my wheedling could not draw from him the size and precise nature of the arms cache; and, as for its burial place, the first time I dared ask him was the last. Twenty years later, he died without letting go of his secret, possibly because there was by then no one left to whom he could usefully tell it.

It was only as I wrote the foregoing that it came to me with hilarious clarity where the arms were and still are to this day and why my father had been the ideal man to bury them. Without meaning to do so, he even gave me a clue that day at the front gate. My mother, who became a tigress whenever she got wind of a conversation that did not include her, flung open the front door and asked if we would prefer to be carried in to our tea, or have it carried out to us. As my father and I walked up the path there was time for a last question. 'Yes,' I said, 'but if there were guns to be buried —'

'Tell the shaggin' town, why don't you?'

'I mean, why did they pick on you?'

He smiled unexpectedly. 'God, but you're a comical boy. Sure what better man could they pick?'

In those days, I had no notion where the arms were, but I

knew where I wanted them to be. My brain was seething with the great satirical novel. It would be a latterday *Valley of the Squinting Windows*, and its time was ripe. The year was 1949, and there were six thousand books on the banned list, with as many more yet to come. Mr de Valera, spurned at last, was sulking on the Opposition benches, but the country remained in thrall to his vision of comely maidens dancing at any given crossroads as a kind of cultural millennium. His ideal might never come to pass – the weather alone would see to that, never mind that the native diet of bread and potatoes would hardly produce a corps de ballet of comely maidens – but the dream was mandatory. It was a rejection of all that, by dint of being foreign, was corruptive. More importantly, it was asexual and, on that account, just possibly not immoral. If the Pope was Christ's vicar on earth, Mr de Valera was Archbishop McQuaid's in Ireland, in which capacity he saw to it that whenever his Grace sneezed the country's nose ran for a month.

When I thought of my book I modestly tried to keep the word 'Swiftian' at bay; still, and to face facts, greatness seemed to be unavoidable once I had complied with the small formality of writing it. It never occurred to me that, throughout the land, a legion of weedy youths were sitting hunched over kitchen tables or shivering in linoleum-paved bedrooms, each one fashioning the great satirical novel or play. Whichever it was, it would topple the idols and unwhiten the sepulchres. It would expose the venality of the gombeen men and the urbane tyranny of the priests. It would, for all time, put Ibsen in the ha'penny place.

My own novel was to be set in a small town artfully called Drane, but understandably pronounced 'Dreen'. It took for its departure point the story of Honor Prendergast, her twins and the saga – at least it would be a saga in *my* version – of the iron gates. To this, like a literary Escoffier, I stirred in another ingredient: a sub-plot which told of a veritable mountain of high explosives, buried since the Civil War and still volatile. And, in a master-stroke of narration, this gigantic bomb would exist at the exact point where the gates would be built. I had my *dramatis personae* in readiness, with the Canon at the centre of the web as a village Richelieu. And, rather than make a show of my father, I gave his role to a local character: a drunken, one-armed I.R.A. veteran named O'Connor, painting the lily by making him one-eyed and one-legged as well.

When it was time to start, I laid in a stack of pilfered minute paper from work. The irony of using civil service stationery to launch an attack upon the rotten shorings of society did not occur to me: I was simply trying to save a few pence which were better spent on Alan Ladd and Donna Reed in *Chicago Deadline* than on ruled notebooks. My writing table was a flat-topped trunk in my bedroom. Its disadvantage was that I could not get close enough without barking my knees against the front, so in the end I sat sideways. Banishing from my mind such Lorelei as the billiard hall, the Roman Cafe, and the sea-front girls with nuns' eyes forever downcast, I began.

I had written an entire chapter before the discovery came that I had not the faintest idea of how to write.

It was not a matter of skill or artifice, or even the Holy Ghost's failure to descend. To say pompously what was plain truth: I had not yet begun to live. I was waiting to become a person, just as my friends and I waited for jobs, or a new suit, or money from nowhere, or the end of a hated virginity. We looked about us for the future and saw no sign. We waited, dimly aware of an instinct that warned us to do no damage to the waiting room. A wanton act, born of despair that a door would ever open, might mean the forfeiture of one's passport, so that the waiting room would become forever after a living room.

Our needs were diverse. Jackie Whiston wanted a job that would take him away from the corner of Marine Road where he stood the year round: sometimes with his face upturned to the sun; at others, trying to blow winter from his fingers. Dan Cleary was wild with grief that, on his two pounds a week as apprentice to a watchmaker, he seemed never likely to marry Nora Kavanagh. When his parish priest warned him of the perils of long courtships and Dan protested that he had no money, the reply was a genial, 'Erra, boy, sure all you need is a bed and a frying pan!' Joe Byrne yearned to go to Birmingham, where his father worked in exile. Oliver Mongan's ambitions were not so earthbound: he wanted to be Tyrone Power and, failing that, to marry Joan Fontaine; there were moments, however, when he lowered his sights and confessed that, at a push, he would settle for any girl who had a nice chest and was sincere. As for me, I caught the 9.07 to Westland Row each morning to sit with thirty others in a room where I could feel my life withering. I lived for the day when I would be quit of the Land Commission and could think of no other way out than by writing. It came as an unpleasant shock to discover that words, simply because they were *my* words, did not come forth golden-born.

If *Sex on Thursdays* ever had a claim to exist, it was as a child of a time forever gone. Written today, even if written well, it would be a curiosity: an assembly of grotesques that once were real and seem funny only from the safeness of distance. If anything is worthy of recall, of the casting of a net into the past, it is perhaps that time of waiting and how we passed it.

As for my father's arms cache and why, of all people, it was entrusted to him, there can have been no better hiding place than beneath three acres and a half of lawns, an orchard, flowerbeds and a meadow, where the gardener happened to be a stalwart of the I.R.A. rank and file. Like myself in the matter of the civil service writing paper, my father's Commandant would probably have seen no irony in burying the guns in the garden of 'Enderley', the home of members of the Society of Friends, even had he known that, with Catholic owners, it was later to become 'Santa Maria'. Perhaps it proves that even arms dumps may be ecumenical.

2

In our town, people die but are not permitted to grow old. Once, a few years ago when I was still a smoker, I became conscious of an old woman glaring at me in the local newsagent's. Addressing the morning air, she said: 'I know the root up the arse his mother would-a gev him, standin' there with a cigar stuck in his fat gob.' Then, as a kind of envoi, uttered with a hatred that was almost sensual, she added: 'An impudent pup the like of him.'

The pup was in his mid-fifties at the time and his mother was fifteen years dead, but that, as far as the old woman was concerned, was the splitting of hairs. I was one of a younger generation than hers and always would be, just as I would forever be my parents' son, or rather – and it made the debt greater and my treacheries more heinous – their adopted son. I might as well never have grown up, married, lived abroad, and written plays under a rashly taken pen name. Now I was home again, where I was Jack Keyes and the local cottage industry was the craft of shrinking distended heads. Here, the world's opinion counted for nought. Of those who foolishly thought themselves exempt from the judgment of the town, there were a hundred voices to say 'I know him' in tones as final as they were unforgiving.

Over the next year or so, I saw my elderly critic here and there in the town and usually in deep conversation with a crony. As our eyes locked, I would veer across the street like a fishing boat making for a lee of the jetty, but the abuse would follow me the length of the Bus Lawn or down Convent Road.

'There's the whelp now,' I and half the town heard her say.

'God, but isn't his poor mother better off where she is, lyin' in the wet clay of the Kill of the Grange, than to have that cur fornenst her.'

The day came when I saw and heard her no more, and all one knew for certain was that if she had died it was not – considering her vocal powers – from lung disease. I was given no respite from torment, for her duties were at once taken over by another old woman, rather in the manner in which the secret formula for a liqueur is passed on from a monk on his death-bed to his appointed heir. Her successor, plump and trim in a grey coat wisping with borders of pale fur, hailed me by name in Castle Street and said: 'I'm the daughter of "Oats" Nolan.'

I thought, for an insane moment, that she was announcing the title of a song which she proposed to sing to me there and then. Instead, she went on: 'You put my father into your play, *Da*.'

I said carefully: 'I mentioned his name in it, yes.'

She said: 'Nick Keyes, oul' eejit the like of him, took you in out of God knows where and put a roof over you when your own wouldn't have you. He brung you up, so he did, and gave you a name, and the way you paid him back was, you put him in a play. Your poor mother was disgusted be that play.'

I should have left her with the last word, knowing that she would take it in any case, but I could not resist delivering what I foolishly thought to be the perfect quelch. 'That's odd,' I said, 'seeing as how she was seven years dead when I wrote it.'

Her eyes were bright splinters of contempt. Her heel twitched, ready to be turned upon. 'Well then,' she snapped, 'she was disgusted by something else you wrote.'

Probably she was. Patrick Kavanagh once said that anyone who writes a poem that a policeman can understand deserves whatever he gets. As much may be said of a writer who chooses to live in the village where he grew up; and his worst crime lies not in the nature of the words he sets down, kindly or wounding, but that they were set down at all. To take a man's character over a game of Twenty-Fives, or to sip slander from the lip of a pint glass, is no more than human nature, and in any case your victim is at that moment probably saying as bad or worse of you. It is between neighbours, if not friends. To parade him naked in a book or a play for the world to see is an indecency. And it is less than no excuse to protest that you did it out of affection and in praise: you will be leered at for cuteness and told: 'Oh, I'm sure it waş. Jasus, do you see the green in me eye? It's blackguarding, what else?' And then the clincher: 'Sure why else would he write it?'

What is not so easily answered is why my grey-haired tormentors even now strike a faint chill of fear into the heart. Perhaps I suspect that they may be in the right of it and that, for all my worldliness, which in truth is not much, I am the 'whelp' they take me for. Or it may be a legacy of the days when, although my friends and I were in no sense delinquents, the elders of the town knew us to be what they called 'proper go-boys', bent on whatever sins best belonged in the dark. Of our enemies, the priests were the most easily fooled. They came towards us, enveloped in a priest-smell of incense and talc; we simpered, stood upright, saluted and said 'Good evening, Father,' and they smiled, saluted back and knew you to be good lads at heart.

Just as a cat will leap on the lap of the one person in the room who hates animals, I have always and disastrously been a magnet for my natural enemies. When I was fourteen, Father Creedon threw me out of the confessional for not knowing the *Confiteor*; later the same year, during a religious knowledge lesson at Harold Boys' School, he had almost suffered a stroke when, wholly in a spirit of theological enquiry, I asked: 'Please, Father, what's adultery?' The war with Credo, as we called him, had, however, begun even earlier.

To my grief and the grief of others, I have always been what Americans call a joiner. A psychiatrist would probably say that, having been rejected by my natural mother, I was attempting to find a place where I might 'belong'; whatever the cause, within ten years I was thrown out of the altar boys, the choir, the sea scouts, the Local Defence Force, at least one dramatic society, and Butlin's holiday camp.

It was actually my mother's idea that I should 'join the altar', and become – in her eyes at any rate – a kind of pygmy priest. Once a week after tea the church clerk, Dessie Swords, taught the new boys how to pronounce clumps of Latin responses, which we then learned by heart. No one told us what any of it meant: only that when it was all memorised we would be permitted to serve at Mass. Meanwhile, on special occasions and as a kind of show of strength, we would emerge, like formation dancers, from the sacristy, each boy a mother's dream-come-true in lace surplice and scarlet soutane, and sit out of harm's way in a pew off to one side of the high altar.

I remember, and with reason, a Sunday afternoon marked by a form of devotions known as the Golden Hour. This was rather like several of the once-monthly Holy Hours rolled into one. The altar was hardly visible behind banks of flowers, and there were so many candles that it took Dessie Swords ten minutes to light them. The church was crammed to the doors. Even my father, who bore us off to the Picture House every Sunday of the year, had been shanghaied, my mother saying that, if she could make a sacrifice for God, my father could make one for her. 'It's missing the serial I mind,' he confided to me. 'Now we won't be able to folley the shaggin' thing.' I could not have agreed more. No one had told me that becoming an altar boy meant having to renounce Flash Gordon. 'You begged to go on the altar,' my mother said, lying through her teeth. 'You tormented me, and sign's on it, the altar is where'll you'll go if I have to swing for you.'

And so, with seven others, I stood in the sacristy in the red soutane that was our equivalent of dress uniform. It was not unlike waiting in the wings of a theatre: from the body of the church and above the throb of the organ we could hear whoops, wheezes and coughs. Then Father Creedon, always vast and, today, dazzling in his vestments, came up behind us and we started off in double file: eight small ponies drawing a golden coach. Nothing quite prepared us for the blaze of candles, their smoke stinging the eyes, or the sickly scent of the flowers. Already the packed church was almost airless and, as we crossed to the pew, a familiar fear gnawed at me.

In those days I fainted a great deal. Or, rather, I would become weak in any confined place – although never, strangely enough, while at the pictures – and, as faces swam about me and the room stood on its head, would go staggering out, crashing bruisingly into door jambs and walls until, once in the open air and blind to all onlookers, I would assume a foetal position on the ground, grass or concrete, rained on or dry. Looking out now at the wall of faces, among which somewhere on the four-penny benches were my parents, and feeling the wave of heat, I all but succumbed to an urge to lie down and curl up there and then. It seemed unlikely that I would survive the Golden Hour which, tossing its head at earthly time, usually lasted an hour and three-quarters.

Thirty minutes of this were occupied by Father Creedon's sermon. He was a portly, majestic man who seemed to over-flow the pulpit. His pink hands conducted angelic choirs. His speech was orotund and slow: an ocean swell that rose and dipped. From somewhere in the congregation a snore rasped: a harsh, metallic snort that became a death rattle as the soloist was nudged awake. Wedged in the altar pew, I had begun to get over my initial panic and to feel that I might, after all, survive the afternoon. It depended upon whether there was a Benediction, for Father Creedon was famous for swinging the thurible like a fast bowler coming up to the crease, and even his own not insubstantial bulk had been known to shimmer and vanish in the haze of incense. My fear was that the overpowering odour might fatally tip the balance in my own case. As the sermon boomed on like distant guns, I whispered to Billy Costello sitting next to me: 'Will there be Benediction?'

From the pulpit Credo said: 'And then at that simple village wedding feast, Jesus turned to His beloved mother and said will the boy who is talking on the altar please leave.'

He had changed course from Cana to Dalkey without as much as a hiccup, and so it was only when his massive head swivelled towards the altar that what he had said sank in. Five hundred pairs of eyes, which a moment before had been glazed and cataleptic, now brightened and looked with interest at the altar boys. I felt my heart slow down and knew that the blood had drained from my face. Perhaps it had not happened; perhaps I had dozed off and dreamt it. And yet if so, why was Father Creedon silent? His hands grasped the velvet cushion at the pulpit's edge. He spoke again, loudly and with the deliberation of a hanging judge: 'I said, will the boy who is speaking on the altar *leave*!'

The last word was uttered with such a roar that when a tram rumbled past just then its noise seemed no more than an echo. A tremor, part unease, part delight, went through the congregation, and I bitterly regretted not having fainted earlier on. Ten thousand Father Creedons could not have made me rise and walk off the altar, disgraced before the town, and so I sat and tried to look not only innocent but unconcerned. This might have worked had not the other altar boys cunningly absolved themselves from suspicion by turning to stare point-black at the pariah. I felt the blood rush back to my face in double measure as if to make up for its defection, and the bowel-loosening thought occurred that Credo might actually descend from the pulpit and expel me by force. Instead, having piled a second eternity of silence upon the first, he turned away, his face glowing like an angry moon on the parishioners, and said: 'And Jesus told his mother "Woman, you know that my time has not yet come." '

It was a reprieve, or rather a stay of execution. The looks I now received from the other altar boys told me that Credo would probably maim me for life once the Golden Hour was over. I began to feel ill. To alleviate the symptoms, I attempted to think, not of future terrors, but of happy moments in the past, but all I could remember was that I had disgraced myself in front of the town, my own parents included. I thought of taking a tram into Dublin after tea and starting life over again with a new identity.

After an eon or so, the water had been turned into wine at Cana, and Father Creedon squeezed his way out of the pulpit and returned to the altar, flicking in my direction as he passed a look that was like the kiss of a bullwhip. Dessie Swords came from the sacristy and assisted him into a vestment of some magnificence. Its silver threads threw back the candlelight, as did the Celtic cross, entwined with shamrocks, which was worked down the front and back in gold. It was a long garment and Dessie acted as train-bearer as Credo moved to the altar steps where, all in one superb movement, he knelt, disembarrassed Dessie of the train and flung it behind him, where it spread out fan-like on the steps without the minutest wrinkle or fold. It had been said in the town, and with pride, that there was not a priest, or a bishop either, who could come within an ass's roar of Father Creedon's expertise at manipulating a chasuble.

He began to pray. I was doing so myself, swearing to God that if He kept me from falling into a dead faint I would give up telling lies and kneeing my mad aunt Mary in the behind as she walked past. God, as ever, knew when He was being sold a pup and answered me with the sight of Dessie Swords producing a smoking thurible and handing it to Credo. I became even weaker. The shame of being frog-marched, unconscious, off the altar, thereby becoming the most notorious twelve-year-old in Dalkey twice in one afternoon, paled when set alongside my need to breathe the clean air of the chapel yard. I knew that I had turned deathly white; the saints in their niches shook their haloed heads at me, and Christ on His cross disengaged one perforated hand and pointed it towards the way out.

I have only the account of eye-witnesses for what happened. I got to my feet, staggered towards the sacristy door, and tripped over Father Creedon's train, draped as it was down the altar steps. Then, in an attempt to prevent myself from falling headlong, I caught hold of him by the shoulders. At this point, accounts differed. Some said that I mumbled 'Sorry, Father,' others that in my delirium I said 'Sorry, Credo.' All were agreed that he ceased praying and looked around, first at my feet, planted on his golden train, then at my face. He flinched, so I was told, with appalled recognition, as if he had been slapped on the back by the Angel of Death.

As I left the altar, the tail of Father Creedon's vestment wrapped itself like a squid around my foot. I kicked it free. Next thing, there was cold air and the comforting rasp of gravel against my face. Once the dizziness had gone, there was barely time for a foray back into the vestry, while Benediction was still on, to change out of the soutane and swap my altar slippers for shoes. I was at home, pretending to read the *Hotspur*, when my parents came in. My mother said nothing at first, but took the pins from her hat and bore it, held high in both hands like a monstrance, to the wardrobe. My father opened the *Sunday Dispatch*, then looked at me over the top. He said: 'Who was the pup that was talkin' on the altar?' Without a moment's pause, I told him: 'Billy Costello.'

'There, Mag,' he said. 'Didn't I tell you it wasn't Jack?'

My mother gave me a searching look. 'Are you all right?'

'Yeah.'

'You look pasty-faced. I dunno what curse-o'-God bee got inside you that the be-all and end-all of your life was to go on the altar.' (Her shamelessness really knew no bounds.) 'Y'ought to give it up if you're not able for it.'

I did not tell her that the altar had, in effect, given *me* up. At school, I came in for a barrage of jeering ('Hey, Credo's lookin' for you!') and there were mock swoons wherever I went. Morty Mooney came up and said, meaning it: 'Jasus, I thought he was going to hit you with the thurible.' And an unforeseen consequence was that my father met our neighbour, Tweedie Costello, and said: 'Isn't your young lad a holy terror for talkin' on the altar.' Tweedie was so wisplike that a summer breeze would blow him over, but whenever one of the Costellos misbehaved and was found out, the screams went the length of our lane. At the news that his son had been read out from the pulpit, he rushed home, picked up the nearest object to hand, which was an iron wrench, and flung it, catching Billy in the small of the back.

All the Costello children were red-headed and took after their mother, who was built like a house, and probably the martyred Billy duly gave me the thumping my lie deserved. If so, the memory is effaced by what happened a few days later. I was coming out of Mammy Reilly's newspaper shop, when a man shoved me up against the wall with such force that my head banged. I knew him to see: he was one of the town's elders. He collected Christmas and Easter dues and was a prefect of the men's sodality. At Corpus Christi he was among those chosen to carry the canopy over the Eucharist. Once, when there was whispering at Mass, I had seen his head rise like that of a bird of prey disturbed over its kill, and flinched as his pale eyes went in search of the heathens. He wore gold-rimmed glasses and a dark suit with small badges in the lapel. As he shook me, spittle hit my face.

'Filth,' he said in a whisper that was worse than a shout. 'Young bowsie. Desecrating the house of God. But Father Creedon is a match for you. He'll fix you. *And* your like.'

Once the shock had passed and I realised that he was talking about what had happened at the Golden Hour, I no longer heard the words, only the hatred. A white foam began to appear at a corner of his mouth, then, as if finding himself in an unclean act, he thrust me from him and walked away with quick female steps. The nakedness of his loathing stayed with me. I saw him again years later in a train compartment; he was in conversation, defending Irish war-time neutrality. 'We don't want Americans here,' he was saying, 'debauching our women.'

If I had not at once recognised him by his appearance I could not have mistaken that voice, which still bore witness that its owner had been to, and perhaps still lived in, one of the bedsitters of hell. It was as if I had rounded a corner and suddenly come upon an accident victim, the innards exposed. By then, Dalkey was no more than my dormitory; I stayed out of it each day for as long as my pocket and my mother's patience would bear, and I was not to see him again, but thanks to him I have never without revulsion heard the term 'God-fearing' used as if it were a Christian virtue.

As for Credo, I was to fall foul of him in years to come, but at least one potential disaster was avoided. A short while after the humiliation of the Golden Hour, two older boys came up, one on each side of me in the school yard. Their age was fourteen, and so they were as near to being men of the world as made no difference. They talked to me as an equal, offered me a bag of sweets and told me to take two. I was flattered. The conversation turned to Father Creedon. One of them said that I had made a bad enemy, that from now on he would have a down on me. The other agreed; he told fearful stories of Credo's appetite for revenge, saying that he had been transferred to Dalkey because in his previous parish a boy had hanged himself. I swallowed the story more easily, because my mouth had gone dry with fear, than I could swallow the sweets.

'If I were you,' one boy said, 'I'd get on his soft side.'

'But how?'

'Before he comes looking for you,' the other said.

Again, and I was now becoming frantic: 'All right, but how?'

They walked with me for a time in silence, their brows furrowed with kindly concern. Then one said: 'I know. The next time you go to him in confession—'

'To Credo? No fear.'

'No, wait. What you do is, you go into the box, you say "Bless me, Father, for I have sinned", and then you tell him that you've committed self-abuse.'

'Pardon?'

My two new friends carefully explained to me what self-abuse was. If you slept on the linoleum instead of in bed, or gave up taking sugar in your tea, or washed in cold water for a week, and if you offered it up, that was pure proof that you had mended your ways and wanted God's forgiveness. It was like doing a school examination in Irish: you got five per cent extra marks straight off for good intentions. The name for this kind of mortification of the flesh was, logically enough, self-abuse.

And so for the next few days I washed in cold water, although to be truthful it was little more than a few dabs of a face cloth. Then, assuring God that this was only a part-payment, with more purgations to follow, I set off for confession. Father Creedon was not one of those clerics who believed in silent prayer, and as I entered the church I could hear him moaning out a penance: 'You are to say five decades of the grand and glorious family rosary. *Ego te absolvo* . . .' When he had given absolution, adding – unconvincingly, I thought – 'God bless you', a little woman, stooped from age and a lifetime of toil, came out of the confessional. As she hurried down the aisle to say her penance before the side altar, I felt my nerve break. There was the possibility, I thought, that Father Creedon, being a contrary kind of man, might find no great virtue in my several days of diligent self-abuse. In the end, I funked it and went to confess my sins to Father Clarke, who as usual refused to listen to them, saying instead and with the height of jollity: 'Are you sorry? To be sure you are. Three "Hail Marys" and one for meself. Bless you, me child, and off you pop.' Nonetheless, at the back of my mind I felt that my daily chastisements of the flesh should not go to waste.

My chance came some weeks later when the Redemptorists arrived for the yearly mission. From Monday until Friday they struck terror into every heart, with descriptions of the hellfire which the God of infinite mercy had prepared for us, and on Saturday evening the town went, shivering, to confession. When my turn came, the slide between priest and penitent was slid back with such violence that my heart leaped. I began to speak, but a mixture of shyness and fright overcame me. I faltered. 'C'mon, c'mon, c'mon,' the missioner said, not unkindly, but as a man whose supper time was getting no nearer. This had the opposite effect, and I began to babble, peppering him with sins.

'Whoa there, whoa! Slow down, Neddy,' he said with a chuckle. He was not nearly as frightening in the confession box as he was in the pulpit. 'You're not racing at Leopardstown.' I could hear a snigger from the crowded pews outside. 'Now tell me, how old are you?'

'Twelve, Father.'

'Twelve? Begob, that's a great age. You must be bursting with sins to tell me.'

I knew that he was playing, if not to the gallery, then certainly to the listening benches, and, as far as I was concerned, more power to him. If it meant staying on his soft side, I was more than happy to let him be the one who got the laughs. However, and like the showman he was, now that he had softened up his audience, he switched to an earnest note.

'You know that Penance is a sacrament, don't you?'

'Yes, Father.'

'To be sure you do. Good lad. Therefore we must treat

it with respect and not go rushing at it like a bull at a gate. Have you me?'

'Yes, Father.'

'Grand, so. What's your name? The first name only, now.'

'Jack, Father.'

'Jack? Aren't you the great man. Right, Jack, trot them out. As calm as you like, now. What depredations have you been up to?'

My chest swelled like a pouter pigeon's. This missioner was as nice a priest as a fellow could hope to meet, and it was evident that I had a good leg of him. I rummaged in my mind for whatever would please him, and at once it came to me. I was not one to hide my one and only poor light under a bushel, and so I said it loud and clear, not only for his benefit but for that of the eavesdroppers outside.

'Please, Father, I did self-abuse.'

I know it sounds absurd to say so, but there are different kinds of silence. At one extreme there is the mellowness, not unlike that of a good claret, when old friends come together and savour the pleasure of there being no need to speak. At the other there is the silence which exists only because of the terribleness of what might otherwise be said. The latter was the kind that ensued in the confessional, although, ever the optimist, I put it down to the missioner being momentarily speechless from admiration.

After a time, he whispered: 'What did you say?'

'Self-abuse, Father.'

'*Yes.*' It came out angrily, as if he were reproaching himself for causing me to say twice what should not have been said at all. 'And you say that your age is—'

'Twelve, Father.'

It was dark in the confession box, but my impression, peering through the wire grille, was that he had buried his face in his hands. He groaned softly and said 'Oh my God', which I took as my cue and at once launched into the mandatory act of contrition: 'Oh, my God, I am heartily sorry—'

'Stop!' Then, more calmly. 'Wait. This . . . thing. You're certain? I mean, you know what it was you did?'

'Oh, yes, Father.'

'My poor child.' Then, clutching at the only straw in sight, he said: 'And you say you did this thing just the once?'

Of course I had said nothing of the sort and so I hastened to make his day, even at the risk of immodesty. 'No, Father. Two times every day for a week.'

A deep sigh went through the confessional. He said: 'My child, do you want to become a degenerate?'

'Yes, Father.' Good manners impelled me to add 'Please'.

Quite sincerely, I thought he was offering to make me a member of an élitist society of Catholic children, much as, at school, one was put in charge of the ink-wells, and, as I have said, I was nothing if not a joiner. My reply caused him to sit upright and squint at me through the grille, all but putting his nose through the cruciform gap in the centre. In the voice of one who has suddenly espied, not a straw to grasp at, but an entire haystack, he said: 'Tell me about this self-abuse.'

I did so. He gave a sigh of a different sort and laughed out loud: a short bark of a laugh that was more relief than merriment. I could not see what was so funny and was, in fact, disappointed that he said no more about making me a degenerate. He did not even let me tell him my sins, but said: 'Will you clear off out of this and say one Hail Mary. You divil, you.'

When I came out of the box, every face was turned towards me. Not until then, I realised, had they suspected that a candidate for sainthood dwelt in their midst, and so I dropped my eyes modestly, put the palms of my hands together, the fingers pointing heavenwards, and walked down the aisle trying to look next door to canonised.

It was a full two years before I found out what self-abuse was, and another two years before I found out that the name for it was 'self-abuse'.

By then we had begun to move out into what we saw as the wide world, partly because wings are for spreading, partly because of our need to escape. The priests, as I have said, were not a threat: they looked about them for angels, and we made sure that angels were what they saw. As for

47

the police, we kept out of their way. They instilled us with fear, which was no doubt exactly what they intended. Even the one we called the 'Cat' McDonald, of whom we walked in terror, was the kindliest of men (so we found out years later) once his policeman's mask was off. Our crimes were few: robbing windfalls from an orchard, or bicycling along the footpath known as The Metals, were the worst of them. For myself, I had been law-abiding ever since, aged eight and on my way home from school, I had run behind a milk cart, turned the brass tap and was at once engulfed in a Niagara of white. The milkman sprang into the roadway and was after me as I fled screaming. For perhaps a hundred yards the pursuit hung in the balance, then I began to draw ahead. Ignoring the invitations from the rear to 'C'mere 'till I burst you', I took the corner of Rockford Avenue at a tremendous lick and could not believe it when, dead ahead, I saw my mother at the end of our lane, waiting for me.

'It's not up to me to tell you how to rear him, ma'am,' the milkman said, all but flinging me at her, 'but the weight of a hard hand never spoilt any child's rearing.'

It was a theory with which my mother concurred. As she flailed at my legs with the cane handle of our feather duster, she said bitterly: 'And you're the one I thought was going to be a priest.' It was the first I had heard of it.

I think that what we most feared was not the priests or the police, but ourselves: that we might some day become like Mr Mundow, who took offerings at the fourpenny door and looked exactly like his name, or Mr Finnerty, who once upon a time put his hand up women's skirts and now ran the Christmas savings club that was nicknamed the Diddlum. The town was their world. They believed that outside it there were dragons, to be kept at bay until death enabled them to stand down and at last stop worrying. They cared only for old ways and old songs; if they praised a book it was probably Charles Kickham's *Knocknagow, or The Homes of Tipperary*, which they had read in the long ago when there was time for books, and they would one day read it again, please God. In those days and ever since, whenever they lay on top of their wives in a silence that denied they were next or near a bed, never mind actually in one, they did so unfailingly in the dark and, to make assurance double sure, with their faces pressed into the pillow. Now, one of their sons was in the bank, another in Toronto, and the eldest girl in the Benedictines. They found safety in old phrases. They said: 'Sure aren't we all in the hands of the Man Above?', and Mr Finnerty knew, but never spoke of it, that the brown paper gathering dust on top of the wardrobe contained his burial habit, bought by Mrs Finnerty from the Little Sisters and kept in readiness because – and that was another tried and true saying – the day never dawned but had someone's name on it. They were not philosophers, but, if put to it, would say that it was better to do nothing at all than to risk doing wrong. They measured out their lives in droplets, like three-times-a-day medicine.

At the other extreme, it was easy to become like my uncle Sonny and his comrades, who would forsake the lee of Foley's corner only for the shelter of Gilbey's when the wind was from the north. Now and again, when signing on at the labour exchange, they found to their dismay that the corporation needed labourers for the laying of a sewage pipe, or a nightwatchman to mount guard over the pipe itself. Otherwise, they stood at one corner or the other, musing upon the conundrum of life, wondering who had done them down and how, when by birthright and an innate superiority they should have been on the pig's back for life. They talked about horse-and dog-racing and the Wicklow Regatta. They never ran out of bones of contention, for, when a topic was at last dead and buried, it was only so that it might one day be exhumed from the grave, refreshed and ready for another outing. Their eyes missed nothing, and few walked the gamut of Castle Street without incurring their judgment. Jer Rooney was a proper gauger, and Jack English was a hook and a chancer, as were the whole seed and breed of him, while for Mr Dignam, whose son Charlie won a scholarship, my uncle Sonny reserved the very nadir of his contempt. 'He'll get on,' he would say with a look that told you he had Mr Dignam's measure, 'he'll be kep'.'

Sonny was my mother's younger brother. In middle-age, he

49

had married a laundress named Kate Fortune with whom, as my father liked to remind us, much to my mother's vexation, he had been keeping company since old God's time. Opposites, so they say, attract, which may have been true of Sonny and Kate, for she was a tall hairpin of a woman, while he was short and stocky, even if one made allowances for the gammy leg. The theory of opposites was borne out in his case by an apparent infatuation with a woman named Maddie Devlin, who was even taller and more gaunt than Kate Fortune. Her face, racked by martyrdom, was cadaverous. She had a dark moustache and there was a hirsute mole on her cheek. When she was not working at the pork butcher's she was forever either going to or coming from a meeting of the Children of Mary. Her way homeward to Sorrento Road led her between the Scylla and Charybdis of Foley's and Gilbey's. As she passed, Sonny would not accost her or even speak; his feelings went too deep. At her approach, he would swing into her path on the good leg and give her an unwavering look of his dark eyes, which were the pilot lights of a passion that Maddie, if she but chose, could turn up like a gas mantle. For her part, she took a tighter grip on her prayer book, moved her lips in an unheard ejaculation which was probably designed for such occasions and went hurrying past, her eyes fixed on any object except Sonny.

I once called out 'Hello, Maddie,' and she went to Kalafat Lane to tell my mother that I was making a jeer of her; so, since she never took open exception to Sonny's silent courtship, it may be that in a remote and unvisited corner of her mind she enjoyed it. He and Kate are dead these many years, but I saw Maddie in the town yesterday, and she looked away, knowing that not only was I still a pup but now an apostate as well. She looked not a day older, except that the moustache had turned white.

My first small step away from the world of my parents, Uncle Sonny, Maddie Devlin, Mr Mundow and the rest of them came with an incident as small and as terrible as buying a ham sandwich in Da Lundy's cakeshop. I was fourteen and had just won a scholarship to the Presentation Brothers, which to Sonny was proof positive of what he had long suspected: that, like young Charlie Dignam before me, I was above myself and too good for decent poor skins like himself. He harboured the belief that an adopted child who knew neither where he was got nor how he was got ought at least have the manners to lie low, instead of calling attention to himself with scholarships and codology. To me, going to Prez, as I learned to call it, had one drawback. When I was at Harold Boys' national school in Dalkey, I would run to catch a tram every Monday and Friday afternoon at three, climb to the upper deck and, like a jockey on a horse, spur it onwards to Dun Laoghaire. There, ensconced in the Picture House, my mother was waiting with my lunch in a paper bag: sandwiches of white pudding, milk in a Baby Power bottle and Scots Clan caramels for afters. Lesser heavens have been lost than that one: sitting in the front row of the sixpennies, choking from trying to eat and at the same time laugh at the saints of our innocence: Edgar Kennedy and Hugh Herbert and the great Edward Everett Horton. At Prez, however, the school was not over until 4.15: too late for the afternoon show. My mother knew better than to decree that I simply give up going to the Picture House except on Sunday afternoon; pictures were too much a part of our existence. More than a passion, they were a kind of surrogate life. And so, with tea eaten and more often wolfed down, I was permitted to go out in the evenings.

There was, of course, a proviso. Let the sky fall and the seas turn to beef tea, but I would come straight home the instant the pictures were over. 'Half-past ten sharp,' my mother said, 'or that front door will be bolted.'

'Grand,' I said, uppity from excitement. 'Then I can stay out all night.'

'Shut your mouth.' She skewered me with a look, the while mobilising her troops, who as usual were not long in arriving. 'Well, that's the price of me,' she said, 'oul' eejit that I am, for being soft with you —'

'Look, it was a joke . . .'

She was unstoppable. One might as well bid a bullet to return in mid-course. '. . . giving you your own way in everything. Spoiling you, denying you nothing. And for what

thanks? Oh, they all told me, me good neighbours. "He'll turn
on you," they said. "You'll rue the day." '

It was a familiar tune, played this time not in anger, but from
worry that some danger might befall me on my journeyings after
nightfall, and, instead of waiting until the recital had ended, my
father was rash enough to make a contribution of his own. 'Sure
of course he'll come straight home, Mag. Where else would he
go?'

At once she swung her guns away from me and trained
them on him. 'Well, trust you,' she said, picking up the teapot
for no other reason than to slam it down again. 'Trust you.'

'Trust him,' my mad aunt Mary said, sensing that she
was on a winner.

'Trust me to what?' my father said. 'What ails you?'

'While you're at it,' my mother told him, 'why don't you
tell him *where* he can go instead of the pictures? Why don't
you trot it out?'

My father was as bewildered as I was. 'For the love
o' God,' he roared, 'trot shaggin' what out?' I knew that
he was becoming flustered, for he at once rephrased this
and said: 'Trot out shaggin' what?'

My mother gave him the scalding look of one who has been
trapped into saying more than she intended. 'You couldn't keep
your mouth shut if it paid you,' she said.

'Not if it paid him,' Mary said.

'You hold your tongue,' my mother said.

Plainly, there existed some orchard of forbidden fruit between
Don Laoghaire and Dalkey of which neither my father nor I was
aware. Into my mind came a vision of the kind of western saloon
one saw in the pictures, with unshaven ruffians playing cards,
silken women tucking dollar bills under their garters, Brian
Donlevy, slit-eyed in black suit and string tie, and Marlene
Dietrich singing 'See what the boys in the back room will
have'. It seemed unlikely that there would be a saloon in our
neighbourhood, even after sunset, and in any case I would in
all probability not have been admitted.

And so the matter was dropped. Later that evening, however, I heard my mother, still in a bad temper, muttering to

herself as she cleared the tea things. She was saying: 'Time enough for him to go chasin' after trollops, takin' them up the back roads, doin' God knows what and destroyin' himself over them.'

I all but guffawed, and small wonder. What was tormenting her was the notion that I would fall into the clutches of some Delilah from Sallynoggin, perhaps, or Glasthule. It would have made a cat laugh. I had better uses for my time and few pence than to spend either on a shrill, complaining creature who would tell her mammy if you said 'Jasus' or 'feck', who wanted to walk on footpaths instead of the grass, and who hated cowboy pictures and thought that blooming old Barbara Stanwyck was great. Not only were girls God's worst mistake, but, into the bargain, they hated you. I wondered if my mother had a slate loose. Later, much later, I realised the truth: she had opened a door for me into the future, had herself looked through it and was jealous.

The new regime began. It took a while to get used to seeing films in the evening: the people around you seemed different and there was the uneasy sensation of night deepening outside. And so for a few weeks I gladly observed my curfew, hurrying home as through a hostile land. One evening, as I got off the tram in Castle Street, a fellow I knew asked where I was going.

'Home.'

'What for?'

While I was trying to think of an answer that made sense, he said: 'Have you got fourpence?' Next thing, I was led into Da Lundy's shop, where in the daytime you bought sweets, broken chocolate and rock cakes. At night, as I now saw, there were three small tables with gingham cloths. The fellow took my fourpence and added fourpence of his own to it. He said: 'Two ham sandwiches and two glasses of milk, please.'

I was appalled. You bought sweets and chocolates and perhaps a doughnut in Da Lundy's; what you did not buy was *food*. Food was provided by your parents; it was what they were there for: to see that you had clothes and school books and a boiled egg at tea time. Once, Johnny Quinn, who lived at Number 5 in our lane, had put a finger to his lips and led me to Mrs Threadgold's house. When she answered the door, he made the kind of mewling whisper you heard from a tinker woman with her hand out for a penny, and Mrs Threadgold brought us a slice each of bread and jam. The realisation came that, without meaning to, I had become a beggar. My mother prided herself most of all on being what she termed a great manager; others would tell you admiringly that she was the devil for style. The beating I received for turning the milkman's tap on would have been a caress compared with what she would have given on learning that I had shamed her and taken food from a neighbour. Now, if I were to tell her that I had actually bought a ham sandwich, she would have said 'Anyone would think I didn't feed you' and tend her hurt for a week.

As the milk and sandwich were brought and I sat at the table, with its rough wood showing through a tear in the gingham, the feeling of guilt gave place to one of being an unabashed sybarite. I had never in my life experienced such sophistication. It was the sweet life, easy street, clover, the pig's back.

Only adults, I was aware, paid for their food. The mistake I made in Da Lundy's was in thinking that paying for my food made me an adult.

3

I was a snob. Instead of accepting the decent anonymity of the Christian Brothers school in Dun Laoghaire, I had foolishly opted for the cachet of Presentation. Because it was smaller and closer to home, my new classmates soon knew that they had a cuckoo in their nest. The cuckoo's father was a gardener, and his home – if such birds had homes – was a two-roomed cottage in a back laneway. It was called Kalafat Lane or Anastasia Cottages, as one preferred, but whenever I was asked where I lived, I remembered the *Magnet* and the Fat Owl of the Remove, who promoted his home from Bunter Villa to Bunter Hall. Accordingly, I gave my address as the not so lowly and quite imaginary Anastasia Terrace. It fooled nobody.

There were other terrors. On my first day, the roll was called, and to my dismay I heard the name 'John Byrne' being read out. I sat, not answering, then and when it was twice repeated. Later, in the school yard, I was summoned indoors. The superior, Brother Berchmans, was poring over the roll book. He jabbed a finger at the hated surname, and his adenoidal voice made my adopted name, Keyes, sound like a soda-water syphon. 'Kizz, is this you?'

I nodded. I knew that to be what they called illegitimate was an occasion for deep shame. There had been a sin of some kind, and because of it you were not the same as children who had parents. I had heard neighbours and ladies in the town tell this to my mother (my mother in Kalafat, that is), not in so many words, but by some pitying murmurs such

as 'Wisha, God love him' and 'Weren't you great to take him!',
accompanied by the movement of a hand which made to touch
my hair, but desisted just in time. My mother would not dare
to defend bastardy; instead, she behaved like a woman whose
child is known to have committed murder, but who against all
reason declares him innocent. When the Costellos up the lane
gave me a book for my eighth birthday and wrote my name
as John Keyes Byrne on the flyleaf, such was her fury that I
thought she would get gaol for them. Now, Brother Berchmans
looked at me with scorn – whether for my cowardice or my
flawed pedigree, I did not know – and said: 'Very well, Kizz,
we'll keep your dark secret.' Then, crossing out a name on the
roll, he wrote another. For a moment, the skeleton was safely
back in the closet, but all my stratagems could not hide Kalafat
Lane and the two rooms. Had I strutted into the school yard and
cocked a snook at what the others thought, they would probably
have left me alone; but instead of strutting, I skulked, and they
sensed my shame as a dog is said to smell fear. For a year, until
the sport grew stale, they doled out my punishment, and, at the
back of my mind, deserving it, I took it as my due.

At the end of my four years in Prez, Brother Berchmans
sent word that I was to come to him. As usual, he looked at me
in the manner of one in whose path a dustbin had overturned.
Perhaps I do him an injustice, but the impression persists that
he and Lady Bracknell were siblings under the skin. Probably,
he was of the opinion that, whereas to be a scholarship boy who
lived in a condemned cottage in a back lane was a misfortune,
to be illegitimate as well could be reasonably construed as
carelessness. He had a flat, white coffin of a face, with a nose
that resembled the gnomon of a sundial and had earned him
the nickname of 'Schnozzle'. He took me for a half-trot walk
around the school yard, his robes slapping in the breeze like a
wet sail. Trying to keep up, I was enveloped in a smell of
angry carbolic.

He began by saying: 'You are no doubt aware, Kizz, that
as of this day your scholarship to Presentation College is at
an end?'

I said 'Yes, Brother' and waited for him to embark on the

kind of stern valedictory which, in a Warner Brothers picture, a prison warden addressed to a two-time loser whose latest stretch had been served, and to which the standard response, usually delivered by an uncontrite George Raft, was: 'So long, Warden, see you in choich.'

Instead, what Schnozzle said was: 'We of Presentation have friends in the Department of Education.'

It was as if he had spurned the role of prison warden for that of Conrad Veidt as a Nazi agent, silkily reminding a humble old watchmaker – usually Ludwig Stossel – that the latter still had relatives in Germany. In my case, however, the words were less a threat than the prelude to a reluctant accolade. 'Our friends tell us, Kizz,' Schnozzle went on, 'that you have attained third pless' (he meant 'place') 'in Ireland in the Intermediate Examination.'

The Inter Cert was, as the name implied, a scholastic half-way house. Two years further on, the Leaving Cert, once obtained, would open the door to university. It was a threshold I had no thought of crossing: for one thing, I loathed school; for another, it was time I gave up living off my parents; and, for a third, I could hardly afford to take a tram into Dublin, never mind the cost of transporting myself into Trinity. (The question of attending the younger, Catholic university, U.C.D., could never arise; I was, as I have said, a snob, and as such clung to the belief – and, to my continued happiness, still cling to it – that in life there exist two classes: first class and no class.)

Schnozzle looked at me with his customary distaste. 'However, Kizz, before you bask in the glow of your great accomplishment, let me express the humble opinion that you could and should have achieved no less.'

His opinion was not in the least humble, but it was well-held. I had sat for the Inter Cert on three occasions. On the first, I had failed; on the second, I had scraped through. I should then have moved up a rung into Fifth Year, but on the first day of the new term I wandered into my old classroom and sat at my accustomed desk. It was from timidity, a fear of seeming to thrust forward, only to be pushed back for the impertinence.

I waited for one of the Brothers to say: 'What the hell are you doing in Fourth Year, you thick, you? Go next door.' Not one of them uttered a word: presumably because none of them noticed. I stayed rooted where I was for another year, until I could have passed the Inter Cert, with honours and in my sleep.

Schnozzle and I had completed a round of the school yard when he came to a sudden stop. I saw emotions, as contrary as hares and hounds, go chasing across his face. Then he said, getting it over with like a man spitting out gristle in one lump, and the devil take table manners: 'In view of what some may see as reflecting credit upon the school, even if there are those of us who will beg to differ, the Presentation Brothers are prepared to keep you on here free of charge for two extra years.'

Boys yelped as they ran around the school field. Liberation was in the air. It was the last day of term, and in a matter of minutes Brother Joseph would appear on the school steps, blow his whistle and shout 'Will ye get off home, the lot of ye!' For myself, I was like a man who, after four years of imprisonment, was standing at the gaol gates, his belongings under his arm, only to receive a message asking if he would very much mind returning to his cell for another two years.

I became aware, through my dismay, that Schnozzle was still talking. Rather than look up at that white, slab-like face, I lowered my eyes and noticed for the first time that his feet were enormous. I heard him say that I was lazy, that I lacked application, that the world and his wife knew that my days were spent in picture houses. He spoke of this golden opportunity, of how by seizing it I could repay the sacrifices made by my parents, good people that they were. He even made mention of another scholarship, this time to university.

The thought of my penal servitude being extended, not by two years, but a possible six, was a pain so exquisite that I looked at last up into his face. For no reason I recalled how, during my first, far-off week at Prez, he had forbidden boys kneeling at prayer to rest their backsides against the benches behind them. The word he had used was 'posteriors', which I had not previously heard, and so I smiled in appreciation of what I took to be a piece of Micawber-like grandiloquence. 'You think it's funny, Kizz, do you?' he said, for the first time but not the last, liquefying my bowels with the inevitable prologue to a caning: 'Git ahtside the door, plizz. Ah'll be aht in a minnit.'

He had looked at me then with the distaste of an epicure confronted with scrag-end, and his expression was not much friendlier now. His voice, however, had acquired a small match-flame of warmth. My future, he said, hung in the balance; I would do well to think long and hard, to stop being a boy, to grow up. 'You are a schemer and a dodger, Kizz,' he said, 'because you think of myself and the other Brothers as adults who are therefore enemies, to be feared and outwitted. Hear this or you are lost: we do not live in separate worlds, do you understand me?'

I replied, without understanding him: 'Yes, Brother.'

He dismissed me on a practical note. 'If you decide to accept this most generous offer, your parents need bear no financial brunt. The college will accept the schoolbooks you already have in exchange for the new ones you will require.'

He went flapping away from me across the yard. Forever after, whenever I have heard or read Tennyson's line 'For the black bat Night has flown', the image in my mind is that of Brother Berchmans.

We broke up early, soon after lunch, and I cycled the hundred yards or so from Prez to the Astoria. There were only one or two others waiting for the curtains to squeak apart to the combined sound of a fanfare and the crowing of the Pathé News rooster, and I sat in the sevenpennies thinking of Schnozzle and his offer. It was true that my mother could not wait for me to find a job and supplement the four pounds ten shillings my father earned weekly tending Enderley's three and a half precipitous acres. And yet I knew that today's news would bear witness before the world that she had reared a genius. At the thought that the Presentation Brothers would further educate me, free of charge, towards a vague but indisputably golden future, she would first of all tell the ceiling that as sure as God my codology would land us all in the Union, adding that my uncle Sonny was right about me having a smell of myself: that Gentleman Jack had become too grand for the likes of my father and her. Then, having had her grumble, she would with the ferocity of a tigress set about making any and every sacrifice to ensure that I stayed on at school – and if it meant that my father, who was already past sixty, must go on working until he was a hundred, then so be it.

I have two selves. One, like a stranger, stands apart and watches the other, and now this second self saw that I was weakening. The miseries of the past had already begun to recede; I thought instead of my mother's pleasure and of hearing her say, just this once, that I was a credit to her. In a daydream, I even walked the cobbles of Front Square in Trinity. It was too much. I roused myself, and both selves combined to confront the less nebulous problem of new schoolbooks for old. My intention had been to sell the old books, and I had made particular plans for spending the proceeds. The money had, as the saying went, its hat and coat on. In fact, only an hour previously, I had cleared out my desk at Prez, and—

An iron fist clenched shut upon my heart. It had come to me where the precious books were – or should be – at this moment: crammed tight into the saddlebag of the bicycle that I had left leaning against the side wall of the Astoria. It took me a year-long fifteen seconds to be out of my seat, through the Astoria's tiny foyer and into the lane. Not only were my schoolbooks already gone, but the thief, whoever he was, had had the labour-saving notion of taking the saddlebag as well. I quite deliberately chose to regard the theft as a straw in the wind. At home that evening, I wrote a letter to Schnozzle thanking him for his generosity, but declining his offer on the grounds that my conscience had told me to put aside childish things and (brazenly perverting a line from Yeats) dance attendance on my parents' old age. He did not reply. Having spent his adult life dealing with boys, he could probably smell a hypocrite a mile off.

I began looking for work straight away. Rather, it was my mother who did the looking, and, seeing no difference between one job and the next, she made me answer every advertisement in sight, whether in the 'Help Wanted' column of the *Irish Press* or on a postcard in Mammy Reilly's shop window. Once, she sent me to Bray, where an electrician needed an apprentice. After five minutes, he assured me solemnly that, were he to take me on, I would electrocute myself within the week. I was desperate for work, not only for self-respect, but because a job meant money, and money meant girls.

I had developed a taste for women during the years at Prez. This was remarkable, considering that at the age of fourteen I had taken Mrs Hammond's daughter, Gloria, on an outing to Dublin: an experience which, but for my natural resilience, would have made me a lifelong celibate.

It was my mother who, in a fit of apparent insanity, arranged that I should take Gloria to the pictures. Given her jealousy of other women, I have no idea why she connived at such an event, unless it was done in the knowledge that Gloria and I loathed each other. She lived in the same lane as my grandmother, and I could not have been more than nine when she stuck her tongue out at me as I walked peacefully by, licking a ha'penny ice-cream cone from Toole's shop. In the craft of effectively sticking one's tongue out at another person, the first requirement is that a discreet distance should be kept between the sticker and the stickee, but Gloria, with a woman's contempt for rule books, came so close that I was able to take hold of the neck of her frock and drop not only my own ice-cream down its front but also the cornet I had been sent out to buy for my mad aunt Mary.

'Where's Mary's ice-cream?' my mother wanted to know when I arrived at my grandmother's a minute later.

'I dropped it,' I lied.

'Oh, the shaggin' cur, me lovely ice-cream,' Mary groaned and tried to run me down with the old pram in which she kept her collection of dolls.

Just then, there was a banshee's wail, and, dragged by her mother, Gloria came up the garden path with gobs of ice-cream trickling down her legs. Justice was rough and immediate, but I would gladly have done it again. Gloria was a termagant, a shrew and a fury – in short, a girl – and now, five years later, because of an unholy alliance between my mother and hers, I was to be shackled to her for an afternoon. I could have said, half meaning it, that I would die first, but two bribes were tendered and accepted: money for the pictures, and my first trip to Dublin unaccompanied by an adult.

When I called for Gloria, she was scowling, and I remember that she wore white ankle socks, for her mother told her not to forget that they were 'fresh on' today. 'Now, you'll mind her?' Mrs Hammond implored, handing me a bag of mixed sweets. I said yes, aware that Gloria was the kind of strap who could look after herself in a pit of snakes. As we set out, I looked up Sorrento Road and saw my own mother at the end of Kalafat Lane, giving me the kind of heartbroken wave one keeps for the last glimpse of a loved one sailing for Australia.

We had the day's first falling out as we boarded the Number 8 tram with 'Nelson Pillar' on the destination board. Gloria wanted to sit downstairs, whereas I, a trail-blazer at heart, preferred the open space at either end of the upper deck. Neither would yield, so we went our separate ways, and, as the tram swooped and sang down Bulloch Hill, I felt the wind hard on my face and saw the overhead trolley spit flame against the wires. As I browsed through Mrs Hammond's mixed sweets in the consciousness that an imperfect world could not offer much more happiness than this, the conductor appeared from below. He did not say 'Fares, please,' but stood rocking on the balls of his feet and grinding his teeth. His troubles on such a cloudless day were no concern of mine, and so I merely asked for two return half-fares to Dublin. He took my shilling, gave me the tickets and twopence change and suddenly said: 'Are them the sweets you stole off that poor young one?' Before I could answer, he snatched the bag, called me a right little bollix and bore the sweets downstairs to Gloria.

I had my revenge on the trip when we reached Dublin. As we alighted in the shadow of the Pillar, the air strident with the groans and clangings of the trams and the cries of the old ones selling fruit and flowers, Gloria set an unmistakable course for the Savoy Cinema. I shouted after her: 'Where are you going?'

She turned and looked at me as if I were a skivvy from the country who had had the impertinence to ask her if she had washed herself. She threw me a crust of an answer. 'To see *Smilin' Through.*'

I remembered having sat through a previous version starring Norma Shearer donkey's years before, when I was six, squirming with embarrassment while my mother wept buckets. Now that I was fourteen and my own man, I would eat my grandmother's soapy potatoes before seeing it again, this time with Jeanette MacDonald ullagoning about the little brown road winding over the hill. I told her: '*I'm* going to the Theatre Royal.'

She said: 'What's on there?'

I told her: 'Humphrey Bogart in *The Return of Doctor X.*'

She stood between the fruit-stalls of the shawlies who were screeching 'T'ree ha'pence deh luvly apples, tuppence deh ri-ep pay-ars' and bawled at me in a voice as hoarse as theirs: 'Humphrey Bogart? That's an old gangster picture.'

'No, it isn't,' I told her in the informed voice of a regular *Picturegoer* reader. 'He takes the part of a vampire.'

She screamed as if she had just seen one. It was partly the scream of a thirteen-year-old girl to whom horror films gave nightmares, and partly the envenomed howl of a virago who had realised that I was holding the purse strings and could call the tune. She hurled threats at me all the way to O'Connell Bridge: she would tell her mammy and my oul' one, her daddy and my oul' fella; she even mentioned an uncle of hers who was a sailor and due home for Christmas. Once across the Liffey, she began wheedling. She told me seductively that *Smilin' Through* was in what she called glorious Technicalcolor. She said that I could have some of the sweets – no, all of the sweets, and she would treat us to the kind of ice-cream high-up people ate out of tubs with wooden spoons. I wavered; then, knowing that she would not only welsh upon her promises, but do so with a witch's cackle of triumph, I marched up the three front steps of the Theatre Royal. Realising, at last, that the iron had entered my soul, she yelled 'I hate yeh!' and hit me with the white handbag she had received for her Confirmation.

A minute later, we were watching a kind of variety show called *Apple Sauce* that preceded the film. The Royalettes

63

danced; a skyscraper of a man named Noel Purcell came on, first as a woman, and later in a black coat and glasses as Mr De Valera; a fat woman and a scrawny one did Fred Astaire and Ginger Rogers; then a painted volcano appeared and a woman named May Devitt sang 'One Fine Day' dressed in a kimono. There was a quiz called 'Double or Nothing' with Eddie Byrne; finally, an organ came up out of the ground, was played and went down again, and *The Return of Doctor X* began. Gloria had kept quiet during the show, but now, even before the first victim's blood was drained, she was half-way under her seat. The film, as it happened, was only middling, which made my victory a Pyrrhic one. She would blame her nightmares equally on me and Humphrey Bogart, and Mrs Hammond – a tall, bony woman with a sharp, stuttering tongue, a long reach and knuckles of iron – would either clout me or tell my mother. And yet I had won a prize of sorts: never again would anyone in his or her senses suggest that I go out with a female. A kind of peace glowed within me, and, in the spirit of one who might as well be hanged for twenty sheep as a single lamb, I took out a large packet of Craven A and lit one after the other, ignoring a voice from under the next seat that said: 'And I'm going to tell your oul' one you smoked as well.'

She did, later on. We queued, not speaking, in the rain for our tram home and arrived in Dalkey like a couple of drowned mice. Soaked as she was, Gloria did not turn into her laneway, but followed me up Sorrento Road to my front door. I slammed it on her, but she turned the handle and marched straight in, with a cry of 'Mrs Keyes, Mrs Keyes!' Carefully waiting to burst into tears until she was sure that my mother was at home, she launched into a seemingly endless recitative, in the course of which she never once paused for breath, but connected the details of my various crimes with a gasped ' . . . an', an', an', an', an' then he . . .' When she mentioned, which was true, that I had gone on smoking Craven A until an usherette came and threatened to put me out into the street, my mother fetched me a dirty look. Meanwhile, my father, half-way through his te ., was looking at Gloria as if she had just come down the chimney.

My mother, at last forcing a way through the wailing wall, asked: 'Did he hit you?'

The question took Gloria so by surprise that she stopped in mid-cry. 'Wha'?'

'I'm asking, did Jack lay either hand or glove on you?'

'*Him*?' The she-devil all but burst out laughing. 'Him, hit me? God, I'd burst him.'

'In that case,' my mother said, 'how bad you are! So will you go off home like a good girl and dry yourself. Your mammy will be worrying.'

I had rarely known her to be capable of such calm good sense. She took a towel and dried Gloria's hair, then set her on the way home. When the door was closed and the sniffling had died away, she turned to me and said: 'Was the picture any good itself?' Then, before I could answer, she snapped at my father: 'You drink your tea.' She seemed quite unperturbed by Gloria's tales of woe; probably, she was relieved that I was now certain to remain a bachelor for life. As for my cigarette smoking, next day she actually bought a packet of ten Gold Flake and planked them down in front of me with a virtuous: 'And them's the last you'll get from me!'

My aversion to women was destined to wear thin. At school, Dinkie Meldrum showed me a smuggled copy of the war-time *Men Only*. It contained a nude photograph, demure by today's standards, of a woman kneeling, her hands modestly in her lap, her hair covered by a kerchief. Her breasts might have been carved in marble, but from the moment I caught sight of her my years as a mysogynist were over. For three days, I would waylay Dinkie and say off-handedly by way of concealing the molten lava in my gut: 'Show us that old picture again.' He would do so, whereupon I would shake my head, hardly believing that poor immature devils existed who actually derived pleasure from looking at naked women. Then, chuckling sadly to myself at human folly, I would walk away, trying not to buckle at the knees.

I was, as I have said, a joiner. While still at Prez, I enlisted in the sea scouts and, later on, the Emergency Communications Corps and the Local Defence Force. From the first of these,

I was expelled; in the case of the second, I was issued with a bicycle and resigned when I fell off it and bent the front wheel; as a raw recruit in the third, I ruined an all-night manoeuvre and was told afterwards to go home and wait until I was sent for: which I never was.

It was my scoutmaster who first took me to the theatre. He was a slim, bald man named Richardson. He had a quick, almost girlish walk, and I never saw him address his wife, a plain, timid, frizzy-haired creature – without snarling. He took me to see Joan Hammond in *The Magic Flute* at the Gaiety, but it was war-time, and she refused to sing because the German ambassador was in the audience. Instead we were given *Ernani*, and I was fascinated to see that the leading tenor was suffering from a nose-bleed and spent the entire performance with his head thrown back, his face buried in a bloody handkerchief as he sang 'Solingo, errante misero', not to the implacable Silva, but to the flies.

On another evening, the Skipper, as we called him, took me to see Myles na Gopaleen's comedy *Faustus Kelly*, at the Abbey. It was poor stuff, and I was not at all taken by F. J. McCormick in the title role. I thought him dry and pompous; it was only years later, when I saw him as Fluther Good in *The Plough and the Stars*, that I realised where his genius lay: he became whatever character he played so completely that there was danger of confusing the role and the man. On the tram homeward, the Skipper suggested that we have cocoa and discuss the play, but instead of taking me to his house on Albert Road he led the way to our scout hut near the Forty Foot. He put a billycan on the primus to boil. We sat.

'It's weakening, you know,' he said.

I thought at first that he meant cocoa. It took me a while to realise that, without prologue, he had launched into a lecture on the perils of masturbation.

'It isn't manly. A true Scout will despise it for what it is: a habit that saps the energy and rots the brain. Never mind about it being a sin: that's Canon McGough's department. No, what concerns me is that it turns fine lads into contemptible weaklings: cowardly go-by-the-walls. Not to mention that it's a waste of precious seed. We're each of us given only so much, you know.'

I silently implored the water to boil and willed him to change the subject to *Faustus Kelly*. Quite apart from wanting to know what he thought of F. J. McCormick, the steadiness with which he watched my face was unsettling. I tried not to flinch and felt a tic leap high in my cheek.

'Boys who masturbate think that nobody knows. They do it where no one can see, in locked rooms, in bed and in the dark. They think they do it in secret. Well, more fools they.' He gave a small, shrill laugh that did not reach his eyes. 'Any doctor can tell in an instant. He can look at them and say straight out: "That boy degrades himself." Will I tell you how?'

I said miserably: 'Yes, Skipper.'

'I mean, do you want to know?'

Teachers' pets are to be pitied. Sooner or later, if they are not to fall from grace, there is a reckoning to be paid. I was the Skipper's favoured one, envied by the others and justly resented, for I had few of the conventional scouting skills. I was too weedy to handle a heavy oar in the racing skiff and so, by default, became the coxswain; I could not swim or climb a rope or put up a tent or build a camp fire, never mind cook on one. What I excelled at was word games and whatever else needed a quick mind, without physical strength or dexterity to go with it. It was a quality that appealed to the Skipper; I was a match for him. Now, on the edge of a dark *terra incognita*, I looked back at him dumbly.

'Well, do you want to know or don't you?'

I heard the faintness in my voice as I told him yes.

He said: 'Right, I'll show you. Open the front of your trousers.'

I stared at him.

'Well, come on. Didn't you say you wanted to know? Just take your thing out and I'll show you.'

A whisper. 'I don't want to.'

'You what?'

'I don't want to, Skipper.'

It was as if his old dog, a spaniel, had snapped at him.

67

His face was suddenly new to me: a stone mask of dislike. He said: 'The reason I like Micky Farrell' – our patrol leader – 'is because he's so open and above board and doesn't make strange.' He extinguished the primus. 'That water will take all night to boil. You're out late enough as it is.'

A few days later, our troop was in the hut waiting to come to order for one of our twice-weekly meetings. In passing behind me, another boy flicked his finger and knocked my cap off. When I whirled around, he dodged backwards and fell over the Skipper's dog, which had just preceded its master into the hut. We were at once called to attention, and the Skipper, his face and bald head scarlet with rage and hatred, ordered me to step forward and delivered a shrieking, five-minute tongue-lashing, at the end of which I was expelled from the 3rd Port of Dublin sea scouts for hooliganism. I was framed.

4

My first job was as a clerk in the offices of Columbia Pictures
in Middle Abbey Street. My four years at Prez had atrophied
into a kind of limbo, and the prospect of working for Columbia
evoked agreeable images of Frank Capra, *Mr Deeds* and *Lost
Horizon* and, at a less rarified level, *Blondie*, Charles Starret
as the Durango Kid and Warren William as the Lone Wolf. The
actuality was a public office in Middle Abbey Street from the
ceiling of which apathy drifted down in flakes. The manager
was Mr Jay, a lank-haired autocrat who affected a Protestant
accent and the languidness of a feudal warlord strolling among
his vassals. Prominent on his office wall was a framed telegram
from Wardour Street in London complimenting him on his effi-
ciency. The message was perhaps the last of an endangered
species, for while I was there he was bombarded almost daily
by telegraphed threats, insults and goads from the same source.
His secretary, Miss Grace, sucked up to him shamelessly and
loathed the rest of us. For a time, her habit of leaving by one
door and seeming to return by another an instant later and in
a change of dress made me wonder if I was having blackouts;
then a kindly soul explained that she had a twin sister who
dropped in every day. The only other person I remember, and
with good reason, was a shapeless girl called Dolores who sat
opposite me. She favoured floppy twinsets and seemed herself
to be floppy underneath them; one was conscious of heavy,
untrammelled breasts. She and I took turns at operating the
small switchboard, but otherwise hardly spoke.

My pay was thirty shillings a week, and every day at

lunchtime I would cross O'Connell Bridge to the Goodwill Restaurant opposite Trinity. It was a far cry from eating a ham sandwich at Da Lundy's. There, for one-and-sixpence, you were given chunks of bread with soup so thick that a spoon would not sink in it, followed by a stew that was a bubbling archipelago of mutton, carrots, swedes and spuds. For a penny extra, scalding tea was splashed from a great metal jug into both your cup and lap, favouring neither. You sat at a long, bare table, and the cutlery was all but flung at you, but you were nourished, and in the war years and after, there was more to eating than avoiding hunger. It was a time of plague. Old people called it consumption, the young, T.B., and everyone had friends or family who had died of it. With a hypochondria that has been a loving companion down the years, I could not catch a head cold or stand on a weighing machine or feel a twinge in my chest without seeing myself, gaunt and hectic, expiring in a sanatorium at Peamount or Blanchardstown, and so, rather than run the risk of falling into a decline, I wolfed down the Goodwill's stew, gristle and all.

For all its virtues, it was not the kind of eating house where one lingered over a *demi-tasse*, and there was always time to walk in the little back lanes between Dame Street and the river and go hunting in secondhand shops for a *Blighty* or a *Men Only* that had somehow escaped the censors. Usually as I walked, with the mutton like a stone in my craw, I would try to work out what had become of me.

I knew of only one person who was deluded enough to regard my thirty shillings a week life as enviable, and he was my friend, Oliver Mongan, who lived his own life, not in the real world, but in the Picture House, the Pavilion and the Astoria. When aged eleven, he had fallen through a kind of tear in the educational net and had not been to school since. Instead, each morning he would sit at an upstairs window, and use a pearl-handled revolver to shoot me dead on my way to Prez. He and I had not previously spoken, but one day and to be obliging I clutched at my abdomen and bit the mud of Tubbermore Avenue, and it constituted a kind of introduction. We became best friends. I learned that his mother, who had gone astray in the head after winning £500 in a crossword competition, had taken him out of school, and he was now educating himself. He read *Teach Yourself Psychology* and the works of Emile Coué and Dale Carnegie. He had also joined the Rosicrucians and was learning how to harness and utilise the energy of the cosmos. He believed that, sooner or later, he would be able to bend others to his will by sheer force of personality, and I had his word for it that he would not put this power to evil ends, but use it for the good of mankind. Already, he had acquired a steely penetrating look which he employed sparingly, aware that overuse might blunt its efficacy. Meanwhile, he lived and breathed films even more than I did and had a trunkful of clippings from *Modern Screen* and *Picturegoer*. To him, working in a film renters' office was like dying and going to heaven. It was no use telling him that the place was mean, that its people were sullen and defeated; nothing would do him but to believe that it was a rung, if a lowly one, on the ladder to Hollywood and, in his own case, the long-planned marriage to Joan Fontaine.

Oliver had so unshakeable a sense of his own destiny that I regarded him as a superior being, and his envy afforded me a glow of pleasure. Even so, it hardly justified a lifetime spent with Columbia Pictures or 'The Marvel of the Industry', as it styled itself. The staff were treated as clock-watching malcontents and on that account became so, and the pay, even in the winter of 1945, was insulting. In the event, however, I had even less of a future there than I imagined.

One January day, a grey shawl of rain came down the Liffey from the west, and I thought to go back early to the office and peck out on one of the typewriters the beginning of a short story. (I started at least one story a week, confident each time that, if I could only finish it, Frank O'Connor and Sean O'Faoláin would fold their tents in despair.) As I entered the public office I heard a female voice coming from the alcove where we hung our coats. Evidently, two girls were having a gossip, and it occurred to me to tiptoe over, and leap in front of them with a heart-stopping yell. And so I crept softly to the alcove and made my leap. As for the yell, it hung frozen and unuttered.

Columbia employed a number of 'reps', whose task it was to travel the country hymning the glories of, and taking orders for, Warner Baxter in *Crime Doctor's Strangest Case* and the Three Stooges in *Crash Goes the Hash*. We, the deskbound, envied them as free spirits, and one of them – their doyen, in fact – was at present in the alcove furiously coupling with my bespectacled *vis-à-vis*, the amorphous Dolores.

She was hiccupping as her back thudded against the door leading to the basement. When they saw me, they faltered in their exertions, then quite literally ground to a halt. I stood as if petrified, one forefinger uplifted and my lips still rounded for the 'Boo!' that never came. Probably, I looked like an idiot, but at least I had the consolation that they were not in a mood to say so. As the earth showed no inclination to open beneath my feet, I went to my desk, picked up a pencil and began to scribble on the bare wood without the formality of using a sheet of paper. I was eighteen and almost certainly felt more guilty than they did.

The 'rep' came over to me, and I saw that in adjusting his dress he had skipped a buttonhole so that his flies pointed outwards in a false tumescence. He gave me a raffish Errol Flynn smile.

'Listen,' he said. 'Be a good man and say nothing. You don't want to get the girl into trouble.'

As green as I was, I could still recognise a remark that dictated its own riposte, but even if I had had the audacity to deliver it, there was no time, for he went skipping out into Middle Abbey Street, leaving me with Dolores. She came over, tugging at her skirt, and to my horror I caught a glimpse of old-fashioned pink knickers, mercifully elasticised just above the knees. She sat on her accustomed chair, looked demurely at me through her bottle lenses and said: 'Did you see that fella gone out?'

I nodded, dumbly.

She said: 'Nobody here likes him. He's always trying to talk to me.'

Next day, something worse happened: she began to twinkle at me. Every time I looked up, she was smiling, and once she actually cupped a hand around as much of her bosom as it could contain. It was for a time perplexing, for her wantonness deserved no less than that she have the decency to blush, or at the very least to look away. It was not until later, when I was having lunch at the Goodwill, that the fog lifted and I suddenly knew the reason for the smiles and what I had mistaken for an itchy chest. She had decided that the only way to ensure my silence was by seduction. Whether this was to be in the nature of a bribe or an entrapment was no matter: either carried with it the same terror. The main course that day was shepherd's pie, and I thrust it from me, for once uncaring as to whether I caught consumption or not. Back at Columbia Pictures, she was still smiling. Once, while passing by my chair, she ran her fingers lightly up my spine.

Three months previously, I had sat for a civil service examination and, by coincidence, the results arrived that same weekend. I had won a temporary clerkship. My mother was in a daze of excitement: to her it was the next best thing to my having discovered a vocation for the priesthood. The civil service was respectability incarnate, and anyone who worked in it was, *ipso facto*, a genius. My mother's sister, Chris, had married John Bennett, who was in the Land Commission. In time I was to find out that John's grade was that of Paper Keeper, which was looked upon as an even lower life-form than Clerical Officer, but Chris comported herself as if he were the Minister for Lands. It could justly be said that her marriage to John had marked the first non-Sunday appearance of a collar and tie in the Doyle family, and she never allowed my mother or Uncle Sonny to forget it. Now, a generation later, if one overlooked my uncertain pedigree, the torch had been entrusted to me.

'Of course,' Chris took care to remind my mother over Twenty-Fives on the Sunday evening, 'he'll only be temporary. Not like John.'

'What differ?' my mother said. 'Isn't he made for life?'

She would have disdained to recognise the word 'temporary', even if she had known what it meant. As far as she was concerned, once my foot was inside the door of the civil service I was predestined to end up running the country. She

73

was unshakeable in this, just as she knew that, had I instead chosen the priesthood, I would have been the first Irish pope.

She gave me a look of maternal pride mixed with incredulity. 'Made for life he is,' she said again. 'Tell him, John.'

'Oh, just so,' my uncle said, his face shining.

Everything about him shone: his pink cheeks, his bald head that was pinker still, his gold-rimmed spectacles, his scrubbed fingernails, his shoes. Years before, when I was small, he had worn spats. His soft, courteous voice belied his youthful nick-name of 'the Curser' Bennett. My aunt's unfeigned devotion did not prevent her from managing him with the ruthlessness of a Chinese warlord, coldly telling anyone pass-remarkable enough to put their spoke in that it was for his own good. He was too adoring to protest; in fact, he was the gentlest of men, and it pained me to announce in his presence, never mind in front of my mother, that I did not want to go into the civil service.

To an appalled silence, which I knew would not last long, I tried to explain that, while I could easily escape from Columbia Pictures, becoming a civil servant was like climbing into a coffin and pulling the lid shut after you. This observation provoked a modest spectrum of comment.

My father said that I was a comical boy.

My aunt emitted a tinkling laugh that sounded like an entire orchestra of celestes and made me want to pick up the flat-iron from the fender and hit her with it.

My uncle said with great politeness: 'Well now, do you tell me so?'

My mother said coldly: 'What codology is this?'

She said a great deal more than that, with my aunt contributing the occasional leitmotif. I was unnatural, my mother said, I did not know what I wanted, I would rue the day, this was the thanks she got, this was the price of her, Sonny was right, himself (my father) was not good enough for me, any more than she was. Ironically, my uncle John, in an attempt to restore calm while her rage was as yet merely at gale force, was the one who sealed my fate.

He said: 'Excuse me, Mag, excuse me for interrupting you. But we have only the one life to live, and one road to travel—'

74

'Now don't talk foolish, John,' my aunt murmured. Being herself a literal person, she believed that figures of speech were not good for him.

He leaned towards her. 'What I mean, Chrissie, is that maybe Jack has inclinations of his own. Something more to his liking.'

'He's been offered a bobby's job,' my mother snapped, 'and he's turning his nose up.'

'With the greatest respect, Mag' – no one had ever taken offence at my uncle John and ever would – 'why don't we let him tell us what it is he wants to do?'

'Do you mean let him pick and choose?' she said. 'Much pickin' and choosin' *we* were ever let do. *We* done what we were told.'

She gave me the old familiar look that had a knife in it, then, with her lips closed to the size of a full stop, waited for me to tell her what was a better job than the civil service. My uncle John, risking another reprimand from my aunt, again produced a small metaphor. 'To be sure,' he said, 'Jack's the one who'll follow his star.' He, too, waited.

What I wanted was to become a writer, but I dared not say so. My mother read racing novels by Nat Gould and maudlin romances that were chosen for her by the girl in the tuppence-a-book-a-week shop, but I knew that no tendril of her mind had ever strayed towards the concept that books had authors, never mind that the writing of a book might be a way of life. I had no faith in myself: only longings and the knowledge that if my fever – the desire to write – proved not to be accompanied by the disease itself, then there was no life for me. The hope was so threadlike that one splutter of derision could have snapped it, and so I did not speak up, only sat and looked sullenly at the playing cards spread on our kitchen table and for the moment forgotten.

My mother, sensing victory, punched the side of one small fist into an open hand. 'You'll take that job,' she said, knowing now that I would. 'Be me song, you will!'

Later I consoled myself, rightly or not, that there was more to it than weakness. Bernard Shaw, who had cabbage water for blood, crowed that the true artist, meaning himself, would let his mother drudge for a living sooner than work at anything but his art. I was a weedy adolescent, too myopic to look for horizons. I lacked not only ruthlessness, but also the kind of arrogance which, in the young Shaw's case, saw the world in terms of no one's needs but his own. Another factor was that I had been adopted. My name was Byrne; my foster parents' name was Keyes (it was to be another ten years before I would hopelessly confuse matters by taking a pen name as well); and I had grown up in Dalkey as Jack Keyes. For all my mother's carryings on, she and my father doted on me, and affection is the deadliest of nets. More to the point – and art and artists bedamned! – there was debt that hung over me like a raincloud. And so I gave in, but I found a scapegoat. With my liking for a well-rounded tale, I chose to pretend that of two evils the civil service was the lesser. Columbia Pictures, even at thirty shillings a week, was bearable, but not when one thought of one hundred and forty pounds of elasticised and determined feminine flesh. And so I exchanged Middle Abbey Street for Upper Merrion Street and, shifting the blame from my parents, my aunt and uncle and myself, dumped the lot on Dolores.

Within the week I was sitting at a desk – or a table, as I learned to call it – just up the street from my uncle John. There were perhaps thirty others in the room, which was painted orphanage-green. Its cheerlessness was too absolute to have been accidental; despair semed to have been knowingly mixed in with the paint and ingrained in the dark wooden floor tiles. There was not even a wall calendar as a sign that humans had passed that way; the only small unruliness came from a torn screen on which were pinned a dozen holiday postcards. At the other side of the screen was a woman who, more than any other at that time, was to influence my life. Her name was Kay Kelly. She was our typist and, on my first day, caught sight of the misery on my face, mimicked it most cruelly and within ten minutes had become my friend of ten years. Being myself only eighteen, I took her to be all of forty (she was thirty-two). She was slim; her hair was brown and bobbed. The screen was her way of cutting herself off, not only from draughts, but from the sight of the Staff Officer, Mr Drumm. Once, when she came over to my table for a chat, he arose from his chair and said pointedly: 'Good morning, Miss Kelly.'

She gave him a summer meadow of a smile. 'Good morning, Mr Drumm.'

His nostrils flared, and what had been underlined was now italicised as well. 'I said *good morning*, Miss Kelly.'

It took her a moment to realise that she was being ordered back to her typewriter. She laughed aloud: an unforced bubble of amusement that caused his Adam's apple to jolt to attention. It was as if she had committed the unimaginable *lèse-majesté* of telling him that he was a caution and needed only a clown's red nose to bring the house down. She swished across the room, still laughing.

'What are you going to do with yourself?' she asked me on that first day, her eyes wide. 'And ah, God, no, don't say you're going to be like that crowd of jack-asses, stuck for life in a bog hole.'

She nodded towards the other clerks, most of them middle-aged, who, so as not to wear out their blue serge, had donned the jackets, now ragged and spilling their innards, that they had worn on their first day, perhaps before the 1916 Rising. I did not hesitate, but told her what no one save myself knew. She did not even blink.

'A writer?' she said in a whisper. 'Aren't you great?'

I felt wetness come into my eyes that someone had more faith in me than I myself had. Then she put the icing on my cake and the sun in my sky. 'Can I type your manuscripts?'

Every day, I would catch the 5.14 home from Westland Row and bolt my tea, which, in that last year of what we called the Emergency, was coarse war-time bread and a slice of over-the-ration boiled ham ruthlessly cadged by my mother from Mr Cussen's shop ('God, ma'am, do you want me to starve me own childer?') This was accompanied by the daily and unvarying ritual of intimate discourse with my parents.

My father: 'Well, son, an'thin' strange or startlin'?' (I never knew where he had picked this up.)

Myself: 'No.'

My father: 'So how's the job?'

Myself: 'All right.'

My father: 'Oh, the Land Commission's a great place. Sure you don't know yourself.'

Myself: 'Uhh.'

My mother (muttering): 'Hasn't a word to throw to a dog.'

Then, after a minute, or more probably not that long, at the cold-water tap in the scullery, I was out by the front door, ignoring both the bakelite holy-water font and the shout from my mother: 'Bless yourself before you leave the house!'

My friendship with Oliver was dying a natural death. He had begun what in those days was known as a steady line, and the girl, one Maureen O'Reilly, quickly and correctly recognised me as a natural enemy and embarked on the time-honoured female strategy of divide and conquer. Also, I had recommended Oliver for my job at Columbia Pictures, but to no end. Perhaps, when interviewed by Mr Jay, he had rashly made known his intentions towards Joan Fontaine; at any rate he had been shown the door, and both he and his mother decided that I was to blame. 'You must have dirtied your bib in some way,' Mrs Mongan said balefully. 'Why else would anyone say no to Oliver?' It was a rhetorical question, and for once Oliver disagreed with his mother, never mind that, in the opinion of the town and as a result of her crossword win, she was as daft as a brush. A chill set in.

I found new, less exotic friends. 'The Lads', as they called themselves, went to the pictures or the snooker hall, or for walks when payday, although bidden, would not come. Adventure was not welcome in their lives. Every Sunday and on one weekday evening, each of them went out with his steady girl friend, who was warm, loyal and loved him to distraction, and would sever his head from his body if he dared place a hand above her knee or upon the cliff-edge of her bosom. One day they would marry. My own ambitions were less admirable. Courtship could wait; what I desperately craved was easement from a throbbing libido. The Lads and I talked about girls – not their 'steadies', God forbid, but the pert creatures who paraded

78

in pairs and threes along the sea front – and about what we would do to and with them if only given the chance; what they did not suspect was that I alone meant every word.

Luckily, perhaps, for me and for my mother's fears, I met with little success, 'little' in this case being a euphemism for 'none'. Once, in George's Street in Dun Laoghaire, a girl gave me a sidelong look. As I followed her around a corner into Clarinda Park, I bounced into a navy-blue wall that turned out to be the unyielding front of a policeman. 'Are you following that young one?' he asked. I tried stepping to one side, and so, as if we were waltzing, did he. 'Well?' he said.

My civic spirit was outraged by the suggestion that chasing girls was in some way illegal. For one of the very few times in my life, I told a policeman the truth. 'Yes, I am.'

He clamped a hand on my shoulder. 'Well, get after her, boy, and the best of luck. The little bitch has been asking for it all day.'

Once I had got over the shock, I skipped past him, almost dancing. Naturally, given the kind of luck I was having with women, my prey was by now nowhere to be seen. Clarinda Park had opened and devoured her. I flew blindly in all directions, like a bird trapped in a chimney, then went home and day-dreamed about her for a month, imagining in the most sudorific detail the hours of animal passion that would have ensued had I caught up with her.

Dun Laoghaire policemen were, by the way, a libidinous lot. Once, I was passing the Garda station shortly after midnight, only to be laid hands on by two Guards who were leaning against the spiked railings outside. For a moment, I saw myself as an innocent victim of police brutality, then I realised that they were positioning me between them. 'Stand dere and feast oor eyes on dat,' one said in a ripe Cork accent. I looked and saw a woman taking her clothes off in a bedroom of the Avenue Hotel opposite.

Occasionally, I would stay in town after work and sit in the gods of the Gaiety where for sixpence one could see a double-bill, with Micheál MacLiammoir in *The Man of Destiny* and Hilton Edwards taking forever to expire in *Tsar Paul*. The

Lads were not playgoers, but I persuaded them to accompany me to *John Bull's Other Island*, with Hilton as Broadbent and Micheál as Larry Doyle. The show ran late, and, because there was a tram strike in progress, the others left to catch the last train while I sat to the end. Earlier that day, I had bought a secondhand copy of the play and on the ten-mile walk home kept stopping under street lamps to memorise bits of Larry Doyle's speech in Act One. By the time the lights went out a few minutes after midnight, I had it off by heart and chanted it to myself until, with the night sky already lightening, I fell in through our front door to a cry from upstairs of did I know what time it was.

One day at work a fellow named Moroney asked if I wanted to join an office dramatic society to be called Lancos. In those days I was too cowardly ever to say no, and so I gave him sixpence every Friday and even went to see their first production, which was Patrick Hamilton's *Gaslight*. It is a thriller which I even then found to be not the least bit thrilling, but Kay Kelly, who took a freakishly un-Irish pleasure in the success of her friends, thought it marvellous.

'Buy me a coffee,' she said afterwards. 'Here's the money.' Before I could speak, she said: 'Wasn't it smashing?', and, before I could reply to *that*, she said: 'I think plays are great. Listen, will the pair of us join Lancos?' She answered herself in the same breath. 'Yes, we will.'

I told her: 'I'm already a member.'

She said: 'Well, you sneaky thing,' and led me to Cafolla's for our coffee.

A week or so later, she came up and said: 'It's all arranged.'

'What is?'

'Lancos. I joined. We're doing a programme of one-act plays and I'm producing a French yoke called *Villa for Sale*, and you're to play the part of the man.'

Of the various deaths I had died in the course of my nineteen years, that one was the deadest. She mistook my instant pallor. 'Don't worry about it,' she said. 'It's not actually *in* French.'

I closed my eyes and saw an audience on their feet, not

applauding but throwing things. A feeling, not dissimilar from the nausea I had felt while trampling on Father Creedon's chasuble, came over me. Kay prodded me in the chest until I looked at her. 'Stop fretting. You need it. It'll be *good* for you.' I made no protest, no plea. For one thing, to her whatever I said would have been as insubstantial as fog; I knew that had she wanted to, she could have talked me into leaping out of our third-floor window to fly on carbon paper wings the length of Merrion Street. More disturbingly, I realised that my shyness had a devil inside it that wanted to show off. That evening, I read the 'French yoke'. In fact, I read it twice in case there was a waiter or a comic gendarme whose fleeting appearance I had missed the first time. The one-acter had been written by and for Sacha Guitry so that he might tear up the scenery as a sophisticated *boulevardier* named Gaston. He shared the stage with no one except three awestruck females, and the play ended, as I recall, with:

WIFE *(a querulous creature)*: Gaston, what have you done?

GASTON *(smirking airily)*: I? Earned a hundred thousand francs and a Corot!

(Curtain)

Rehearsals began, and I came to know others in the group. There was Róisín, who had a magnificent lip-curling sneer and would one day play Hedda Gabler to my Tesman; Eva, who was small, demure and wicked and could act the rest of us into the wings; Jimmy Keogh, who ad-libbed and interspersed his lines with verbal sound effects such as 'boinng' and 'gedoink'; and Denis and Jeannie, who were courting, which was just as well, for his voice was contralto and hers, by way of compensation, was a pleasant baritone. We rehearsed twice weekly in a barren unheated room in Gardiner Row, just across from Findlater's Church. Kay's idea of being a producer (nowadays we would say 'director'), was simply to look on and not only gurgle with laughter at every line I stammered, but actually to hold her sides and groan, 'Stop, stop.' This would have helped my self-confidence immeasurably, except that nobody else laughed. One evening, she volunteered a stage direction: 'Take your time here before answering. I know! Why don't you stroke your beard?'

'Ah, Jasus. What beard?'

'Don't be bold. I mean, the beard you'll be wearing. How else will we disguise it that you're too young for the part?'

Her brazenness, considering that it was she who had shanghaied me into murdering Sacha Guitry in the first place, was almost worthy of my mother.

When the first night came, I was catatonic. Someone drew red tramlines on my forehead in a futile attempt to simulate middle-age, and Kay stuck clumps of hair on my chin and upper lip. As the moment came for my entrance, she pushed me towards the stage and said: 'Oh, yes, I meant to tell you. I've used a new chair.' Before I had time to ask her to render this into standard English, a French maid, barely identifiable as Bridie White of Forestry, flung open a door in the set, gave me a saucy curtsey and said: *'Bon jour, monsieur.* Please to come een.' It was at this point, somewhat late in the day, that Kay pressed the buzzer that was the doorbell, causing Bridie to hiss in an un-French accent: 'Ah, Christ, Kay.'

Theatres no longer have footlights. This one did, which meant, mercifully, that the glare kept me from seeing the audience. They were not, however, out of earshot, for I heard the giggle of recognition that greeted each of us as we entered. Someone hissed: 'It's John Keyes Byrne from Collection Branch.' Meanwhile, there was the sensation of having walked into a room which had a sun lamp for a ceiling and was missing a wall. Bridie informed me that Madame would be down presently, threw me another curtsey and was gone. Lifting a bemused eyebrow like Clifton Webb in *Laura*, I took off my homburg, slapped my gloves insouciantly into it and made to place my walking stick on the tallboy as instructed. It was then I realised that, since the dress rehearsal, Kay had turned the set into a nightmare of feminine decor. There was chintz all about; every surface, including that of the tallboy, was crammed with tiny ornaments: vases, a snuff box, a cup and saucer, a candle-snuffer, china kittens. I found myself stopping, holding my stick like a billiard cue and aiming through the clutter. Not one ornament rattled, and a voice from the audience called out: 'Well potted, sir!' A roar went up. Some applauded.

A moment later, Pat Cafferkey came on as the lady of the house and invited me to take a seat. It was then that I saw what Kay had meant about using a new chair, for what Pat was indicating, to her own dismay no less than mine, was a child's rocking chair placed squarely at stage centre. Perhaps Kay had known exactly what she was doing, for, as Pat and I looked at the thing, the audience began to hoot. As the laughter escalated, I rode it instinctively. With no expression on my face except Arctic coldness, I sat very slowly, very carefully, on the tiny rocking chair. Out front, female civil servants were having seizures.

One of the most quoted lines in the history of film comes in *Forty-Second Street*, when Warner Baxter tells Ruby Keeler: 'You're going out a youngster, but you've got to come back a star.' *I* had gone out a petrified adolescent and had come back a ham. The only flaw in the evening came after the performance. A man appeared backstage and Kay, having congratulated me once again, took his arm and went off with him. I was deeply hurt, not because I had a crush on her, but because with the selfishness of the young I thought I owned her. It had never occurred to me that she would be feckless enough to have a life of her own. She was the only one who with utter certitude believed that there was nothing I could not do. A dabbler herself, she opened the door of theatre for me, and if my soul was not destroyed by the years in Merrion Street, I had her to thank.

The opportunity never came. One morning, I entered the office to find Mr Drumm sitting on the edge of his table as he regarded a cluster of women clerks who were squeaking furiously. He was in ripe form. As I signed the attendance book, he said: 'Mr Keyes Byrne, we need not go far to divine the cause of the cluckings in the hen house. There is a note in that particular cacophany that unmistakably betokens the presence of an engagement ring. I should say that our Miss Kelly is leaving us.'

And so she was. A month or so later, she shook hands, told me to keep up with the writing and went off to an eve-of-wedding party for her women friends only. I never heard from her again, but after two years her best friend, Peggy Mulligan, came in, her eyes red from weeping, to say that a month after giving birth to her second child, Kay had died of cancer.

I have a sort of half-fancy of one day arriving at the heavenly gates to be met by her, saying: 'Come on in, hurry up. We're doing a play, and I talked God into being the Protestant minister.' She would, too.

5

Mick, who became my best friend in the Land Commission, worked in a small office in Hume Street which he shared with, among others, a woman so nervous that she jumped in the air whenever he slammed a ledger. At our first meeting, when I was there on official business, he asked, apropos of nothing: 'Did you ever hear tell of Pavlov's dogs?' I said: 'Yes, why?'; whereupon he opened a heavy record book and banged it shut, and I saw a red-faced, tweed-skirted woman levitate, screaming, from her chair. Mick's boss was a bald countryman named Walsh, who had arteriosclerosis and was determined, for the sake of his pension, to stay in the service up to and far beyond the end of whatever usefulness he had had to begin with. Brooding upon his own troubles, he had never connected the slamming of the ledger with the woman's sudden leap in the air. Now, I saw him throw a ruler at her with a shout of 'Are you at it again? Shut up, you banshee, you.' In the Land Commission, eccentrics were the rule rather than the exception; even so, the people in Mick's office seemed to me to have more than the ordinary madness. I learned, in time, that not only did Mick carry anarchy around with him like a germ, but also he infected others.

He had a round, babyish face that gave him a more than passing resemblance to the film actor, Eddie Bracken, who usually played fumbling milquetoasts. Mick, on the other hand, had a military bearing and was a lieutenant in the Local Defence Force, our equivalent of the British Home Guard. He came from the hamlet of Lissycasey near the village of Corofin in County

85

Clare, and our friendship was a collision of opposites. I was a townie; he was country. I was timid; he was brash. As a born romantic, I hoped for the best; as a realist, he awaited the worst. I was a weed who slouched along and was so puny that, even now, whenever I attempt to wear a coat over my shoulders cloaklike, it slides off. He, on the other hand, did not so much walk down a street as lead a victory parade of one, chest out, chin in. He had a brazenness that mocked the taking of offence. Once, we went together to donate blood at Pelican House, and he dutifully answered the list of questions: had he ever had T.B.? whooping cough? smallpox? When the catechism was done, he assumed the look of a village idiot and volunteered: 'I had syphilis twice . . . but I'm better now!' Everyone thought this a scream; had it been I who said it, the consequent silence would have been colder than the plasma on its shelves in the vault.

Even when hardly out of his teens Mick was an accomplished womaniser. I envied him his conquests and his way of sweeping girls along effortlessly, nodding his agreement as they declared – meaning every word of it – that they were going nowhere with him and besides what did he take them for? With hindsight I wonder if, like most Irishmen, he really liked women. Certainly, they adored him, but the act of sex itself may have been a way of showing them up for what he believed them to be. The easier they were, the deeper went his contempt, the more brutal was his rejection. One evening, he called to my house, leaning his bicycle against the front wall. He had been out to Bray where he had picked up a Scotswoman on holiday. Among the gorse bushes on Bray Head he had made to kiss her, whereupon she had said 'Och, for God's sake, kid's stuff!' and pulled him down to her. Afterwards, they had walked into the town and, on catching sight of the Roxy Cinema, she said coyly: 'A true gentleman would treat a lassie to the pictures.' 'Fair enoughski,' Mick said. 'I'll just go and park me bike.' He left her to wait for him by the box office, wheeled his bicycle around the corner, climbed on it and pedalled the six miles to Dalkey and me. I listened to the saga open-mouthed. He finished it by saying: 'I was this side of Killiney by the time I remembered

86

I had these.' He reached into his pocket and produced a pair of woman's knickers.

I was at first shocked beyond measure; then we sniggered. Finally, laughter set in and the pair of us fell about my parents' front garden, guffawing like the young jackasses we were. If I did not see what he had done as brutish, it was perhaps because his exploit had come to me at a remove, and, to use the words of Synge's Pegeen Mike, there was 'a great gap between a gallous story and a dirty deed'. Also, to us, as to our contemporaries, sex education was a thousand dirty jokes, told on street corners and in queues for the pictures. Sex itself, we had been told from the pulpit, was too sinful ever to be romantic, which was probably why we saw females as rather frightening creatures who were not quite human and therefore needed not to be so treated. One windy Sunday afternoon on Dun Laoghaire pier, I saw a girl's skirt blow up, revealing an undergarment that had a large, unmatching patch on the seat. A fellow named Joey Fitpatrick caught sight of it, too, and, although he and I detested each other, he ran over to me, hand outstretched, to celebrate the momentous sighting.

As for Mick, he was the eldest of four brothers. They lived in a tall house in Rathgar with their father, a schoolmaster, and a diminutive aunt named Moll, who tried to impose orders on the bedlam. I can still hear the cry go up of 'Hey, Moll, throw us an oul' ciggie' and see her, complaining for the sake of appearances, as she fumbled for her packet of five Woodbines. Their mother had died when the youngest was born, and Moll had come up from Clare to keep house. Perhaps it is plucking what O'Casey called 'magnificent meanin's' out of nowhere to say so, but I wonder if the death of a mother is not often looked upon as a kind of desertion for which all women must thereafter be punished. If so, it may go part of the way to account for the callousness of Mick's philandering; equally, it could well be home-made psychiatry at its most glib. No matter; what did concern me in those days and for two decades to come was that Mick and I, who were relatively harmless while apart, had the effect, when together, of a detonator upon a bomb.

We were walking by the canal late one evening when I

became aware of a call of nature. 'Piss there,' Mick said, indicating the gable end of a cottage. I thought the place too public for safety and said so.

'Ah, for God's sake, who's going to see you at this hour?' He pointed to a dark stain on the wall. 'Anyway, somebody's been there before you. You have a slash. I'll keep nix,' he said magisterially.

He looked both ways, up and down the canal. I set about my business and was in full spate when I noticed that a policeman had come around the corner of the cottage behind Mick's back and, with massive calmness, was already leafing through his notebook.

'I have ye now, oo dirty bugger oo,' he said. 'Gross indacency in a public place.' He took a ballet step backwards. 'And don't go oorinating on my shoe or 'twill be assault as well.'

I would probably have been sent on my way with no more than a warning had Mick not put his spoke in. 'Hold on there, not so fast. What ever happened to fair play?'

It was as if two of the guard's birthdays had unexpectedly come at once. He smiled upon Mick. 'And who might oo be?'

'Never mind about me. What I'm saying is, you're not going to shanghai him on a trumped-up charge.'

'Mick, shut up.' (This from me.)

The guard waved me to silence. He might have been Toscanini quietening the woodwinds. He said to Mick: 'A trumped-up charge, is it? I suppose you'll tell me that 'twas liminade he was pouring agin the wall?'

I had seen Edward Arnold as Daniel Webster addressing a jury of the damned in a film called *All that Money Can Buy*. He was an earthquake incarnate, but Mick put him in the ha'penny place as he propelled an arm, a hand and a forefinger towards the stain on the wall. Ripples furrowed the black canal water as, in a voice of thunder, he clinched the case for the defence. 'That pee is . . . *not* . . . *all* . . . *his*!'

To my surprise, the guard actually seemed impressed. 'Do you tell me?' he said mildly. His brain seemed to be working slowly, but in the desired direction. 'Right, so,' he said, licking his pencil. 'Grand. So tell me, how much of it is his?'

The upshot was that I was marched by the scruff of the collar as far as Portobello Bridge, with Mick trailing behind, chanting over and over 'I'm his witness', but keeping at a safe distance, just in case it occurred to the guard to charge him with obstruction. As for me, I could already see a headline in my parents' *Irish Press*: DALKEY YOUTH FINED FOR INDECENCY. When we reached the bridge, I heard Mick call my name.

'Listen,' he said. 'I'm off home. But don't worry, I won't see you stuck. They don't know who they're messing with when they mess with us. We'll give them lackery.' He added 'See you' and walked away up Rathmines Road.

The guard was as surprised by the defection as I was. We watched Mick lope off under the street lights. 'That fellow's a sleeveen,' he said. It was a pejorative word meaning a little mountainy fellow, as treacherous as he was unpredictable. Of a sudden, Mick was the real villain, and so my role became that of victim, whose worst sin was consorting with bad company. The guard assumed a gruff voice, said, 'Listen here to me, boy, for Jazus' sake,' and lectured me for ten minutes on the fine art of relieving oneself in public without giving scandal. Then he asked where I worked and, when I mentioned the Land Commission, told me stories of his upbringing on a farm at Ballyagran near Kilmallock. By the time we parted company and he said 'Safe home, now,' I knew that I had missed my last tram. Resigned to walking the ten miles home, I had turned down Richmond Hill, when a voice said 'Howayah?' and Mick appeared from the shadow of a front garden.

Before I could scald him with a look and go swiftly past, he was by my side, keeping step. 'I knew that if I acted the mean louser and did a bunk he'd feel sorry for you. I bet he did, too. Sure he was an oul' softy.'

I looked at him angrily, about to roast him for a Judas. Then I saw that his face contained nothing but transparent honesty and that what I had taken for betrayal was simply one countryman outsmarting another or, more exactly, a Clareman besting a Limerick man. All I could say to him was: 'I've missed my tram.'

'Sure I'll lend you a bike,' Mike said.

I went home with him and pedalled off at high speed an hour later, a glow in my breast from tea and friendship. Mick trotted after me to the corner of Dartry Road and called out to me, five seconds or so too late, that the bicycle had no brakes.

Dr Johnson said that being hanged in a fortnight concentrates the mind wonderfully. The same may be held true of writing a memoir: faced with a blank page, one asks the whys and wherefores of what for years has gone unquestioned: why, for instance, two people as dissimilar as Mick and I should have come together. From the start, he played one role, I another: I knew, for example, that if we were in the same room and he happened to break wind, I was the person at whom people would sniff. It never for a moment occurred to me that I might more safely go through the world with a less volatile friend: one who was not flint to my gunpowder. The answer was that with him, I became airborne. Too timid to trust to my own wings, I used his. For his part, his wildness pushed him towards self-destruction and, being aware of it, he made of me the lifeline that connected him with earth. I gave him a mooring.

He, too, was a member of Lancos, but as an actor he had two defects. One was that he refused to look at you, in the eye or elsewhere. It was as if, with the best of intentions, his gaze had started out towards your forehead, but grew tired on the journey. You looked at him and saw two unfocused buttons, which in moments of acute histrionic emotion, turned upwards like the eyes of a dying El Greco saint. His other handicap was that, on stage and off, he favoured brown army boots which were size 10½. Whenever the time came for his entrance in a play, he was invariably in the dressing room nursing a bottle of stout or shoving the leading lady amorously against a wall. A chorus of whispered cries would go up – 'Mick, you're on!' – and the entire audience would hear the thunder of his boots as he charged towards the stage. On one such occasion an actress froze as he crashed on, taking half the door with him.

Her line was a vexatious 'Do you always come upon people by stealth?', and it stuck in her throat. Mick, thinking that she had forgotten her words, tried to be helpful by saying 'I'm sorry I snuck up on you by stealth,' and it brought the house down.

When I was twenty-two, he caused me to be thrown out of Butlin's holiday camp at Mosney in County Meath. I have never been the kind of person who bounds from his bed with a glad heart to the Tannoyed cry of 'Wakey, wakey!' or who, except under extreme duress, would wear a cardboard Edwardian moustache and sing 'Nelly Dean', but a rumour was sweeping Dublin to the effect that, where sex was concerned, Mosney made Messalina's Rome seem like a Carmelite convent.

It was common knowledge that Englishwomen, their morals in flitters from six years of war, were coming to Ireland to eat farm eggs and butter, unrationed steaks and any young Irishmen they might find. In going to Mosney, my intention, as one of the last-named, was to be as findable as I was edible. It was a coincidence that Mick was at the Gormanstown army base at this time, doing his annual reservist training, and that the two camps, holiday and military, adjoined each other.

I arrived on the Saturday afternoon with perhaps two hundred other holidaymakers and was no sooner off the train than I noticed public toilets labelled 'Lads' and 'Lassies'. As I walked towards the former, a redcoat cried out 'He'll get lost!' This generated roars of mirth from the new arrivals, and I spent fifteen minutes in the toilet waiting for either the crowd or my blushes to go away. It was as inauspicious a beginning as I had feared, notwithstanding the assurances from my colleagues in the Land Commission that my luck was about to change for the better and that I could not fail to return from Mosney either with gonorrhoea or in a test tube.

My chalet mate proved to be a man from Coleraine who was on his second week at Mosney. We had no sooner shaken hands than he asked me if I liked women and, without waiting for an answer, informed me that he had a midnight assignation with a Miss Morris and a Miss Watson, both from Manchester. They had gone, he said, to Dublin for the day, planning to return by the last bus, and had invited him to drop in later and bring a friend. Seeing as how (and I can still hear his Northern accent) both women were, true as God, as hot as mustard, would I oblige? My senses swam. I had hardly set foot in Mosney, and already my virginity was all over bar the panting.

After dinner, the minutes crawled as I waited for midnight when Miss Morris (or perhaps Miss Watson) would make me hers. At last, unable to contain myself for excitement, I thought to pass part of the time by walking the mile or so to the front gate of Gormanston camp to leave a note for Mick. Recovering from manoeuvres with the regular army, he would, I knew, be delighted to learn that my own fortress was at last about to fall. I went out by the front gate of Mosney, and it was as if I were quitting a kind of Shangri-La, for at once rain began to fall in swaying curtains that swept across the flat fields. At the camp gate, I gave a note to the sentry and squelched back to Butlin's, and it was not Shangri-La after all, for the rain kept falling. It made bulls' eyes on the swimming pool and sighed across the Kiddies' Korner and the putting green, then combed through the crab grass and the sand dunes, to become one with the sea. I was soaked through and went straight to the chalet to change my clothes. In the gloom, a naked figure was sitting on my bed.

Never reluctant to clutch at straws, I thought for an instant that the mountain had come to Mahomet and that Miss Morris (or Miss Watson) had returned early from Dublin and, try as she might, had been unable to bank the fires of her passion until midnight. Then I saw that my unclothed visitor was Mick.

'Howayah.'

'What are you doing here? And why are you in your pelt?'

Mick placed my bed pillow modestly upon his lap. 'I was wearing me civvies, ready to go for a jar with the lads. Then I got your note, so I took the short cut by the beach. I got pissed on.'

I switched on the light. Steam was rising from his clothes which he had carefully piled on the other bed. Already the bedspread was soaked. I asked again: 'But what brought you here?'

He said: 'I just thought it might be nice to see you.'

Of course he was lying fit to damn a saint. The person he thought it would be nice to see was not me, but Miss Morris (or Miss Watson). He wanted her for himself. I had been a fool to send the note, and twice the fool to put my chalet number on it. Now I thanked heaven for the rain, for without clothes to wear, he could not follow me to the Englishwomen's chalet, ply them with a fake broth-of-a-boy accent as thick as a doorstep of soda bread ('Now that's a *real* Irish brogue!' they would certainly exclaim, loving it), and steal what was mine, if not by right, then certainly by need. As I changed into my good suit he watched me as if there were only one bottle of stout left in the world and I were drinking it. He said: 'Have you e'er an oul' rag I could put on?'

Coldly: 'No.'

'Well, at least could you dry me suit so's I can go home?'

That seemed reasonable. Anxious to be rid of him, I gathered up his clothes and took them to a nearby building which from its hot breath as one went past I had guessed to be the laundry. On the way, I met a girl who had sat opposite me at dinner. She was dressed up for the evening dance and asked me where I was taking the pile of clothes. It was then that I made yet another mistake. I told her, making a meal of it, about Mick crawling along Mosney beach in the rain and through the barbed wire. 'And if I don't bring his suit back,' I said, chuckling suavely, 'he'll never see Gormanstown again.' She gave me a razor blade of a smile and went on her way.

When I returned to the chalet, my new friend from Coleraine was there with Mick. He was in a foul temper, which had not been improved by the discovery that his bed was all but awash.

'You can sleep there tonight,' he told me, 'for I'm damned if I will.' He added, venomously: 'And you needn't think that either of us is sleeping any place else. We've been shat on from a height.'

He had just come from the chalet occupied by the Misses Morris and Watson. They had returned from their day in Dublin in a state of advanced drunkenness, and the latest bulletin was that Miss Morris (or Miss Watson, perhaps) had been sick into their washbasin, which had promptly clogged up, and that she was now insensible. The Northerner said in disgust: 'I'm going to the Pig and Whistle.' Seeing the dejection on my face, he told me: 'Cheer up, old son. Sure if we don't get them tomorrow night, we'll get their likes.'

For me, there was to be no tomorrow night. Mick went back to camp at two in the morning, shivering in a suit that was still damp; and at lunch time a redcoat came and asked if I would be so good as to call to the Commandant's office. As I left the table I heard the girl from the previous night say: 'That's fixed him.'

The Commandant was British, with flat Brylcreemed hair, and looked as though he should have been in charge of a destroyer in a war film. There was perhaps ten pounds in banknotes and silver on the desk in front of him. He pushed it towards me, then delivered himself icily, as if I were an Ordinary Seaman who had disgraced the ship.

'My information is that you have assisted an unauthorised person to infiltrate the camp. That cannot be permitted. The unused portion of the cost of your holiday is here refunded. The camp police will escort you to the Dublin train.'

I felt like Richard Attenborough in *In Which We Serve*, and even more so when he bade me a clipped, Noel Coward-ish 'Good day'. I was stunned. To my certain knowledge, nobody in all of history had ever been thrown out of a holiday camp; one would as soon be expelled from Mountjoy Prison for hooliganism. On my way back to the chalet, I remembered what the Commandant had said about the camp police, and knew that I must at all costs avoid the crowning shame of being dragged bodily out of Mosney. I packed, ramming my clothes any-which-way into a suitcase, and was slamming the door behind me when two men dressed in blue tunics came around the corner. They were between me and the way to the front gate, so I ran towards the sea, past the paddling pool and the donkey rides. A few people looked around. Terror is the fastest of all runners, and the policemen fell back as I reached the beach and made for Gormanstown camp.

I cannot remember how I made contact with Mick, but I was smuggled into one of the huts and given a cot for the night. That evening there was an impromptu concert in my honour, the high point of which was a soldier, quite naked except for a tin helmet, dancing by candlelight and languidly making his bayonet serve as an ebony walking cane as he sang 'Me and My Shadow'.

Next morning, Mick advised me to go north to Belfast instead of Dublin and home. 'The Orangewomen,' he said, 'have their tongues hanging out for it. You can't miss. Only don't let them know you're a Catholic. If they ask you, say you're a Proddy-dog.' And so I hitchhiked to Drogheda and from there took a train across the border.

It was my first time out of the Republic – or the Free State, as the Northern Irish called it and still do. All was new to me: the Union Jack flew on Royal Avenue; the police wore bottle green and carried guns in tiny holsters. The accents were harsh, the words frugal and workaday, not Sunday morning words as in the south. Everywhere, there were men and women in service uniforms. Even in those days, long before the murderers and their bombs, Belfast was at small risk of being mistaken for a seaside resort, and so I exchanged its red brick for a pleasant guest house in Bangor, nine miles away. On my first morning there, I walked towards the sea front and, along a pleasant sunlit avenue, came across a girl being held at bay by a snarling dog.

She wore a dark uniform. Red hair flared out from under her peaked cap. She was green-eyed. I see her still: a creature out of the better kind of dream. I picked up a small stone and threw it at the dog. Considering my eagerness to play the role of a knight charging to the rescue, the animal was fortunate that I did not pull a garden gate off its hinges and throw that at it as well. At any rate, it fled. The girl gave me a long cool look and said: 'Thanks. Mind, you needn't have bothered.'

Not knowing what to say, I gave her a great tongue-tied shrug.

She said: 'I suppose now I've been picked up.'

I went red and shrugged again, this time almost dislocating my shoulders. We strolled together for the best part of an hour, and, once my accent told her that I had come from the 'Free State', she was friendly and inquisitive in the dry northern way that seems not to give a hang whether you answer or not. The moment came when she said: 'I have to go now.'

'Will I see you again?'

It was her turn to shrug. 'Try Castle Park tomorrow evening.'

Given my appalling luck, I was certain that she would not turn up, but she was there, trim in her uniform, strolling across the grass as if the park were somehow hers. 'It's yourself,' she said with a mocking but not unkindly smile 'the wee mon that saved me from the wolves.' At five feet, eleven inches, I was anything but a wee mon, but I let it pass. We sat beneath a tree and watched the sun go down. We seemed to be the only people in the park, and, after a time, she put her face up and said: 'You'd better get a move on. They close the gates at sunset.' I kissed her, and, what was even better, she kissed me back. Made reckless by success, I unbuttoned her tunic jacket, but when I attempted to do the same to her white blouse she took hold of my wrist and, without seeming to try very hard, held it in a grip that came close to snapping my hand off.

'None of that,' she said pleasantly.

Cunning young devil that I was, I thought to defuse the moment with idle chit-chat. 'By the way,' I said insouciantly. 'I meant to ask. Which of the services are you in?'

'I'm not in the services,' she said. 'I'm in the police.'

It is acknowledged among my friends that whenever I make a mistake I do so in style. I mean that in saying that she was 'in the police', she was too self-deprecating by half. I discovered this later when, on saying goodbye with what began life as a bold peck on the cheek and ended up with a poltroonish handshake, I asked if her parents approved of her choice of profession. She said: 'Well, my father does. But then he'd have to. He's the Chief Constable of Belfast.'

On the train back to Dublin, my virtue as intact as ever, I remembered her with affection and found it easy to forgive Mick for causing my expulsion from Mosney. If bitterness crept in at all, it did so only on one occasion each year for the next decade, when at Christmas I unfailingly received a card inviting me to return to Butlin's for more fun and sun.

*

Love came to Mick with the unexpectedness of summer hailstones. Her name was Angela; she was petite and dark. She told Mick that she was the illegitimate daughter of a well-known tenor, who conceived progeny among his female admirers as readily as he would launch into yet a fourth encore of 'My Mary of the Curling Hair'. On Dun Laoghaire pier one evening, Mick asked me if he should marry her. I was so taken aback that before I had time to segue into my impression of a tribal elder (I was, after all, a year his senior), he came to the nub of his problem.

'You see, what if Angela takes after her oul' one?'

'Pardon?'

'I mean her mother. She let some old ram go all the way with her. I mean, otherwise Angela wouldn't be here, would she? So supposing it was handed down from oul' one to daughter, like. The . . . ah . . .' He swallowed, and the word, when it came out, did so like a foreign body. ' . . . the immorality.'

I looked at the harbour waves, as grey as the stone pillars of the two yacht clubs: the one at the pierhead for bank managers and chief clerks, the other for the kind of ascendant Catholics whose wives affected Protestant accents. Across from us, the mailboat's engines throbbed and the deck lights came on. Mick, it dimly seemed to me, was speaking out against wantonness in women.

'The evenings are drawing in,' I said, just in case I had misunderstood.

'Yeah.' Now that I had allowed him his second wind, he went on. 'I mean, what if it's in the blood and if Angela turns out to be . . .' – he took a breath, and his voice actually trembled – '. . . unfaithful to me?'

Time would teach me that it is commonplace for womanisers to insist upon chasteness in their intended life partners. Mick was, however, out of the ordinary run. It was not Angela's morals that were troubling him, for he and she were, after all, coupling happily whenever darkness or privacy, or both, permitted. She was as sexually avid as he, and he would not have wished her otherwise. It was part and parcel of his contrariness that what ailed him was that, twenty years previously, his future mother-in-law had wanted for virtue.

He continued as if I were not there. 'Of course, for all we know, Angela's mother might have gone all the way only the once. The old get might have given her drink.'

'Why don't you ask her?' I said, trying to be funny.

'Too late. She snuffed it.' Love, blind as it is, does not often see a joke. 'And look at it the other way. A fellow might as easily marry a girl whose oul' one had been getting her oats morning, noon and night, tongue hanging out for it, the town bicycle, like, only she never got caught.' Mick was brightening by the moment. 'Do you know what I think? I think that a girl like Angela's ma was 'ud actually have to be a right innocent to be put up the pole. Would you not agree?'

I said yes, but a trifle absently. The theory that a promiscuous nature could be passed from mother to child had never before occurred to me. Now I began to wonder if my own irregular birth could be the reason for my permanent, if so far unsated, randiness. It was not a possibility that I was likely to discuss with Mick or anyone else, for I would have killed rather than let it be known that I was adopted; in any case, Mick, now that he had ensured Angela's lifelong fidelity by convincing himself that her mother had been more sinned against than sinning, was moving further along his marital agenda. Still using me as his sounding board, he discoursed on ways and means of renting a back basement in Belgrave Square on his clerical officer's pay, which was only a few shillings more than I earned as a temporary clerk. 'If I was to take a spare-time job,' he said, 'and if Angela could put up a few bob as well, then we could swing it in six months.'

He became the evening manager of a filling station. Each afternoon, he would leave his office in Hume Street a few minutes early, pedal like a maniac around St Stephen's Green and up Harcourt Street and arrive on the blow of five, to sit in a glass booth on the forecourt until one in the morning, taking money and giving change. Meanwhile, Angela found a job in Belfast demonstrating gas cookers.

Mick was in charge of three urchins who worked the petrol pumps in exchange for tips. They robbed him blind. He saw them doing so, thought of banging their heads together, but instead felt sorry for them and simply looked on. At the end of the week, he discovered that, as the person in charge, he was expected to make good any losses. Accordingly, his entire pay was forfeit, and, with a warning to pull his socks up, he was forgiven an additional five-and-ninepence. He tendered an Irishman's resignation: which is another way of saying that he did not bother to turn up on the Monday. Meanwhile, Angela, to her delight, was earning twenty pounds each week. In those days, it was the kind of wealth one described more fortunate beings as 'rolling' in. A year of this, she wrote to Mick, and, never mind a back basement in Rathmines, they could put down the deposit on a house. He showed me her letter, keeping his hand over what he called the lovey-dovey bits. 'Tell the truth, is she the berries or is she not?' he asked, pink with pride. He went on about what a bloody great girl he was marrying, and how it was once in a blue moon that a bird was not only an oil painting but had brains as well, but even as he said it I noticed that something had gone wrong with his mouth. In a time long before the word came to be used in the sexual sense, Mick was a chauvinist. Love, admiration, carnal desire: all turned to ashes against the realisation that Angela was earning five times as much as he.

He knew he was a fool for minding; he knew, too, that the money was no more than a means to the glorious end of their soon being always together. He told himself for God's sake to have more sense. Then it came back to him how, after a week in the filling station, with his civil service collared-and-tied mates leering in at him through the window, he had ended up with that deficit of five and ninepence, and the humiliation came eating at him like a rodent. His common sense told him that the money was a blessing; his gut instincts spat at it for an insult. At first, his resentment was unfocussed; then it nagged at him that Angela, even without meaning to, had belittled him. 'Women!' he said, with a sideways grin that pretended to make light of it. 'I know what they're like. Sure Angela's no different. One day she'll use it for a stick to beat me with.'

When I argued with him, he packed me off to those far

suburbs where I was no longer his confidant, at least where Angela was concerned, but I knew that he and she had begun to have fallings-out. He found pretexts for being short with her and, stiff-necked with pride, never as much as hinted that, by earning more than *he*, she had impugned his manhood. I can see his face at this distance: the deceptively weak mouth set hard in the determination to be wrong at whatever cost. As for Angela, being female and in love, she flew, like a homing pigeon, to the conclusion least flattering to herself: that he had tired of her. She came down from Belfast at weekends and sobbed all the way home, late on Sunday.

Mick and I were in a Lancos play at the time. It was Joseph Tomelty's *Is the Priest at Home?*, and one day he rang up to ask if I would meet him for a drink before that evening's rehearsal. It was an unlikely request: we rarely drank, if only because we could not afford to, and when I arrived at whatever pub he had named, I saw that he was carrying a cardboard suitcase. He said: 'Have a jar. I'm off to Dun Laoghaire to catch the boat.'

'The boat? What boat?'

'What do you mean, what boat? The Holyhead boat. I'm getting out.'

He told me an unlikely tale of how, while on his way home the previous evening, he had been accosted by two gurriers, both the worse for drink. Words led to thumbings of the nose; then one of them attempted to kick Mick in the privates, whereupon he had picked up a half-brick – and here I knew it to be a cod of a yarn, for such missiles did not famously abound along Upper Rathmines Road – and flung it. According to his story, it missed its target and went through a chemist's window. Now, to avoid a court case, he was on the run. I asked him why. Had he been recognised? Did the police come? He became vague, ordered whiskies for us both and said that his crippled boss had, like a decent skin, lent him forty pounds, enough for a new start in London. Mick lacked the imagination to weave lies from whole cloth, so I knew that, sure enough, there had been some kind of jack-acting the previous night, but that he had seized upon it as an excuse to escape from the linoleum-runged treadmill of the Land Commission; from his home, which had lost its heart when

100

the old aunt, Moll, had suddenly died a year before; and, most of all, from Angela, who had taken from him his God-ordained role as master of their lives. He ordered more drink. I was not used to spirits, and within an hour we were both legless. I remember telling him with ossified gravity: 'You're making a balls of it. Wrong end of the stick. Man who's . . . who's emigrating ought to be going *to*, not running *from*.' I then sang a spiteful chorus of 'Run, Rabbit, Run' to myself while he was in the lavatory. By the time I streeled after him to the bus stop I could hardly stand upright, but performed small figures of eight, using my hands to stroke the air, like a swimmer staying afloat. A conductor's bell rang twice, and, with a briskness that was the sting of an open hand across the face, he swung himself on board and called out: 'See you, so. I'll drop a line.' There was a cough and a consumptive shudder from the bus, and he was gone to Dun Laoghaire and the mailboat. To the end, I had not believed he would do it. I began to bawl.

It was a lamentable sight for those who chose not to look away: a young man, dead drunk in the middle of O'Connell Street, maudlin tears streaming down his face as, by trying not to weep out loud, he made noises that were immeasurably worse. I looked for my handkerchief, knowing that it was in Dalkey in my good suit. An old woman in a shawl came over to me. 'What's up, son? Are you in trouble?'

I told her with an enormous hiccup of grief: 'Me . . . me friend's gone to England on me.'

She gave a smile that embraced not only me but also the grief of the world. 'Ah, sure God and His Blessed Mother pity you this night.' Then, with an abyss between the saintliness of the tone and the venom of the words, she added: 'An' sure God is good, and the whoor's melt won't have a minute's luck.'

Within a year, Mick was married, but not to Angela. The same mulishness that brought him to Holyhead and beyond kept him from ever returning home, even for a holiday. 'When you leave a place forever,' he told me, insincerity shining from his brow, 'you can leave it only the once.' I saw him six times over the next thirty years, and each meeting was a disaster, usually because we could not let the occasion pass without celebration. I have often been the worse for drink, but only with Mick have I ever been an Irish drunk, with all that that implies: the rowdiness, the messing, the spilt drinks, the cold looks from strangers, the weaving from one pub to the next, the mawkishness that alternates with aggression, the moments of truth that are whole hours of barefaced lies. And, with the years, Mick never relinquished his role as my evil genius.

I met him for the last time in 1969. By then, I had for ten years been a full-time writer and was living in London. Mick telephoned me; he was in Clacton-on-Sea, training to become a teacher in, of all places, a reformatory. A recent television comedy series of mine had achieved a mild *succès de scandale*, and Mick said that if I would drive down and say 'a couple of words to a few of the lads' it would be a feather in his cap. To put it more brutally, for want of a real celebrity I would do to be going on with.

Whenever called upon to speak in public, I have always thoroughly rehearsed the most spontaneous of my remarks, but on this occasion I had a mental picture of myself sitting in a common room, toying with a glass of less than dry sherry and not so much lecturing four or five of Mick's colleagues as enjoying an informal discussion. One of them, tapping the dottle from his pipe, would courteously suggest that television was ('Let us be honest, sir . . .') sedation for the retarded; whereas I, just as Johnsonianly ('Come, sir, if you watch television you refute your own argument; if, on the other hand you do *not* watch it, then how can you possibly . . .'), would with a victor's quiet smile outflank him at every turn. At any rate, I thought it unnecessary to prepare notes or even to hit upon a theme.

I took a wrong turning in Clacton, and when I at last found the training college Mick was at the gate, hopping from one foot to the other. 'C'mon, c'mon,' he said by way of greeting, 'they're waiting for you.' I could not understand the fluster: I was there, after all, to chat with 'a few of the lads'. Mick rushed me up a path and through a concrete labyrinth, and I heard a sound as unmistakable as it was familiar. It was voices: several hundred of them chattering away fiercely as they waited for a performance to begin. I could even tell from the timbre that the show was late in starting and that the audience, captive to begin with, was in restive mood. I looked at Mick, not believing what he had done. One of his fellow trainees remarked afterwards that my face had gone chalk-white. All Mick said was: 'Sure you'll be great.'

He lied: I was not great. To begin with, the audience, wherever they had come from and however entrapped, was the kind that defies conquest: there were two hundred adults and as many schoolboys, so that to enlighten one half was to bore the other. In the event, and invidiously, I bored them all; at one nightmarish point it came to me that I was enmeshed in the coils of a Henry Jamesian sentence and had not the least idea of where or how it would finish. Afterwards, there were no questions from the floor and the audience filed out with the dispirited air of holiday-makers coming home from a fortnight of rain. I stayed for a single glass of sherry that was not so much less than dry as more than sweet. Mick was for once subdued and did not protest when I pleaded an evening engagement in London. I think he felt that I had let him down.

I did not hear from him again until nearly twenty years later, when a chatty letter arrived from New Zealand, looking for 'all the news' from Dublin, as well as the amateur rights to my play, *Da*. Mick was still acting and probably staring his co-stars unflinchingly in the forehead. A fitful correspondence ensued, and I asked him if he would mind having his story told in a book – this one. His reply, as I expected, was: 'Fire away, only don't come the hound.' Later, we again lost touch. Today, while I was actually revising these pages, a letter arrived enclosing photographs of Mick and his lady friend, Helen. He is semi-retired and spends much of his time fishing for trout. Life is good. A separate letter was enclosed from Helen, saying that I would find my friend little changed. By way of demonstrating that the leopard's spots are where they have always been, she mentions that Mick recently had surgery for haemorrhoids and was afterwards grossly overcharged for a jar of laxative which was no more than bran with a sweetener. His response was to telephone an M.P. while the latter was making a radio broadcast and not only aired his grievance, but also acquainted all of the South Island with the more recondite details of what Helen refers to as his anal fissure. Eventually, a local hospital managed to silence him with a year's free supply of laxative.

Mick lives in a town not very far from Invercargill. I looked it up just now in a gazetteer and discovered that it is not only in the South Island but at the southernmost end as well. It is probably coincidence, but, barring Antarctica, it is as far from Ireland as one can get.

6

Amateur actors have one quality in common with professionals: they take superlatives as their due. I have never in my life praised one of them so lavishly that it for one moment crossed his or her mind that I might be overdoing it. Even so, our group – Lancos – was not bad. We attempted O'Casey, Ibsen, Arthur Miller, Eugene O'Neill and the brothers Quintero. Some of our members belonged, too, to the grandly named Dublin Repertory Company, which in fact had no repertoire at all, but favoured allusive plays from the French of Jean-Jacques Bernard, Jean Sarment and François Mauriac. Its presiding genius was a window dresser named Chris Clinton. He rubbed his nose furiously while directing; and his pet words were 'diffident' and 'crystallise'. Reticence was his high altar, and his most frequent instruction was 'Could we have less of the Sweeney Todd?' Plays such as *Le Printemps des autres* and *Le Feu qui reprend mal* were exquisitely boring and, on that account, much admired by the critics and that sizeable minority to whom merely being entertained was as vulgar as eating the heel of a loaf or potatoes with the skins on, and to my surprise I was asked to play Blaise Lebel, the sinister tutor, in Mauriac's *Asmodée*, translated as *The Intruder*. As a piece of miscasting, it bordered on the lunatic. If I had a talent, it was for playing comedy, and I was never funnier than when trying not to be; but, with an amateur's iron ego, I said yes at once, thereby not merely courting disaster, but putting an engagement ring on its finger and naming the day as well.

Asmodée is the story, if one can describe it so strongly,

of a young Englishman who comes to spend a summer with a refined French lady and her daughter. The latter, in the manner of French *ingénues*, has been kept in tremulous ignorance of the world's baser ways, and it is in the nature of things that the young couple should fall in love. They do so; but the mother, a widow, finds that the boy has in all innocence caused passions, long dormant, to come awake in her own bosom. We infer this from her moments of atypical bad temper and a tendency, in the middle of a translation into English, to revert to her native French with small impatient *moues* and murmurs of *'Tiens!'* Not far away is the sinister tutor, who is loved unrequitedly ('Blaise, how can you treat me so?') by the governess, a querulous creature. His amorous sights are set, however hopelessly, upon his employer, the widowed chatelaine.

The young Englishman was played by Tadhg (pronounced 'Taig') Murray, whose acting skills were tempered by a reddish, bony nose, cavernous nostrils, a receding jaw which perpetually sagged in seeming stupefaction, and a swooping Cork accent which turned the simplest prose sentence into a Verdi aria. He lived and died a bachelor, not because he was a homosexual, either overt or latent, but because the landlady of his digs took better care of him, so he said, than a wife ever could. He was the inventor of SPRAWL (the Society for the Prevention and Repression of the American Way of Life) and would pretend that his holidays in the country were recruiting drives. Every summer, I would receive a telegram from West Cork or the Aran Islands saying: 'SPRAWLING ALL OVER THE PLACE.'

We ran for a week at the Peacock, a pocket-sized theatre one floor down from its mother-house, the Abbey, which leased it out to reputable amateurs who, as such, could be trusted not to besmirch the mantles of Synge, Yeats and Lady Gregory. (O'Casey did not as yet merit a mantle; for, by remaining alive, he had failed to comply with the first Irish criterion of greatness.) In the second act of *Asmodée*, the following interchange occurred:

GOVERNESS *(distraught)*: Blaise, is this goodbye, then?

LEBEL *(in a manner that bodes ill)*: On the contrary. You will see me again very soon. *(He goes.)*

My exit obliged me to traverse the width of the stage. As I did so, the image came into my head of Groucho Marx, leering, waggling his eyebrows, tapping his cigar ash and quitting Margaret Dumont's presence at an obscene lope. I did none of those things, but the mental picture must in some way have communicated itself to the audience, for they fell about. In the wings, Chris Clinton stared at me. 'What did you do?'

'Nothing.'

We listened in bemusement to the audience, who continued to shriek in happy memory, but of what I had no idea. On my next appearance, I was greeted with the throb of pleasure which welcomes the return of a well-loved comic who brightens an otherwise cheerless play. Somebody applauded. A lady whispered 'He's come back,' and in that small auditorium her voice was a thunderclap. At once I heard the concerted groan, far worse than the unkindliest of laughter, of a hundred people trying *not* to laugh unkindly. I was supposed to stand at my employer's elbow while she wrote a note summoning her daughter. Peering over Kitty O'Brien's shoulder, I saw that she had written in block capitals: 'FOR GOD'S SAKE WILL YOU STOP IT!' She put the dot under the exclamation mark so savagely that the pen went through the paper. Aloud, she said 'Monsieur, have the kindness to give this to Mademoiselle Elise.' As I walked towards the door, someone whistled Laurel and Hardy's theme tune. Everyone was suddenly having a good time, with the exception of the critic of the *Irish Times*, who next morning said that a talented company's brave attempt at a piece of dramatic filagree had come to nought because of an inept performance in a key role. He named names.

By the time I read the review, I was on the 9.07 a.m. train to Westland Row and work, and it was too late to turn back. All that day, our office echoed to jovial cries of 'Has anybody seen my *Irish Times*?' or 'What's on at the Peacock this week?' That evening at the theatre, everyone was so kind and pitying that I might have had a bereavement. Tadhg Murray consoled me musically: 'Deh *Times* has its hash and parsley, boy, don't mind it. Sure you were shovelling out caviare to deh shaggin' general.' The second-night audience was thin and dispirited, and my exit, which had previously brought the house down, now drew no more than a solitary snigger. The week dragged by, and on the Saturday, when I thought myself free of *Asmodée* for ever, Chris Clinton summoned the cast. Rubbing his nose as if it were Aladdin's lamp, he announced that, to recoup our losses, he had arranged for a Sunday night performance at the Little Flower Hall in Bray, twelve miles from town.

'It'll be a Sweeney Todd audience,' he said, 'so for once let us not be diffident.'

What he was saying was that Bray playgoers had forthright tastes, and, if they could not have the homespun comedies of Lennox Robinson, then they wanted drama that was full-blooded, such as Bryan McMahon's *The Bugle in the Blood* or George Shiels's *The Rugged Path*. The rarefied nature of *Asmodée*, with one Gallic nuance swooning upon another, was likely to cause murmurs, if not aggrieved cries, of 'Codology'. It was hardly, as Chris advised us, an occasion for 'diffidence'.

In the event, we did not commit the sin of over-acting; rather, we put into the play what Mauriac had been so foolish as to leave out. To the devil with pussyfooting: we gave them drama and knew we had a success on our hands when an excited whisper was heard from the audience of, 'God, the mother's in love with the young lad.' As for me, I had at last hit a kind of stride. In the play, my character was a spoiled priest, and on that account the audience, being Irish and mostly Catholic, took a proprietary interest in me. During Act Two, when I was giving what I knew in my bones was a three-dimensional portrayal of a man brought low by sins of the flesh, a child began to cry in the audience. Its mother and a few others hushed it, at which, delighted by what it took for encouragement, it turned up the volume. It and I competed for some few minutes; then the mother, at the end of her endurance, turned upon the infant with a howl of: 'Shut up! Shut up, or I'll get him down to you!' She was, of course, referring to me.

Unless he happens to be playing in Grand Guignol, it is never pleasurable for an actor to find himself brandished like a fist at delinquent children. It is even worse when he is giving a performance which, if there were justice in the world, would

108

draw tears from a turnip. It is a knife-blade in the heart when, seemingly in response to its mother's threat, the infant becomes instantly docile – and that is what happened in the Little Flower Hall. The child's silence was an invitation to the audience to look upon me with new eyes. They happily did so, and my acting career went sharply downhill, reaching bottom with the climactic scene between the tutor and his employer.

'Madame' has discovered that the young Englishman is not for her; she must send the lovers away, pick up the shards of her own broken life and survive as best she can. Seizing his opportunity, the tutor tells her that all is not lost; happiness may still be hers if she will but choose a half-loaf over no bread. To this end, I had what an actor loves most in the world after money: a four-minute speech; and it ended with the words, tenderly spoken: 'Are you listening, Marcelle? Are you listening?'

As the script demanded, there was a suspenseful pause, and then Kitty O'Brien turned to me with ice-blue eyes and delivered the ultimate rebuff. 'I beg your pardon, Monsieur Lebel,' she said, 'but I thought I heard you call me by my first name.'

Humiliated, I was supposed to mumble abjectly and slink off, but before I could do so a female voice from the audience spoke out clearly. Evidently its owner was one of my few remaining admirers, for what she said was: 'Ah, the poor fucker, he's done for now.'

Twenty years later, I took a curtain-call from the stage of the Kurfurstendamm Theatre in Berlin. I had written a play which was not unanimously liked, and booing broke out from the rear of the stalls. I felt the smile on my face become a rictus, and, to survive the barrage, ransacked my mind for an even worse débâcle. Into my head came that Sunday evening in Bray. The audience on that occasion did not boo: they shrieked. They howled like ruptured sewage pipes; utter strangers fell sobbing into each others' laps; a man toppled off his chair.

My first instinct was to get off the stage and out of Bray; then I remembered that this evening marked my last ever performance as Blaise Lebel. I saw myself months – perhaps years

– in the future recalling the ignominy of this swan-song and going red with shame. A cold anger came over me. I was damned if I would allow the Philistines to win; just this once, I would have my way with them. I stood stockstill, now facing the audience, with Kitty O'Brien staring at me, wondering why I had not yet gone. Then, with a daring that was not in my nature, I raised a hand for silence. To my delirium, it worked: the laughter slackened and died away with a last gurgle like the farewell of water in a bath. With the audience back in the hollow of my hand, I turned to Kitty and ad libbed a line, delivering it with consummate dignity.

'Goodbye, madame. I think it unlikely that we shall meet again.'

It was my finest hour and, leaving the stage, I could feel an ovation welling up and about to erupt. Unfortunately, my way off was by way of a flight of stairs, which was no more than three wooden steps, the topmost vanishing behind a piece of scenery. Once an actor had attained this summit and was safely out of sight of the audience, he did a careful about-turn, knelt and just as gingerly lowered himself to stage level. Such was the panache of my exit, however, that I not only took the stairs at a run, but did so two steps at a time. There were, as I have said, three of them in all.

In mid-air, my hands, shooting out for a means of breaking my fall, found and seized upon a length of rope or thick cord hanging from above. I have no idea what it was attached to, but it held and I swung like Tarzan on a vine, not further into the wings, but back on to the stage, carrying a part of the château wall with me. The flat – a sheet of canvas stretched on a wooden frame – fell forwards and sent up a cloud of dust. It was not dense enough, however, to hide the sight of me coming in to land, or of Tadhg Murray, industriously buttoning his flies preparatory to his entrance.

Kitty O'Brien looked at me as if under the impression that I should by now be at the local S.N.C.F. station waiting for the Paris train. Her lips parted as if to speak, but the manner of my return, not to mention the dust storm, had routed all thought from her mind, and her mouth closed again like a steel trap. It would be nice to record that a *bon mot* tripped off my tongue, but all I managed to say was a whispered, 'Sorry Kitty I mean Madame.' It went unheard, but it was no matter. Laughter again billowed from out front and crashed like breakers on an alien shore. I heard a chair fall over. People were saying, 'Stop, stop.' You knew that months and perhaps years from now, old people would wake up in the small hours, think of this evening and choke to death, their elbows stabbing the air in anguished entreaty that a priest be sent for. As for me, there was nothing to do but attempt to leave the stage for a second time. Understandably, I was distraught; otherwise, I would not have gone up the steps again.

My course was set before I realised that the collapse of the flat had revealed the stairs in their pathetic entirety. I was at the top of the three steps in a trice, and stood there like a gold medallist in the Idiots' Olympics. It was an image that may have occurred to members of the audience, for applause broke out. As to the means of getting down, I was for a moment undecided, then leaped boldly towards the wings, hardly noticing Chris Clinton and Tadhg Murray, who, in full view of the audience, were struggling to hoist the flat back into place.

In the last scene of *Asmodée*, the young couple have gone away and the household has resumed its quiet tenor. Madame looks at the recalcitrant tutor, now and forever brought to heel, and says: 'You may read to me, Monsieur Lebel.' Whereupon, taking a volume from the bookcase, I would say 'Flaubert, Madame?' and bring the play to its end by adding somewhat coyly: 'Perhaps *L'Éducation Sentimentale*?' On this Sunday evening, the curtain fell when Kitty O'Brien went to the French windows, looked out into the gathering dusk and cooed: 'Monsieur Lebel, will you come and read to me?' She had little choice because by then, I was already past Shankhill, pedalling furiously towards home and still wearing my stage make-up: a patina of number 3½ Leichner grease paint, eye-shadow, a crow's nest or two, and a satanic white streak in my hair.

My intention was never to return to Bray, but a month or so later an amateur actor, in his *alter ego* of electrician, fell off the roof of the town hall, and at a weekend's notice I was asked to take over his part in Paul Vincent Carroll's *The Old Foolishness*. That was when I first encountered Father Maurice Browne. He was senior curate of Bray, a Tipperary man and greyhound fancier. He was tall, balding, suave and autocratically benign. His walk was patrician, his smile gracious. When you spoke to him, his ear swung towards you so that you could count its hairs, but his pale blue eyes twinkled at passers-by, as if inviting them to witness his readiness to humour even the most lowly of God's beings. His condescension was natural and unforced; as a man of simple faith, he never wavered in the belief that he was doted upon by his parishioners. He had written a novel of country life entitled *The Big Sycamore* and was presently at work upon a play, *Prelude to Victory*, set in the days of the Black and Tans and rabidly anglophobic. He promised to write me what he called a plum role, and, when the time came, I was cast as 'Third Black and Tan', with one line: 'Which w'y did the bawstid double back?' – an enquiry which, when one thought about it, seemed to answer itself.

Like most of Paul Vincent Carroll's plays, *The Old Foolishness* had as one of its major characters a tyrannical canon, compared with whom Edward Moulton Barrett would have seemed not only of sunny temperament but positively waggish as well. In the Bray production, this cleric was played by a mild fellow named Peter Nolan, whom short-sightedness had endowed with a scowl of direst villainy; also, his rented suit, originally of clerical black, had turned green with age and gave him the appearance of a troll. Before the first act was over, a small queue had formed outside the presbytery to lodge a complaint with Father Browne in his capacity as priest, local censor and cultural guru. He came backstage after the performance and beamed upon us.

We were great, he said. Oh, topping; grand, A.1. And there was not an iota of harm in the play. Sure no one minded the man Carroll. What was he and writers the likes of him but poor blades of apostate chaff cut down by the winnowing wind of Heaven?

Possibly, I emitted a small snort of mirth at the alliteration, for his gaze fell on me, calm and smiling.

'Ah,' he said, 'we have a newcomer among us. From the city, I have no doubt.'

'He's from Dalkey, Father,' the group's leading actress, Ronnie Byrne, volunteered, adding: 'He took over from Colbert Martin.'

'Do you tell me? And from Dalkey.' He kept me trapped in the kindly searchlights of his eyes. 'Ah, a grand little town, part of the borough of Dun Laoghaire, home of the West Britons, or do I mean the Little Englanders, what would we do without them? And you're a grand actor, yes, you are. All I was privileged to see of you was in Act Three, but I split my sides. However, the Bray people (sure God love them) are not as well up in the ways of the world as, dare I say it, the inhabitants of the Pale. Not as sophisticated as your excellent self, have you me?'

Artful devil that he was, he waited for an answer and got it: a cowed and barely audible 'Yes, Father.' It was Father Creedon over again, but this time the de luxe streamlined version.

Having settled my hash, he bathed the others in the soup-kitchen glow of his affection. Every one of them lived in the town and was known to him, and he addressed them as if he and they were fellow-conspirators. He told them that as good Catholics all – the three Protestants among them went red with shame and looked at the floor – the innocence of the devout, simple people of Bray was in their hands. Rather than become an occasion of scandal, let them not squander their time and talent on such unworthy babblings as *The Old Foolishness*.

One of the company piped up: 'Sure we weren't planning to do it again, Father . . .'

'Ah, grand.'

'. . . only at the Killarney drama festival next Sunday.'

Father Browne laughed with warm incredulity. 'Killarney? Do you mean it is your intention to perform this play, for want of a better name, in front of poor country people? And this is how the town of Bray is to be represented in the county of Kerry? No, you are making mock of me.'

We all gaped at him. The silence ended when he suddenly said 'God bless you all' and went quickly out of the hall, having first made the sign of the cross at us, concluding it with a lateral gesture that, had his fingers been a razor blade, would

113

have slashed every throat in the place. He was gone before I realised that our play was banned.

'He can't stop us from bringing it to Killarney,' I said, at once earning the snarled reply: 'You don't have to live here.'

Censorship carried the day, and the group replaced *The Old Foolishness* with *Frieda*, a tame melodrama from their previous season. It was the story of a German war-bride who arouses strong, if well-bred, emotions among her husband's Loamshire family, and once again I inherited a role originally played by Colbert Martin, he of the town-hall roof. It was the tiny role of the local vicar, and, being a quick study, I left the business of learning my few lines on the long finger: an hour's mugging up would suffice. I had never been to Killarney, however, and that glorious summer day was spent lolling in a rowing boat on Lough Leane, one's senses blind drunk with the restless light that upon an instant created new mountains and as quickly exchanged them for old.

My words that evening were uncertain, but I wobbled through as far as my exit line: 'Remember what St Paul says: "Be not zealous over-much." ' Instead, it came out as " '. . . be not over-zealous muchly." ' No one laughed; probably the audience assumed that 'muchly' was effetely upper-class English. In any case, the plays at Killarney were no more than an appetiser before the banquet itself: this being the appearance on-stage of the adjudicator, Michéal Mac Liammóir.

I had, of course, seen him countless times at the Gaiety and the Gate. His saints were Wilde and Beardsley. He wore stage make-up in public, varying it subtly with the seasons so that he was not tanned in winter or merely pink in summer, and sported an unlikely wig of jet black. His voice did not speak, but crooned; it told of an explosion in a caramel factory; it flowed over its listeners, drowning all in its path, rolling in languorous flood over the weirs of stops and commas, stopping to draw breath not even between words but within them. He could not or would not pronounce the sound 'ow'; from his lips, a particular sentence, a favourite of elocutionists, would have emerged as a ripe 'Ho no, brrrone co'. He believed in the theatre as a temple of which, an unregenerate Edwardian,

114

he was high priest. The jargon of theatre includes the term 'throwaway lines'; Mac Liammóir never threw away a word in his life.

In the town hall at Killarney, he came upon the stage as we the actors stood behind him. He bowed to us, turned to the audience, placed the back of one hand against his forehead as if to avert a swoon, then summarised *Frieda* in one great non-stop exhalation: 'Ladies and gentlemen this is the kind of play you know the kind of play it is Father's dead pass the marmalade.'

He went on to hold forth upon some of the performances, weaving not so much a tapestry of words, as a verbal Book of Kells, illuminating his manuscript in mid-flight. Of our young leading lady, Annaliese Fuchs, he deduced, correctly, that she was not German but Austrian and, like Professor Higgins homing in on a Lisson Grove accent, actually named the Viennese suburb where she had grown up. He let us off lightly, but as soon as the curtain had fallen he enfolded a terrified Ronnie Byrne in a Don Juan embrace and said: 'Oh, my poor naughty darling, was I awfully cruel to you?' Catching sight of me as I looked on, he said: 'Ah the reverrrend gentleman. You were marvellous, did I mention you?' Before I could reply, he dragged me over to a leather-bound notebook that lay open on his lectern. 'There! That's what I said about you,' he exclaimed for all to hear and slammed the book shut before I could read a syllable.

Years later, while reviewing for *Plays and Players*, I was so intemperate as to speak ill of Mac Liammóir's Claudius, damning it as 'the same old glutinous marzipan'. Although we had not yet met, apart from that moment in Killarney town hall, he kept the clipping in his wallet and would read it aloud on public occasions – once at a luncheon where, mortified, I was present. It was years before he forgave me, if he ever did. Towards the end of his life, I wrote a piece describing him and his partner, Hilton Edwards, as a pair of 'incorrigible Renaissance men'. He wrote me a long, effusive letter quoting from *Twelfth Night*: 'I can no other answer but make thanks, and thanks and ever thanks'; and ended by advising me: 'Jack, never grow old.'

The last time I saw him was at a party. He was thin; his legs had become spindly and weak. He had given up wearing his wig, revealing, to everyone's amazement, a perfectly good head of hair underneath, and had recently undergone an operation for cataracts. A pair of horn-rimmed spectacles now hung around his neck, but he was too vain to wear them in public. When the time came to go downstairs for supper, I saw that he was unsteady on his feet and asked if I could take his arm.

He said, the voice still a word-caressing purr: 'No, darling Jack, but I'll tell you what we can do. As we go down, walk behind me with your good right hand on my left shoulder and your dear face not far from mine. In that way, you can guide me while we pretend to be having a *tête-à-tête.*'

When he died a few months later, he took the precious little that was glamorous about Irish theatre with him.

As for Father Browne, he was later promoted out of Bray and became parish priest of Ballymore Eustace in County Kildare, but still I had not seen the last of him. It was the policy of Lancos Productions to mount two plays each year: one, a glossy affair, done to show our colleagues at work that we were really too good for the likes of them; the second, a crowd-pleaser which toured to country villages, with the profits halved between the local priests and ourselves. Word came from Father Browne that we would not be unwelcome in Ballymore Eustace. A high tea would be provided.

We arrived by bus and went, as directed, to a café where a woman put a cup of tea and a small triangular ham sandwich in front of each of us. A heroic soul asked for another sandwich. 'Only the one has been paid for,' the woman told him and the rest of us, with a look that all but turned the milk in its jug. It needed only Wackford Squeers to explode upon the scene with a cry of 'Here's richness!'

Outside the parochial hall, Father Browne greeted us affably, his eyes fixed, as usual, on a point somewhere down the street. His genius as an impresario was shortly in evidence, to a degree where we had cause to reflect that Rome's gain was Broadway's and the West End's loss. It was a Sunday, and, as soon as the evening devotions were over, his curates and a small band of parish elders assumed the roles of German shepherd dogs, driving the worshippers from church to hall as if they were sheep on their way to be dipped. Only a handful of the poor devils struck out for open country and escaped. The hall filled up to the point where one could not have introduced a cat without the danger of mass suffocation. Those unable to find chairs sat on the bare floor, the window sills and the radiators; a few young gymnasts were actually astride the rafters high up under the roof.

I squinted out through the curtain and calculated that our share of the night's proceedings would go far towards fulfilling our dream of some day travelling to one of the British drama festivals. Father Browne was at my elbow. I said: 'What a crowd. I've never seen any thing like it.'

'Well you may say so,' he replied gravely. 'Oh, a washout.'

I searched his face for a sign that he was joking.

He sighed: 'Well, that's Ballymore Eustace for you. Ballymore Useless is more like. Oh, a hopeless people. They'll support nothing.'

He had had to raise his voice to be heard over the babel from the audience. As he walked away with a smile that King Lear would not have scorned to use, I took another look through the curtains just in case what I had seen the first time had been an hallucination brought on by hunger.

Our play was *Cartney and Keaveney*, a sour farce by George Shiels, a crippled writer who wrote crippled comedies in which cupidity always won and the devil had the best tunes. I played Cartney, a sponging ne'er-do-well who ends up coercing landlord and employer into supporting him rent-free and work-free for life. Rural audiences loved its rascality, and the packed house at Ballymore Eustace cheered us to the crowded rafters. Afterwards, Father Browne conducted the mandatory raffle for two hundred cigarettes.

'Let us now ask Cartney to draw the winning ticket,' he said, eyeing me and chuckling. 'Given the kind of scoundrel he is, he might draw out his own.' Adoring laughter broke out.

And so he himself conducted the draw, announced the winning number, only to see me, brandishing a raffle ticket, come forward to claim the prize. For once, his smile slipped as I accepted the ten packs of Capstan without having the decency to implore that they be raffled again. A few weeks later, he wrote to us, reiterating that the occasion had been a 'washout' and sprinkling vinegar on the wound by adding that our high tea had used up the few miserable shillings taken at the door. His letter was accompanied by a small box of chocolates for the ladies of our company. In a spirit of pure malice, I sent him an invoice for his half of the performance fee. He replied saying that the evening's proceeds, had there been any, would have gone towards the needs of the parish, therefore the question of paying royalties did not arise. The uncorrupted ways of the country, he reminded me, if he could make so bold, were not the ways of the city, where the pound note was God Almighty.

We steered clear of Father Browne after that, which in a way was a pity, for our production of *The Righteous are Bold* would have gone like a house on fire in Ballymore Eustace. It was a melodrama in which a girl returns home to County Mayo after working as a servant in London, where her employers obliged her to participate at a séance. She is hardly back under her parents' thatch than she has spat upon and decapitated a statuette of the Virgin (the play was an Abbey Theatre stalwart, and the programme invariably featured a note saying 'The holy statues broken in this production have not been blessed'). In Act Two, the wise old parish priest diagnoses the girl's problem: she is a victim of diabolic possession. The third act contains the exorcism and ends with the death of the priest, which, in accordance with spiritual swings-and-roundabouts, is deemed obligatory in such proceedings.

Our visit to Blessington on the edge of the Wicklow hills met with such acclaim that we were invited to give a return performance. There was a national petrol strike on at the time, and no buses were running on Sundays; undaunted, the local priests possessed what they called 'a great leg' of the local undertaker and had us conveyed the sixteen miles from town by hearse and two mourning coaches. The brace of curates were the jolliest of fellows and as plump as capons, and had so much enjoyed the play on its previous visit that, without a word to us, they had contrived to enliven the evening with a few special effects. The first of these occurred early in Act Two when I, as the old priest, was putting a flea in the ear of the local doctor, an agnostic. The latter role was played by a man whom I shall call Jim Beamish, a barrel-chested ex-army captain with a fiery military moustache, who happened to be a roaring alcoholic. He had only recently dried out from an eighteen-month rampage and, for a big man, looked as if a summer breeze could be the end of him. His face had a pink, damp look.

'Doctor,' I said to him suavely, 'have you ever heard of a person being possessed of the devil?'

On the instant, there came an apocalyptic clap of thunder and the stage was enveloped in light of a hellish green. The audience screamed in an ecstasy of terror. Cries were heard of 'Oh, Jesus, Mary and Joseph'. The lights flickered and reverted to normal, but Beamish's face remained as green as if it had been dyed. His forehead shone. In reply to my line, he was supposed to say: 'Possessed of the devil, Father? I thought that you of all clerics were immune from such superstitious mumbo-jumbo.' What he actually said was: 'Christ, I'm in the jigs.'

He was not heard out front; the audience was chattering like rooks at sunset, telling each other what an unmerciful fright they had had. I seized the opportunity to try and steer the play back on course and fed Beamish my next line, which was 'My dear doctor, it is a foolhardy man who denies the existence of Lucifer.' At this, the thunder crashed again and the stage was once more bathed in a corpselike green. Beamish began to tremble all over like a condemned tenement when a train goes past.

It was now clear that we had only to mention the devil, Lucifer or Beelzebub for one curate, standing in the wings, to rattle his home-made thunder-sheet, while the other had the time of his life switching on and off the green fairy lights he had so lovingly strung above the stage. Beamish gave every sign of dropping dead at the next thunderclap, and so, thinking frantically ahead, I managed to get to the end of our scene by cutting every further reference to the powers of darkness. In the context of the play, it was like performing *Othello* without the kerchief or *Antony and Cleopatra* minus the asp.

Worse was to follow during the exorcism scene in Act Three. Audiences never failed to thrill to the sight of our star actress, Róisín Ni Nualláin (an understandable alternative to Rosie Nolan), bound hand and foot, writhing on the floor at my feet and spitting out what came as near to obscenities as an Irish parish hall could contain in the year 1954. During the interval, the ladies of the company had with much kissing and cooing and fluttering of eyelids restrained Jim Beamish from fleeing to the nearby Downshire House for a ball of malt, so that he was back on-stage, even if now crushed in spirit and only there as so much human furniture.

We came to what Americans call the 'top of the show'. Roisín, who was a niece of the comedian and pantomime dame, Jimmy O'Dea, had eyes as expressive as his. Also, and as I have said, she could curl her lower lip into the most malignant of sneers, and during the exorcism it came close to resembling a Swiss roll. She snarled and spewed out execrations, her bound feet kicking at whoever came near, while the audience sat dumb and whey-faced with horror. I began the business of casting out the demons: *'Exorciso te, immundissime spirituus . . .'* Out of the corner of my eye, I saw what was unmistakably a double-barrel of a shotgun poking out from the wings.

As Róisín emitted an ear-piercing scream to signal that the devil was quitting her body, there was an explosion that Father Browne could have heard in Ballymore Eustace seven miles away. A ball of fire travelled across the stage, and Róisín, as if by way of suggesting that Lucifer was still within her, achieved spontaneous levitation from a supine position to a height of several inches.

All that remained to happen was for the old priest to expire, presumably from heart failure, and in my condition it required not much acting ability. Jim Beamish, perspiring again, but now to a degree where he was fast dehydrating, managed to pronounce me dead and closed my eyes, his hands shaking so badly that I was unable to read small print for a week. As we took our curtain call, the parish priest of Blessington came on the stage.

Compared with his jovial curates, he was of the old school and had probably first been given nightmares by the Redemptorists when he was six or seven. Calling us Cosmos Productions, he offered his admiration for such a thought-provoking drama; then, without putting a tooth in it, he told the audience that what they had seen was the kind of thing that happened to Irish girls who went to work in England. There were no exceptions, he said grimly. He then conducted a raffle for a bottle of Paddy.

By then, Jim Beamish had left the hall, and although it was now after licensing hours, found a publican who assisted him to alight from the water-wagon, and down the years was never again seen on or in the vicinity of that vehicle. The audience, on emerging into the unlit street, found themselves confronted by the village hearse which, unknown to them, was waiting to take the actors back to town. When a group of us climbed into the rear, some of the onlookers were reassured, others not.

As we drove off, people hung around in small bunches, afraid to walk the country roads home. That was two or three years before the first coming of television, and soon thereafter ghosts and the devil lost their power to frighten. It is perhaps a pity that when ignorance is laid to rest it must often take simplicity with it.

7

Once, at a party, I overheard a woman guest speaking to my daughter, who was then sixteen. She was using the kind of orphans-picnic voice that carefully spoons out a word at a time and has been put by for encounters with small children, mental defectives and people who read lips. 'What,' the lady wanted to know, 'will you do when you leave school?'

'I want to get out of here,' my daughter said.

I had been standing just to one side, glass in hand, smiling a half-smile on which I could either freewheel into the conversation or pedal away from it, as I chose. Before the smile could lose its footing, I bore it and the hurt, cold in my stomach, to the front window of our living room. The immediate 'here' my daughter had mentioned was the house we had moved into on our return from an exile in London. It looked out towards Wales, and on one or two sharp days each winter one could see the white cap of Snowdon, a shard of broken delph trodden into the sea. Off to the south, the Wicklow Mountains, like Edwardians on Whitsun, walked primly along the curve of Shanganagh. As well as our house, we had two acres of grass to lie in, an old tree, soft rain from the south-west and sunlight that stung the eyes. There were worse places to live. In the wider sense, the 'here' she wanted to get out of might have been Ireland as a whole, which was understandable. If, as Napoleon said, *tout soldat français porte dans sa giberne le bâton de maréchal de France*, it is equally true that, pinned behind every Irish First Communicant's rosette, there is a one-way mailboat ticket to Holyhead.

Less easy to face was the thought that she might have wished to be quit of her mother and me. It was unthinkable, and yet, just as every actor will accept as his due his one hostile notice amid an avalanche of praise, I unhesitatingly ran to embrace the idea that my wife and I had somehow failed our darling. All her life, we had tried to walk the razor edge between sternness and over-indulgence; in her teens, we treated her not as the child-that-had-once-been, but as the adult-that-was-soon-to-be. As parents, and not at all by design, my wife and I complemented each other to perfection. She could endure a crippling bereavement dry-eyed, and yet would openly lavish affection upon our daughter, one or two friends and all animals, rodents excluded. I, on the other hand, would sob uncontrollably at *La Bohème* or even at such bathos as Merle Oberon dying in Olivier's arms in *Wuthering Heights*, and yet was so incapable of physically embracing those I loved that I would go to absurd lengths to make plain that my fondness for them was not absent, merely lurking. My wife provided her daughter with food, love and warm clothes, nursed her when she was ill, drove her to school and attended the parent-teacher meetings that I shirked. I saw to it that *my* daughter walked in St Mark's Square, ate sauerkraut in the Alsterpavilion in Hamburg, saw *Robert and Elizabeth* from the front row, and read Maugham when she was eleven and Wodehouse – who was the more serious writer – when she was twelve.

These days, what my wife and I have come to share is less a daughter than a best friend; but for perhaps a week after hearing her so casually say 'I want to get out of here', I caressed my pain as if it were a lover's gift. I have always soon grown tired of my toys, and, once I became bored with being hurt, I grew up another millionth of an inch – it happens even now – and accepted that she simply craved for her freedom. Nothing, as they say, personal. She wanted her four years at Trinity, a roof of her own, and a life and an identity that were hers and not ours. Her bags were already packed. At her age, I had been just as eager to be on my way, but there was a difference. She was impatient for what lay ahead; I was uncaring as to what the future held: I simply wanted to escape from my parents and our town.

One evening, when I was perhaps twenty, I accompanied my father to the parochial hall to play House, which elsewhere was known as housey-housey, but would attain its apotheosis as Bingo. I have no idea why I went with him: possibly there was nothing worth seeing at the Picture House, the Pavilion or the Astoria; or perhaps my conscience told me it was high time I kept him company for an hour. Rather, I think I was making a half-hearted attempt to be part of the town, to put on boots that for once were not too big for me. I was not locally regarded as special, still less as a prodigy, but I had won a scholarship to a school for the sons of bank managers and pork butchers and had made matters worse by soaring far above the Dalkey earthlings and into the civil service (no one realised or, if told, would believe the very real degradation of what my mother proudly described to our neighbours as a 'bobby's job'). Also, I kept my nose in a book as I walked along; I was never out of picture houses and had not a word to throw to a dog. The town's verdict was that if you were eejit enough to adopt a nurse-child, I, in the heel of the hunt, was what you were liable to end up with. The House players were exclusively male; married women were supposed to stay contentedly at home, while the unmarried kind were either out courting or indoors offering up their acne, gift wrapping it for God, with rosary beads as string. I caught sight of my father's friends, Oats Nolan and Gunger Hammond. He went over to talk to them, and I heard him fire off his opening round: an immutable 'Do yous know what I'm going to tell yous?' If any took leave to disagree with whatever it was he told them, he would round upon the heretic with a face like a clenched fist and shout: 'What are you talkin' about, or do you know what you're talkin' about?' De Valera was his god, and sooner or later I could see his cheek-bones turn to a red as dark as yesterday's blood, and, as his voice rose, Father Kearney would cross the floor with an urbane 'Now, men, no politics.' I never knew whether the 'men' was meant in a gruff, comradely sense or was a kind of village apartheid that sited my father and his cronies as being half-way between males and gentlemen. The conversation would at once become a debate on whether today's running at Leopardstown or Fairyhouse had been fast or soft.

Father Kearney, who was to act as caller, positioned himself at the top table, and young Gunger Hammond, who had inherited his father's nickname, distributed small tablets of stained wood, each criss-crossed into squares and with numbers hand-painted in red. Somehow, I was overlooked and put my hand up. When I had caught young Gunger's eye, I said: 'May I have a board, please?'

He gave me one without comment; then I heard him snigger: 'A board!'

What I should have asked for was a 'card', but I had known no better – it was, after all, a piece of wood. Young Gunger moved behind me out of sight, but my ears were like radar, and I heard him guffaw 'Jayzus, a board!' There were a few appreciative cackles from those who were in on the joke, and, whenever he was in my vicinity for the rest of the evening, he would repeat 'A board!' as if it were funnier than Jimmy O'Dea being Mother Goose in the Gaiety. My father, over whose head it was, took note of the eruptions of mirth and made matters worse by nudging me and saying: 'Oh, Young Gunger is a queer harp!'

It was the most trifling of incidents, but if I remember it forty years later it is because I can still feel my cold rage against the town and the sniggerers. I was not, they were telling me, as godly a being as I thought myself. More importantly, I was not of their number and would never be. Years later, I was to write a play called *A Life*, with a central character based on my old civil service nemesis, Mr Drumm. As a young man, he speaks at a public debate and is heckled by a group of the town ne'er-do-wells out for an evening's sport. Forty years on, elderly and embittered, he recalls the experience:

> 'I understood. It was a punishment. I had broken the eleventh commandment. I had tried to be different, to be a clever boy, the born genius. Well, they were not impressed. I had discovered that cleverness was like having a deformed hand. It was tolerated as long as you kept a glove on it. I actually believed that if I spoke well and carried the argument they would admire me. I craved it. I wanted to be One of our Own. Dear God, what a contemptible ambition: to please the implacable.'

Probably, while inventing a past for Desmond Drumm, I had

revisited that evening when I and the town drew up our separate battle lines; then, having inflated what had been a small embarrassment into a major humiliation, I bestowed it on Drumm, using it to alter the course of his stage life for the worst. A writer can have it both ways: he can return to the past, take a small moment that led nowhere, a road down which he dared not travel, and ask himself 'What if . . .?'

What had happened at the parochial hall was an incident, a nothing, a moment of elephantine fun for Young Gunger, who – the only Gunger, now that his father is long dead – passes me daily in Castle Street without a nod, for I am still not One of Our Own. In those days, though, I had a low humiliation threshold. I recall that I once went for lunch to the cafeteria above Woolworth's in Henry Street. It may have been pay day, for I loaded my plate with soup, a roll and butter, grey roast beef, soapy potatoes, ball-bearing peas, and a liquescent trifle. I found a table and set the tray down, only to see it tip over the edge with a Bartok-like discord of plates and cutlery. I could not have believed that a one-and-ninepenny lunch, including a cup of mud-coloured coffee, could have serviced such an impressive area of tiled floor. All conversation died. A hundred tatters of beef hung motionless, like battle banners in a lull, from a hundred forks. The silence could be heard two streets off as I salvaged the bread roll, wiped it on my jacket and bore it away, past the tables, the cane-backed chairs and the gapers. As I reached the stairs, a young waitress followed me. She said 'Ahem' very loudly, possibly because I was not of an age to be called 'Mister'. When I did not pause in my flight, she cried out: 'Young lad, come back. I have your dinner for you.' I flung back at her that I was in a hurry and ran out into Henry Street, brought closer to tears by the kindness than the calamity that had provoked it.

Behind my fury at Young Gunger and the rest of them, there was a sly back lane of my mind where I was already turning my chastisement to good use. It eased my conscience to be the victim, to have it thrown at me – or so I chose to believe – that I was an outsider. Now it was not I but the town who was severing what I hated most: the strings that tied me to home. No one could accuse me of desertion when, in a hundred small ways, I was being set adrift. If I was to be flailed at with briars, I would take care to emerge smelling of roses.

Every Sunday from the pulpit, Father Kearney sang the virtues of simplicity. Faith was to be accepted, not debased by thought. Women were modest, men manly; misfortunes were not to be railed against, but offered up. Our parish priest would have walked barefoot on hot coals rather than contaminate himself by reading the anti-Christ, James Joyce, and yet could not have agreed more passionately with Gabriel Conroy in *The Dead* that ours was a sceptical and 'thought-tormented' age. We should not, he said, seek to ape the ways of film stars in divorce-racked Hollywood. He mentioned, as an example of modern decadence, a recent street brawl between the MGM star, Franchot Tone, and a Monogram B-player, Tom Neal, for the hand and private parts of a blonde actress named Barbara Payton. It did not occur to him that Crutch Kelly from Sallynoggin and Bomber Young who lived on the Bus Lawn had beaten each other to bloody pulp outside Larkin's pub only the previous evening. Harry Young, who was dark of skin, had earned his nickname because of his likeness to the 'Brown Bomber', Joe Louis, but the resemblance stopped there, and Kelly, who had a withered leg, ended the fight by wrapping his crutch around Bomber's neck. To Father Kearney, everyday mayhem, as long as there was not a Barbara Payton to contaminate the proceedings, was not in the least pass-remarkable. Having disposed of Hollywood, he had even less good to speak of England, an abode of godlessness and free-thinkers.

Simplicity was all. It was the bedrock of the faith of our fathers, which, as the hymn attested, was living still in spite of dungeon, fire and sword. To him, yeoman and foeman were indistinguishable. He told us stories of a whole convent school of innocent girls, who were flung over a cliff by the soldiery, and the nuns after them, for refusing to speak well of the Protestant God to the detriment of His Catholic counterpart. Those girls – with, of course, the nuns in attendance – had gone straight to Heaven. The nuns, he assured us, just in case a tittle of doubt should exist, would have gone there even if not thrown over the cliff.

Once, during the annual Retreat, one of the missioners came to Harold Boys' School. He was a Capuchin, a bluff, jovial chap who, while our headmaster, Mr Mullen, looked on, treated the boys as men of the world. For a reason lost in time, Mr Mullen was nicknamed 'Tabac', the Irish for tobacco. He was bald and red-faced, and in moments of stress would dislodge his lower dentures and rotate them gently around the interior of his mouth, with a faint rattling noise as they now and then collided with the stationary top set. He put them in motion when, to his alarm, the missioner invited us to ask whatever questions we liked. 'Fire away, lads,' he said, 'the bolder the better!' To Tabac, it was as if a tightrope walker, bidding farewell to sanity, had set fire to his safety net.

The missioner was in good hands, however. We liked him. He was nice to us, and we were nice in return. We asked him about Heaven.

Would we go there, Father?

To be sure we would. Sure 'twas well known the world over that the Irish had a great leg of God. Were we not His favourites?

And would it be nice there, Father?

Oh, 'twould be grand. Lovely. Sure could it be anything else when it was called Paradise? Now, come on, lads, ask me a hard one.

And, and, and, and, and, when we got to Heaven, Father, what would we do there?

Do there?

In Heaven, Father, all day long. What would we do?

We would have a great time.

But how, Father?

How? Now that was a good one. How? What would we do in Heaven? Ah. Yes, to be sure. We would give praise and adoration to God in His glory.

All day, Father?

Every minute of every day, bedad, and *in saecula saeculorum*!

His smile was a proud beacon of promise, and in its silence we could hear the click of Tabac's dentures revving up. Until then, the missioner had been swathed in the cocoon of our affection; now, instantly, the temperature dropped. We each had our own idea of Heaven. Some saw it as Dalkey Hill, Sorrento Park and the White Rock beach, all rolled into one long swoon of summer days and red sunsets; to others, it was an everlasting picture show, with Buck Jones in one cowboy film and the Three Mesquiteers in the next, and free ice-cream cornets squirted with raspberry syrup handed out in between. Mine was a wild amalgam of south sea lagoons, western ranges and Jekyll and Hyde's London, with myself cast as both Dr and Mr; but even to those whose heavenly aspirations were modest, an eternity of praising God, even though there were few who deserved it more than He, seemed a barren source of entertainment.

Like all missioners, ours was a showman, and he knew that his audience had cooled. His notion of Heaven, our faces told him, was a cod of a yarn. When he saw my hand go up to ask a question, his eyes looked like those of a drowning man who had espied a floating plank. 'Yes, yes, good lad,' he said, urging me to the rescue. 'Fire away!'

It was no more than a year since, as a twelve-year-old, I had confessed to another missioner that I had committed self-abuse twice daily for a week, and I was chary of repeating the performance. But a certain aspect of Heaven had long perplexed me, and now was my chance to sort it out. 'Please, Father, when I go to Heaven will I meet my two granddas and grandmammies?'

Relief two-stepped on his brow. I had shown him a backstairs. 'You will, you will so,' he said eagerly. 'We will be reunited with our loved ones. God has given us His promise.'

His eyes raked the classroom for another question, but I was not done with him yet. 'And please, Father, in Heaven will my four granddas and grandmammies meet their own eight granddas and grandmammies?'

Tabac's early-warning system was a wonder then and is still marvelled at in the town today, forty years after he at last succumbed to stomach ulcers and boys; and my question caused his denture to stall half-way through one of its orbits. The missioner again smiled upon me. 'Oh begob they will.' He essayed a little joke. 'They'll be all together, like Brown's cows!'

'And, Father, will their eight granddas and grandmas meet their own sixteen granddas and grandmammies?'

At this, his smile became strained. 'To be sure,' he said and looked elsewhere.

I was now counting on my fingers. 'And, Father, will *their* sixteen granddas and grandmammies . . .?'

What I was relentlessly conjuring up was an image of a heaven throned with a billion relatives: a nudging, milling, grunting, jostling crowd of them, stretching to the Elysian horizon and going back to the Year Dot and beyond. Eternity would not be long enough for them to find each other, and even when they had done so, the introductions and sortings out would take another eternity on top of that one.

I was taken aback when the missioner, who suddenly bore not even a passing resemblance to a nice man, snarled at me: 'You're so smart you'll cut yourself.'

I looked to Tabac for comfort; he looked back at me, giving none. His teeth, once again on the move, were clattering around like a goods train on an iron bridge. The missioner screwed his skull-cap down on his head as if it were a lid on a jam jar, enquired of our statue of St Anthony holding the child Jesus why he (the missioner) was wasting his time, and allowed Tabac to see him to the front gate. I knew I had done nothing wrong, and yet a score of voices urged me to escape through the window, over the far wall and into White's Villas. Instead, with bowels melting, I sat awaiting the slam of a door, a Krakatoa of a belch, the crashing of bottles as Tabac searched for his milk of magnesia, and the snarl – my summons to the gibbet – of 'Get out here, ye whoor's melt!' The pity of it was that on the subject of Heaven I had had a second question for the missioner, and now it would never be answered, any more than the first had been.

Pope Pius XI had been ill recently, and his doctors were sparing no effort to save his life. Like most popes, he was never more eloquent than when assuring his flock that they were heirs to the kingdom of heaven and the everlasting bliss which awaited those who died in God's grace. I had wanted to ask why he himself, nonetheless, seemed perversely determined to keep out of the place for as long as he could. It was not, I thought, an unreasonable question; in fact, it might well have earned me a few pats on the head instead of the punches on it that I was in for from Tabac.

Unlike the missioner, Father Kearney never invited questions, nor did people such as my parents presume to ask them. They were amazed and grateful to come safely through the world, and they did so by placing themselves under the protection of powers that were both temporal and celestial. Apart from mass on Sundays, they made their Easter duties, and attended their sodalities – my father's, every second Friday, my mother's, every third. There were evening devotions, Holy Hours, Golden Hours, First Fridays and the yearly Retreat; in addition, my father was dispatched to early Mass every morning during Lent, and I was dragged, out of bed, blind with sleep and vicious with temper, to go with him. Whatever the occasion, the message never varied. All unhappiness, privations, and injustices, all hardships, suffering and reverses were to be welcomed as promissory notes drawn on the Bank of Heaven and encashable after death. One did not seek payment in this world. To do so, to resist misfortune, to demand that life should be better, was a slur upon the ultimate justice of God. It implied that the heavenly bank either did not exist or was insolvent.

If the sun shone, you saluted people on the street and said 'That's a grand day, thank God,' and they said 'Isn't it great, thank God' back to you. If it rained, however, no blame was attached to Him. A fine day simply meant that in His goodness He had spared us the downpour our sins deserved. Sunshine was a gratuity, not an entitlement. When I was in the civil service, a fellow clerk cajoled me into attending a one-day retreat run by the Franciscans on Merchants' Quay. There was a slap-up Sunday lunch of spring lamb; the mood was expansive, and afterwards, as a few of us strolled in the garden, an elderly priest brooded aloud on the growing tide of agnosticism and how it could be blamed squarely on pride of the intellect.

'Ah, me,' he said, 'the curse, the terrible curse of modern

131

thought! Thought! That wayward lamb . . .' (given what we had just eaten, it was an uneasy metaphor) '. . . that flees the shepherd's fold, a poor foolish creature that will have no truck with what is tried and true, but instead rushes headlong to the precipice.'

Everyone nodded suavely. I stepped out of myself and to one side and beheld a group of young men in grave and yet heady discourse with a respected elder. We seemed to exist in a bubble world, idyllic and out of time. It occurred to me that Oxford was perhaps not unlike this, except that instead of dreaming spires what towered about us were Dublin tenements. Sunday noises came from the windows: a radio, with Billy Cotton shouting 'Wakey, wakey!', a child being called in from play, a man laughing. Across the Liffey by the Four Courts, a bus coughed its life out. It was not Oxford or anywhere near, and we were walking, not with a senior don, but an old Franciscan whose simplicity only a poltroon would have confounded with deadly argument.

Nonetheless, the temptation was not to be resisted, and so, without pausing to reflect that the same simple old Franciscan could have polished off a dozen of me before breakfast, I delivered my sword-thrust to the heart.

'But, Father, what answer would you give to a misguided person who was to ask you: If thought is so evil, why then di'. God give us the power to think?'

Some of the others looked shocked that I should so brutally open fire upon a sitting target, but the old priest blessed me with the gentle, pitying smile of one who has yet again seen a donkey fall into the most venerable trap in Christendom.

'My son,' he said, 'I would tell the poor creature you mention that God in His goodness gave us brains so that we would have the wisdom to know when not to use them.'

It was worthy of Chesterton.

My parents, if they had had brains, would have buried them in the back yard sooner than tamper with them. If a priest smiled and shook hands with my mother, it was tuppence to talk to her for the rest of the day. If my father blindly obeyed his employers, Mr and Mrs Jacob, it was not simply because they paid his wages: rather, it was because, being non-Catholics who addressed him as 'Keyes' without a 'Mister' attached, they were his betters: the Master and the Mistress, as he called them.

In writing a memoir, one is not only enabled to journey to the past, but must also pay the fare by at last looking in the face what it had once been politic to ignore. I knew that my foster-parents' marriage was not a love match; it had been arranged, and when my mother referred to my father as a 'good provider' I thought her both fair and comradely. Now I must admit that it was the only praise I heard her give him. She resented him as an interloper in her life and, because he was easygoing, thought him a fool. They were not even bound together by children, for those they had were stillborn. My mother saw her life as hard and with few rewards. Once, she entered into negotiations to buy my father a new Sunday suit, to be paid for at a half-crown per week, but the morning came when he, who had always had the constitution of a mule, got out of bed and at once fell back into it with threatened pneumonia. My mother threw holy water on him and sent for Dr Enright who, with his usual sigh of resignation, told her that, please God, the patient would recover. 'Maybe he will,' she said to me when the front door was closed behind him, 'but thank God and his Holy Mother I didn't sign for the suit.' Her affection for my father – or her want of it – was in this case not at issue; she was a realist, who, faced with the possibility of life without a breadwinner, was already counting the shillings.

Her life held several pleasures; one of them was complaining that it held none. Another was that on Mondays and Fridays, when she had done her shopping in Lipton's and the Home and Colonial Stores – her tongue declined to make more of the latter than the 'Home and Cologne' – and bought my father's two ounces of plug tobacco at Sir Thomas Browne's, she would make for the Picture House. It was a redbrick flea-pit where, having entered directly under the screen, you then walked backwards up the aisle to your seat, already goggling at the film. On the wall of the box office there were framed stills from the 1929 part-talking *Showboat*, starring Laura La Plante; they were still there when the Bug House, as we called it, closed its doors and became a branch of Burtons. She loved westerns, gangster films, epics of the North-West frontier, slapstick comedies and dramas of mother-love. She despised so-called sophistication: she would say that Greta Garbo gave her 'the sick', and the sight of a dinner jacket or a night-club interior was the signal for a growl of 'Oul' codology'. She despised love scenes, and her world was never the same again when, in a film called *Riding High*, Gene Autry actually kissed the heroine. 'Oh, the cur,' she said.

In spite of this, she was addicted to romantic novels, although what she enjoyed most were stories of the turf. She left it to the girl in the tuppence-a-book-a-week lending library to choose them for her, but would refuse to read anything written in the first person. 'I want none of your old "I . . . I" rubbidge,' she would say. Of an evening when the house was empty, or she thought it was, she would draw up a chair to the kitchen range, stir the coals into a blaze, hike her skirt up, light one of my father's old pipes, and become immersed in Ruby M. Ayres or Nat Gould. If I came in suddenly, she would thrust the pipe under the chair cushion and affect to read on unconcernedly, paying no attention to the plume of tobacco smoke that arose from beneath her.

I never knew my father to read a book. He went to whist drives and walked the dog across the hill and through the rabbit wood. Each day on his way back to Jacobs' after lunch – dinner, we called it – he would stop off at the bookie's and bet a shilling on an each-way treble for my mother and him. The sort she was, rather than have misfortune come upon her unawares, she would meet it on the doorstep, and my father was hardly around the corner of our lane, home for the day, than she would snap at him: 'I suppose me curse-o'-God horse is down the field again, bad scran to it?' On the occasions when his news was good, he would reply to this by removing his hat and flinging it ahead of him through the open door, whereupon she, knowing by heart what she must now endure, rolled her eyes in the manner of an El Greco saint and moaned that, like Greta Garbo, he would give a body the sick. 'Gimme your hand,' he would say, at which to spite him she would put both hands behind her back. Undaunted, he would reach with awful ceremony into his pocket and plank her winnings down on the kitchen table, one coin at a time and with a look implying that he himself had been not only the jockey, but the trainer, stable-boy and horse as well. And, even if he were to put a million pounds in front of her, she would say stonily, as she always did when the last coin was banged down: 'Is *that* all?'

Their daily newspaper was the *Irish Press* – 'Dev's paper', my father called it proudly; 'That rag!' my aunt Chris would gasp in fastidious disgust – and on Sundays they would take the *Dispatch*, the *Chronicle* and the *Pictorial* among others. Once, when I was nine or so, I was sent to Mammy Reilly's for these, and on my way back a man took me for a paper boy and bought the lot. I was too timid to tell him the truth and arrived home in tears with a fistful of coppers.

My head is like one of the tall milk jugs my mother kept on the dresser crammed with odds and ends: bits of wool, snapshots, racing dockets, a yellowed prayer cut from *Ireland's Own*, buttons, elastic bands, rosaries with beads missing. I have no idea why I should remember a 1940 issue of the *Sunday Pictorial* which, taking note of Hitler's fifty-first birthday, enjoined its war-time readers to partake of the crumb of comfort: 'Napoleon died at fifty-two!' Alongside this was a photograph of a girl almost wrapped in a silken shawl. Its edges did not quite meet, and from shoulder to ankle there was visible a narrow but unbroken strip of flesh, giving the impression that she was naked underneath. My mother glanced at the page without comment, probably because what she saw was the shawl, whereas what fascinated me was not merely the strip of skin, three inches by forty-eight, that I could see, but the vast, merely guessed-at, never-never land that I could not. The censors and I, aged twelve, had dirty minds in common, for the *Pictorial* was banned for salacity not long after.

People of my parents' class did not have friends. My mother had her neighbours and my father his old cronies with whom he would linger a while at the harbour wall, but they did not meet these by appointment, nor did anyone, relatives excepted, come to the house as invited guests. It was not the done thing. To be married meant that the time for foolishness was over with, and friendships, having played their part, were to be put aside. The rules laid down that a man and wife should be sufficient for each other. A bad husband went out to the pub; a dutiful one stayed at home, except perhaps for the occasional whist drive. My parents listened to the wireless, ticked off horses on the racing page, and went to bed at eleven.

One of the black days in my father's life was when my grandmother died and my mad aunt Mary, my mother's sister, came to stay. My aunt Chris who, married to a civil servant and living in a house with stairs in it, was the success of the family, had promised the old woman that when the time came she would take Mary. In the event she reneged. 'John refuses to have her,' she told mother, as if that cherub would for an instant have looked crosswise at her airiest wish. The truth was that her neighbours in Albert Park (she had once given me a fearsome wigging for accidentally addressing a Christmas card to 'Albert Place') and friends on Burdett and Ballygihen Avenues were married to bank clerks and haberdashers, well-thought-of men who, like John, wore a collar and tie on weekdays, and the thought of them finding out that she had a mad sister was too appalling to contemplate. And Mary was not a modest, unobtrusive sort of looney: she made a meal of it: she rolled her eyes, let her tongue flop out like a red leather bookmark, scowled, cursed her enemies, who were legion, and trundled a pram filled with dolls. She used this like a small bulldozer, aiming it unerringly at shins and calves and inflicting such grievous mutilations that one expected to see knife-blades on the wheels. Even without it, she was dangerous. One of the sights of the town was Mary, using her handbag as a mace, the while galumphing along like a rhino vandalising the African undergrowth.

My mother was delighted to take her, pram, dolls and all. She enjoyed putting Chris at a moral disadvantage; now, she could say that, although poor and hard put to it to feed another mouth, she was more of a Christian than her well-off sister, so

136

full of codology that she walked like there was a poker stuck up her. It is just possible that, as a family, the Doyles may have loved each other, but I never saw the faintest evidence of any liking. My father had no say in the matter of Mary living with us. When my mother adopted me, ten days old, she did not even consult him in advance, but simply arrived home by tram one day with a *fait accompli* wrapped in several blankets; so with that as a precedent, he had less than no chance of thwarting Mary's arrival.

Years before, when the last of several still-births had almost killed my mother, a doctor told her that another pregnancy would be fatal. The Church, knowing that celibacy was, in every sense of the word, child's play, gave her the easy choice of chastity or death, and so my father was exiled at night to the sofa in the front room of the cottage they then lived in. After her menopause, he was permitted to rejoin her in the double bed, but Paradise was not long regained. With Mary's coming, he was once again dispossessed and moved back to the sofa, this time lying head to toe with me and unable to sleep for the wall-shaking snores of the runner-in sharing the double-bed next door. It neither lessened nor deepened his dislike of her that she hated him. She hated most people, perhaps all. There were those who said 'Sure God love her' and assured you that the saints in Heaven were putting bunting up in anticipation of her arrival. With the instinct of a ham actor in the rural fit-ups, she played to the hilt the role of afflicted innocent, but to me her capacity for malevolence was baffling; it suggested that the natural state of man was wholly Mr Hyde, with not a trace of Dr Jekyll in sight. My father, who was one of nature's softies, had only to look at her to start grinding his false teeth in rage. He did not court destruction by declaring open war, but he made sure to collide with Mary in doorways or nudge her off the pavement on the way to Mass. Knowing it was deliberate, she would squawk: 'Mag, Mag, do you know what he's after doin'?', and my mother, who could be very grand when out in public and was mindful of the regard of others, would smile sweetly for the world to see, while snarling out of the side of her mouth: 'Shut up, you rip, or I'll swing for you.'

137

Life became not much easier when we moved to a two-storey corporation house in St Begnet's Villas. Mary now had a bed of her own, but it was in the same room as my parents, and the snoring raged on, unabated, a kind of sonar by which I would find my way upstairs in the pitch dark, home from the pictures or the sea front. In waking hours, she would sit, muttering and furiously jerking her pramload of dolls to and fro, like a miner grading ore, while my father, catching sight of her, would munch his tongue in requited hatred. If jealousy was part of his detestation of her, he was self-deluding; she did not usurp my mother's affection for him, for there was little of it worth stealing. Whatever else, it cannot have helped that her presence in his house was a reminder that he had never been master of it. She outlived my mother by some years and him as well, so maybe in the interval of waiting for her to get to Heaven he had peace there for a time.

My parents enjoyed their life within its limits, and as they and I grew older it was their docile acceptance of those limits that, with the intolerance of the young pup, I found hateful. To them, life was to be survived rather than lived, and they gratefully accepted the shelter of the church, the Jacobs, the town and 'Dev'. They surrendered free will, trading it for a whist drive, afternoons at the pictures, a shilling on the horses, the Wicklow Regatta and – as a sop at the year's end – the great toy of Christmas. Sometimes, when my mother was angry at, say, a rise in prices, she would threaten to vote against De Valera's party at the next election, but when the time came she supported Fianna Fail as always. It was not out of loyalty, but from a blind gut-fear of change.

Six years after my father's death, I wrote a play in which I attempted to sort out my feelings for him and lay my anger to rest. 'You were a sheep while you lived,' the self-righteous son says to the old man's ghost, 'you're a sheep now.' I was not so foolish as to expect that he would ever hit out at his life, but I thought he might just once have asked it an aggrieved 'Why?' Only now, remembering an incident that for forty years has lain buried, do I realise why he did not. I was nineteen, and it was the day before Christmas Eve.

My mother was allergic to drink, and the allergy was for some years accompanied by addiction. My father and I came to dread holidays – Christmas, in particular, when an old friend would waylay her in Dun Laoghaire and, taking no refusal, steer her into a snug for just a thimbleful of sherry, or a ball of malt to mark the season that was in it. One sip, and she was lost. So too, for us, was Christmas. She was a bad drunk, with a wasps' nest for a tongue. Once the drinking had begun, the misery would drag on through the holiday and beyond. There were weeks of rows and sulks, of cries for heaven to bear witness that she was persecuted by pimps and informers. The house, no matter that we lived in it, seemed empty and cheerless; along our road, window curtains twitched as my mother came slowly home, hat askew, from another outing. No matter how watchful my father and I were – and he, lacking a cunning to match hers, was useless – our next-door neighbour, Mrs Dunne, would smuggle in Baby Powers and, if I implored her not to, would snap at me that, to suit a pup the likes of me, she was not going to disoblige her good neighbour. After perhaps a month, mortally in debt to Gilbey's the spirit merchants, my mother would become ill and take to her bed for a week, and that was the end of it until next time.

It happened that I intended to spend my first Christmas away from home. The previous summer while on holiday in Limerick, I had at long last given my heart without having it flung back at me. It was first love with a vengeance, and I was in raptures when the girl, Teresa by name, invited me to spend the holiday in the flat she shared with her cousin in Shannon Street. As the time drew nearer, I kept a fearful eye on my mother, but days passed and it seemed as if this would be one of the good years. My life was on the edge of change; the waiting-room door was at last opening, and I took heart from knowing that God, of all people, would have a sense of occasion. On December 23rd, I came home early from the office to pack a bag, say my goodbyes and catch the evening train. As I walked in at the door, she was standing by the kitchen table, one hand resting upon it on thumb and plump fingertips, and as soon as I saw the calm clear-browed look of a woman who had nothing to hide, I felt the old sickness trickle through me like bleeding. I had been a fool to believe it would be otherwise; it was the price of me.

It was unthinkable that I should get on a train and leave my father to cope with her over Christmas, and so I went to the post office and sent off a telegram to Limerick, knowing that it was the end of my romance. By the time I returned to the house, my father was home from work, waiting for a tea he would be lucky to get and doggedly refusing to accept that she had drink taken. I behaved disgracefully. If my future was in bits, I saw no reason why he should enjoy the comfort of self-delusion. I asked him if he was blind. Or stupid. Could he not see what had happened, what we were in for, how this Christmas was lost as well as the others? He smiled, waved a hand at me. Not at all. What was I talking about or did I know what I was talking about? I was a comical boy. Sure the woman was grand. Never better. Not a feather out of her. He turned, eliciting her support. She did not look at him, only at me, the Judas. Then she went on moving about the room as if we were not there, her face set. He picked up his *Evening Herald* and opened it, a hiding place. I tore it away from him. He would not escape. He might not share in my misery, but he would taste of it.

At last, he gave in. He hardly ever lost his temper, straight off, but would begin at first to grumble. He played his old familiar tunes: weren't we all grand and happy and comfortable, owing nothing to no one? Sure where was the sense in, in, in, in? Wasn't she the best in the world when she hadn't a sup taken? The grumbling became anger. Christ almighty, what ailed her that she couldn't let the one week in the year go by without putting shaggin' poison into her? Making a show of herself. Soon, he was ranting and, as always when he lost his temper, he became incoherent. Would he never have a day's peace with her? He would set fire to every public house in the whoorin' town, aye, an', an', an' Gilbey's along with them. She looked at him with contempt, then went from the room and upstairs. It would be a bread and jam tea. The anger dribbled away and became despair. He said 'I dunno' several times. God in heaven, he said at last, but weren't we were a misfortunate family?

I told him with savage calm: 'I don't know why you bother talking to God. There isn't one.'

For a moment, he was about to go rambling on down his own road, then he looked at me and said: 'There isn't a what?'

'A God,' I said.

He stared. To my horror, I heard him say, and it was a moan of terrible triumph: 'You're right. There isn't a God, there isn't a God.'

Once, on Rockfort Avenue, my bicycle had skidded and the brake lever pierced the back of my leg. As the blood began to well, I begged to be given back the past few seconds of time, reclaiming the moment when I had over-twisted the handlebars at the sharp turn into Coliemore Road. Ten measly seconds had seemed a reasonable request then, and it seemed so now. I wanted the words, my father's and mine, unsaid. It was as if he had down the years kept hidden an ultimate knowledge that contradicted all that the town and the world were built on, that went against the sodality and the processions, the altar and the pulpit. He had buried it out of shame, for, if others were wiser and more well-up than he was, then it must be as untrue as it was sinful. Now, of a sudden, it had been said, and he was no longer alone. I had put him in the right.

That time went past; we got through Christmas as we had always done, and what I had said was forgotten, or at least never again spoken of. The stone was put back into place. After a few more years, the drinking stopped. When she was dead and it was too late, I wondered what real harm it had ever done. It was my fault as much as hers: I failed to shake off a bugaboo of childhood: the waking nightmare of seeing a mother become a stranger behind the same face. Children should at least grow up. In my father's case, what I had done was true wickedness, and it was no thanks to me that a vicious word or two cannot as magically shatter lives as it does in a play or a film. By next day he had simply swept away what I had said. Crumbs from a table.

I at least know now and for all time why he, like so many

others, did not ask questions of their lives. It was because the God neither of us believed in tempers the wind to the shorn lamb. Probably, it had been given to my father to know that, for a simple man, the answers are not to be lived with.

8

The apogee of my life as an actor came in 1950 when the newly formed Dun Laoghaire Academy of Dramatic Art – DADA, for short – actually billed me as a guest performer. Even so, I was small fry, for they had engaged a guest *star* as well: a professional actor of great bulk, baleful aspect and empurpled proboscis, who spoke like a distant fog-horn and was on that account known among his peers as Doctor Moo. The play was Paul Vincent Carroll's *Shadow and Substance*. Also in the cast was my friend from the Land Commission Players, Jimmy Keogh, who, even though he was playing a country curate, still believed that the line of dialogue did not exist which could not be enhanced with a 'boinnng' here and a 'gedoink' there. He and I had our sights – but alas, nothing else – on the *ingénue*, whom I shall call Sandra: a wet-lipped eighteen-year-old who habitually stood with legs apart and pelvis thrust forward like a proferred hand. Although with her sultry looks, she was my ideal of the archetypal wrecker of homes, she remained perversely disinclined to practise on mine. The idealistic young schoolmaster was played by Vincent Ellis, who was also a co-director of the academy. He was lanky and stooped, and had a jutting lower lip. Unusually for an actor, he also had a speech impediment. There were kindly souls who referred to it as hardly noticeable, but when he said 'Good evening', it was likely to come out as 'Nyugn eenygning.'

The director of the play was his partner: a small circular lady named Sarah O'Kelly, whose husband, Christy, was the brother of the then President of Ireland, Sean T. O'Kelly. She had a profusion – a veritable *embaras de richesses* – of chins. She walked – I had heard the expression, but had rarely seen it done – trippingly. She held her hands with wrists inward and palms daintily facing the ground, the thumbs, index and little fingers raised, and others curled. She resembled a dropsical fairy permanently on her way to an enchanted glade. In the moments when she was not telling us that this was deportment, she would reminisce of how her eldest child had been born during the 1916 Easter Rising; the climax of the recital came with: 'And God pity me, there I was in the agonies of labour, with the guns getting nearer and Mrs De Valera wiping the sweat from me brow.'

A small string ensemble was to play at our gala first night, and in this connection a musicologist, Jewish by name and in appearance, came out from town. Mrs O'Kelly, awed that a man who did not write out prescriptions should be addressed as 'Doctor', enquired as to his nationality. He bowed and said: 'Madam, I am German.'

She was thrilled to bits. 'Ah, go to God,' she said. 'A Jerry? Aren't you great!' Then we saw her give him the leer of one conspirator to another. 'And, Doctor, listen here to me, don't fret yourself.' And her arm, stiff and straight, shot out from the shoulder. 'We shall rise again!'

She was, in short, an Irish Republican: a breed that may be defined as the sworn friend of anyone, genocides included, who is not the friend of England. She and I were natural enemies. Where it came to acting, I combined my own name with that of my foster parents, so that I was John Keyes Byrne. Mrs O'Kelly enraged me by addressing me during rehearsals as 'Keyes Byrne', without a prefix. I retaliated by endowing her with a nickname. She came to hear of it and, from curiosity rather than umbrage, asked Vincent Ellis: 'Why does Keyes Byrne call me Charlotte?'

He told her, truthfully 'I nging id's neh veemanane for Nygarl Nysawnygn.'

It took her a while to grasp, but with patience she did so, that he was saying: 'I think it's the female for Charles Laughton.'

Ours was not a happy production. Mrs O'Kelly's theatrical experience had been a few walk-on roles at the Abbey Theatre in the 1930s, and what she knew about directing a play was confined to saying 'Enunciate, Keyes Byrne, you must een-nun-see-ate!' and, with every untrammelled pound of flesh juddering, demonstrating how we should walk across the stage. 'Pippa passes,' Doctor Moo said under his breath. Our star, too, had his troubles. For one thing, try as he might, he could not master his lines; for another, the actress who was playing the saintly maidservant, Brigid, was not only too old for the role by a score of years, but she had also been a diva in the Dublin Grand Opera Society and so projected her every line towards the rear wall of the auditorium. At last, Doctor Moo, losing his patience said: 'Will you for Christ's sake at least look in my direction! You're not in fucking *Madame Butterfly* now.' Mrs O'Kelly crossed herself and actually went to stand in a corner where she could pray uninterrupted. Our Brigid burst into tears; Doctor Moo, his huge face a storm at sea that Turner could have painted, set off for the bar of the Royal Marine; and Jimmy Keogh and I stared dry-mouthed with lust at Sandra, who as usual was performing the considerable feat of standing, hands at ease on her hips, and pubes at attention.

The first night was, in effect, the launching of DADA, and, to do justice to the occasion, evening dress was obligatory in the first twelve rows of the town hall. The excitement caused Sandra, whose acting debut this was, to become mildly hysterical, and I could hear her voice as I was making up next door in what served as the men's dressing room. Mrs O'Kelly was clucking at her and saying 'Sure you'll be grand', when the door behind me burst open and Sandra came in. She was wearing a corselet and black stockings held up by suspenders. Before the eyeballs had time to melt in my head, she said: 'I'm going to die, I'm going to die. My heart is slowing down and it's going to stop. Feel it.' I was the nearest person to her, which is perhaps why mine was the hand she took hold of and shoved inside the brassière part of the corselet. Doctor Moo, dressed for his role as Canon Skerrit, stared open-mouthed, the great nose pulsating, his teeth resembling a neglected corner of a

145

cemetery. Sandra's breast was actually heaving, and my hand was full of it. It had never been so full. A nipple poked through my fingers. 'Do you feel it?' she asked, her eyes searching my face.

I told her: yes, I could feel it.

Mrs O'Kelly had followed her in and began to quack: 'Keyes Byrne, get your hand out of there.'

She caught hold of Sandra by the shoulders and pulled her backwards, causing my hand to flop out into the world like a fish regurgitated by a gannet. It was a close run thing: where that hand was concerned, another five seconds and only major surgery would have removed it. In time, Sandra was quietened down and the play began, but for me all that followed was anticlimax. I had been to the mountain top; I had seen the promised land. To be truthful, it was not in any case much of an evening. Doctor Moo still did not know his lines, and soon there was a brown stain on the elbow of his soutane, caused by his leaning on the newly-painted mantelpiece, ostensibly in pained meditation, but actually to solicit a prompt through the fireplace. Sandra was supposed to play the Canon's hoydenish niece, Thomasina; what she gave the audience was Rita Hayworth as *Gilda*. Her stage-fright might never have been; pelvis leading the way, she sashayed on to the stage, swung her hips, sat, crossed her legs and showed her black stocking tops. A groan went up from the unruly element at the rear, and lechery swept down the aisles like a sirocco. As for Vincent Ellis, it was unfortunate for him that Jimmy Keogh's mother was in the audience and had had a drink or two, just in case the hall should prove not to be heated. She knew Vincent, for he lodged with the Keoghs, and she applauded his every exit. His proudest moment came with the line: 'Goodbye, Canon, you will be remembered, if at all, not as a classicist, nor as a priest, but for your love for a poor little miserable child.' He made heavy weather of the sibilants, especially in 'classicists', but burst through into open country with 'ngno lubb foh a moor ngiddle mignable ngniln'. As he turned to go, Mrs Keogh applauded again and shouted, 'Good man, Vincent!' Not recognising the voice and assuming that he was being jeered at, Vincent stood his ground and said:

'Ngo, venny ngnine! Ngaviagn for ngeh ngeneragn.' A friend of mine who had a sister with a cleft palate later told me that what he had said was: 'Oh, very nice! Caviare for the general.' The audience may well not have understood the words, never mind their meaning, but they sensed that Vincent was no longer their friend and humble servant. There was a mutinous rumble and cries from the rear of 'Feck off' and 'Bring back Thomasina.'

The play ends when the servant girl, Brigid, is felled by a half-brick intended for the schoolmaster. As she lies dying, the Canon and the teacher, mortal enemies, face each other over her body, and Doctor Moo heart-rendingly delivered his line: 'Will that doctor ever come? Could we do anything of ourselves? God would guide us surely.' A voice from the back told him loudly, clearly and succintly what to do with regard to Brigid, adding ' . . . while she's still warm.' The advice was loudly seconded, causing those wearing dinner jackets to leap to their feet and glare at the unfortunates who were not, and Brigid's dying speech was drowned by demands, garnished with bouquets of adjectives and adverbs, that those blocking their view should sit down.

DADA did not long survive its first outing. Its second and final production was of Emlyn Williams' *A Murder Has Been Arranged*, and Mrs O'Kelly engaged the services of a producer who had the cachet of working for Radio Eireann. At the first read-through, Sandra took him to one side and told him how ridiculous it was that he should have to travel all of seven miles home after rehearsals. There was a spare room at home, she said, where he could be happily accommodated, and, if this story is to be believed, he was. As for the play, it began inauspiciously with the entrance of Vincent Ellis wearing tights and attempting to enunciate: 'I am the ghost of Caesar Borgia, the world famous poisoner.' Then, in the third act, the set collapsed in a manner eerily reminiscent of *Asmodée* in the Little Flower Hall in Bray a year previously. This time I fell, not off a flight of steps, but from a platform in pitch darkness, and once again, to my joy and the grief of others, there was a dangling rope begging to be caught hold of. An inquest was duly held, with Mrs O'Kelly as the coroner. It took her not long to unmask the culprit, whereupon she pointed her chins to the right and a pudgy forefinger to the left, the while declaiming: 'There, Keyes Byrne, is the door.' As I stalked out, her co-director chimed in with 'Ngungh nygnent!', which I took to mean 'Good riddance!' Three or four others, disenchanted with DADA and glad of an excuse to defect, walked out with me. I later learned that Vincent Ellis, while under the impression that I had formed a murder gang and was waiting for him in the street, sent for the police and demanded to be escorted home. He was in no danger: by then the pariahs were in the Roman Cafe drinking lemon soda and sexually defaming the waitresses.

Within a year or two, Sandra went to England and all that was heard of her was the occasional lubricious rumour which was as outrageous as it was probably untrue; nonetheless, we chose to believe it, if only to day-dream that it was happening to us. Two or three years ago in a pub, a handsome middle-aged woman came up, asked if I remembered her and introduced me to her husband. 'Is that the famous Sandra?' my wife said when she had gone. 'I don't know what all the fuss was about.' Probably she did not, but *I* do.

The DADA business depressed me. While I was glad to be quit of Mrs O'Kelly and her like, the manner of my leaving seemed to prove yet again that, having been born an outsider, I was fated to remain one. It seemed that the hole did not exist that was square enough to contain me. Around this time, I had a friend who managed the Pavilion Soda Fountain on the sea front and was known as Abie from his initials, 'A.B.' He suggested that we cheer ourselves up with a weekend away from home. 'I know,' he said, 'great place.' He let me in on his secret.

I said, almost shrieking: 'Belfast? What do you want to go to Belfast for?'

He looked at me as if at a thick. 'To ride women, what do you think?'

Even as my libido responded like a faithful old dog, I knew it was a lost cause. Nonetheless we set off by train one wet Saturday morning in October, walked with heads bent against

the rain that was driving down from Cave Hill, and I saw Abie
dart into a chemist's shop. He came out grinning, tapped his
breast pocket and showed me the corner of a packet of con-
doms. 'Now,' he said, 'all we need is the women.' It was as if,
having acquired a puncture-repair kit, he assumed that getting
a bicycle to go with it was a mere formality. Next, we went
looking for a bookshop, for he had been told that a certain edition of the *Arabian Nights* was commendably filthy. We found
a shop on Royal Avenue, and the manager enquired as to our
needs. Abie told him and was asked what translation he had in
mind. He had not come unprepared. He reached into his pocket
for the slip of paper on which he had written the details. 'This,'
he said, 'will tell you all you need to know.' With a smirk, he
handed the manager the packet of French letters.

In the evening, we went to a dance hall. Abie had been a
commis chef at the Metropole when he was fourteen and so had
skipped adolescence and what went with it: the street corners,
the girls on the pier, the fourpenny rush with Charles Starrett
as the Durango Kid, the Sunday-night hop and the walk home –
half of it in pitch darkness once the street lamps had gone out
at ten past twelve. When it came to dancing he could not put a
foot under him. I, who stomped about as if I were signalling to
a tenant downstairs, was not much better, but to my surprise
the first girl I asked up – it was a foxtrot – did not seem to
be in the least bothered by my feet of lead. From the moment
we came together, she slammed her hips into mine and began
rotating them as if she were grinding flour. The friction was such
that I wondered how my pelvic area stayed on the cool side of
spontaneous combustion. I hardly dared give house-room to the
thought that my sexual ship might at last have come in sight of
land, but at least I began not to dislike Belfast. My eyes met
the girl's. She smiled and asked: 'Are you up from the Free
State?'

I told her yes.

Still smiling, she remarked: 'You'd be a Catholic, then?'

I had not practised my religion ever since the day, ten
years before, when Father Creedon threw me out of his
confessional for not knowing the words of the *Confiteor*, but

149

her question took me so unawares that I again answered yes.

Her smile did not diminish; rather it broadened. She said quietly: 'I'm a Protestant,' and walked quickly away, leaving me in the middle of the dance floor, vainly trying to conceal her gift to me – an erection. Once I had conveyed my tumescence to a quiet place and, by sitting down and crossing my legs, had tucked it out of harm's way, I found myself not in the least dismayed by the snub. For one thing, it smacked quite enjoyably of martyrdom. To be punished for my faith – which, for the occasion, it now suited me to bring back into play like a dribbling old fountain – made a nice change from being told that I could not dance for skins or was a rotten coort – which was how we pronounced 'court'. For another, bigotry was not new to me: I had, after all, lived for twenty years among Irish Catholics.

There was, for instance, a chap named Michael Keogh, who, since his parents had died, took his Sunday dinner at our house, and had recently wooed and won a girl who was Church of Ireland. The marriage ceremony was to be performed by a Protestant minister, and Michael's best friend, fearful of God's wrath, went to the parish priest of Dalkey and asked for permission to attend. After pained meditation, the ruling came forth: 'Yes, you may do so – but be cool with him.' My mother, to her credit and my own astonishment, asked us if we had ever heard such codology, put on her good hat, left my father and me to fend for ourselves and went off to the wedding and the breakfast afterwards.

Before the evening was over, Abie and I found two girls – both Catholics, since the Protestants would not have us. One was named Belle McLaverty, a big girl with black hair and a mocking Northern laugh; the other, who laid claim to Abie by taking his arm, is less vivid in my mind. Her name was Cara, which means 'friend'. Abie, with optimism as unquenchable as it was unfounded, confided to me with a leer that this was auspicious. He told them that he was the catering manager for Odeon (Ireland) Ltd., and that I was a final-year medical student. We saw the girls to a bus stop, received a scalding kiss apiece and were invited to meet them next day at three.

Our evening was not quite over. Abie and I were staying at the Central Hotel, and he urged me into the Residents' Lounge to drink to our good fortune. The girls, he assured me, were as hot as mustard. It was an expression I had heard to my grief in Butlin's the previous year, as applied to two other odds-on favourites: the Misses Morris and Watson. I signalled to Abie to lower his voice, for we were not alone in the lounge. There was a man drinking on his own. I took him for a commercial traveller, even though it was Saturday and he was unlikely to have been on the road on weekends. He nodded; we nodded back; then, quite out of the blue, he asked us if we had ever been driving at night when the car was suddenly filled with golden light and there was the sound of many voices, all clamorous. I told him that alas, I did not drive. I tried not to look at Abie, who, I sensed, was trying not to look at me. The man seemed not to believe that we had never had such a commonplace experience. He glowered, as if suspecting us of being unsociable. Then, as if by way of proferring the benefit of the doubt, he told us about a murderer he had known.

This murderer was actually as nice a fellow as you could meet in a day's walk, fond of his jar and the bit of crack with his chums. His misfortune was that he had a wife who was a proper bitch. For one thing, she refused to believe him when he told her how, whenever he was driving at night, the car had been filled with— He broke off and smiled archly as if he were too cute for us. He said 'No matter', and told us about how this man had killed his wife by stabbing her through the throat with a pair of scissors.

'He was a bit of a genius,' our new friend said, 'because he convinced the police that he was mad. Of course he was every bit as sane as you or me.'

'Where does the evening go?' I said, standing up.

Abie was on his feet too, but the man was between us and the door. 'Stay,' he said. 'Have a jar.' Softly: 'You will.'

I noticed that his right hand was out of sight in his jacket pocket. Perhaps I imagined it, but the impression that has stayed with me down the years is that I could hear a small metallic snipping noise. We sat again. He rang for the night porter, ordered three lagers and, without bringing his hand into view, told us lovingly how the murder was done. No detail was too insignificant, from the blood-flecked walls to the cat's red paw marks, the dying woman's last gurglings and the banshee wail of the police car drawing near.

He said: 'Guess how long he was in prison for.'

I said: 'Dunno.'

He said: 'You sound hoarse. Have you a cold?'

I coughed and shook my head.

He said: 'Y'ought to watch your throat.'

The drinks came, and he took his hand temporarily from his pocket to pay for them. He said 'Slainte!', took a sip of his lager and said: 'He was found guilty but insane and ordered to be detained at his Majesty's pleasure. Two years, and not a feather out of him. Sure he could have done another two, and a third standing on his head, no bother. Two short years for killing the bitch. What do you say to that for a bargain? Cut price, what?'

Luckily, the pun was unintentional, for if he had laughed I think I would have fainted. Abie, who seemed to have caught my cold, cleared his throat. He knew he was clutching at a straw, but he asked all the same. 'And . . . ah, when is he due out?'

'Amn't I telling you? He *is* out. A week since.'

Abie rose. The man stood up. Abie sat.

'And now, this fella, this friend of mine, he has a score or two to settle.'

It appeared that voices had spoken to the man in his cell in the criminal asylum and had told him who among his neighbours hated him and would do him down. Now he would deal with them, one by one. Some were tale-bearers and informers, others had turned his wife against him, for she had not been a bitch to begin with. All would pay. Listening to him, I began to wonder what colour my hair was.

He stared at us with sudden suspicion. 'Are ye sure certain that voices don't talk to youse in motor cars?'

Leaving Abie to look out for himself, I replied that I did

not own a car. My tone implied that if ever I was so fortunate as to acquire a motor, it would certainly come with a whole choir of voices fitted as standard. He did not seem wholly convinced, but nonetheless guided us through a verbal dossier on the murderer's ill-disposed and, did they but know it, doomed neighbours. On his list were the wall-eyed woman next door, who pretended to cook colcannon but was actually manufacturing poison gas; the man who had trained his dog to defecate in his – the murderer's – front garden; and the local minister, whom he had caught sniggering at him from the pulpit. He broke off to ring for more drink for himself. This time, when the night porter came, he ordered a double brandy. Fear being sometimes the father of courage, I seized on the diversion, sprang up and made for the door with a shout of 'Got to go. 'Night, now.' Abie, seeing my break for freedom, took off like a rocket, and, for a heart-stopping moment, we actually collided in the doorway. Once outside the lounge, we went straight and swiftly to our room and, without saying a word and as if we had been doing it every night of our lives, picked up a chest of drawers and shoved it against the door. Only then did I speak.

'I want to go home.'

'What? It's the middle of the night.'

'Tomorrow morning, then.'

'What about the girls?'

'Hump the girls.'

'We will, we will.'

I knew that his optimism had at last cracked, for he added a fervent 'Please God.' In the end, he talked me round and we met Belle and Cara in the afternoon. On that Sunday in Belfast, the only thing that was open was the sky; rain poured down. I tell a lie: the city fathers, when closing the cinemas and the pubs, had carelessly forgotten to lock up the zoo as well. We wandered about on the muddy pathways, staring at the giraffes and zebras and being stared back at in mutual misery. Then Belle had the idea that we should take a bus to visit her grandmother, who lived in a cottage under Cave Hill. We did so. She was a nice, if shapeless, old woman, sitting in an armchair that occupied most of the kitchen. She wore a cardigan over a torn jumper over an old gansy and had a rug across her lap. She seemed to be a semi-invalid. There was a down-draught in the chimney and our eyes stung from the smoke. When we had had tea with soot in it, Belle asked me if I really was a medical student. I was about to own up and tell her that I was a clerk, perhaps omitting the lowly part of it, when Abie chimed in to assure her that I was another Louis Pasteur in the making.

'In that case,' Belle said to me, 'Granny has a dropped stomach, and would you like to look at it?'

I did not know what a dropped stomach was and I still do not. It was irrelevant, for I would not have wanted to look at her stomach even if it had never dropped. I caught a nightmarish glimpse of the old lady happily throwing the rug aside and preparing to hike her skirt up there and then. A voice began to babble. It was mine.

'I'm not allowed to treat people until I qualify.'

Belle said: 'Sure just looking at her isn't treating her.'

'I can't. I'm not supposed to.'

'Sure who'd tell on you?' As she spoke, she saw the look of panic on my face and did not insist further, but I knew she thought me disobliging for drinking her grandmother's tea and yet begrudging even the most cursory glance at the woman's abdomen. She said, with heavy sarcasm: 'I'm sorry, Granny, he's not supposed to.' Abie had gone pale at the thought of seeing the stomach, but with the danger past his usual pastiness seeped back, and I silently swore to be revenged on him. As we left the cottage, Belle scalded me with her eyes and hissed: 'One wee look wouldn't have killed you.'

For all her roughness of tongue, she was quick to forgive and, on the bus back into town, asked me about Abie, who was sitting with Cara a few seats back. 'Is he all right?'

'How do you mean?'

'Ach, you know. I mean, is he rough with girls, like?'

'Rough, how?'

'For God's sake, I mean *rough*. How many kinds of bloody rough are there?' She lowered her voice. 'Cara's a bit . . . ye know, delicate.'

'Oh, no, Abie's not like—'

154

'Will ye let me finish!' She ransacked her mind for an easy way of saying it. 'She has this wee bit of botheration. It comes and goes, like. You'd know all about it.'

I was about to say 'Why me?'; then, remembering that I was a doctor or as good as, I spoke like one. 'What seems to be the trouble?'

She told me what Cara's trouble was, and said: 'Have a quiet word with your friend, won't you? Tell him what ails her . . . just in case it happens the while he's with her. So's he won't fly into a panic, like.'

I assured her that I would speak to him. 'On the q.t., mind,' she said. 'Don't let Cara hear. The poor creature gets embarrassed.'

We took another bus to where Belle lived on the Lower Malone Road and were shown into the parlour. She said to Cara: 'I suppose I'd better feed the brutes. You keep them company.'

She went out. From where we sat, we could hear her clattering about, and presently there came the sound and smell of food sizzling in a pan. It was unmistakably a fry-up of bacon and eggs; sausages, too, would be part of it, as sure as tomorrow's rain, and perhaps even crumbly rounds of black and white pudding, each as thick as a baby's wrist. An Ulster fry is to northerners as ambrosia to the gods, and the greedy thought leaped in my head of fried potato bread to crown the feast. The sizzling reached a crescendo, and I saw that Abie's mouth, like mine, was watering and out of control. When Belle returned, she was pushing a food trolley on which were four plates, each containing bread and butter, a slice of cold ham, a scallion, quarter of a tomato and a leaf of lettuce. We were too polite to ask about the fry-up. I have no idea what became of it; it is to this day part of my life's mythology: a mystery to outdo the enigmas of Kaspar Hauser, the Iron Mask and the Turin Shroud.

I did not get a chance to tell Abie about Cara's 'botheration'. After tea we played cards, then it was time for him to see her home. He had small, even, yellow teeth, and I saw them bared in a rictus of lechery as Belle showed them out. She returned a moment later, closed the door, flung me matter-of-factly on the sofa and jumped on top. She weighed a ton. She took hold of my necktie and twisted it in her fist until an ocean began to roar in my ears; then she suddenly looked up like a lioness interrupted at her feeding and said: 'I'd better see how the daddo is.' She went out again and was soon back.

To me, Northern Ireland was a foreign country, and I wondered what a daddo was. Somewhat anticlimactically, it turned out to be her father, who was in bed across the hall. At first, I thought the mystery was solved and that his presence in the house accounted for the Ulster fry, but Belle told me that he was suffering from heart disease and ate next to nothing.

'I'll tell you what he does eat: forty Gallaghers a day. Talk about thin, you'd see more fat on a skeleton.' She was angry. 'We put him in the front room because he's not supposed to walk up stairs. Stairs me bum, he's not even let out of bed, but the bloody man would get up if it killed him – and it will! The carry-on of him, you'd think he was in the Olympics. Christ almighty, and him with a heart in him like an eggshell.' She kept from crying by grinning into my face. 'And you needn't worry. I'm not going to ask you to examine him. You're no more a bloody medical student than what I am.'

Hovering between embarrassment and relief, I asked if her mother was alive.

'Oh, aye. She's with me aunt for the one evening she can get out of this kip all week. The poor woman's down to a shadow from nursing him.' This time the tears had to be blinked back. She said 'Ach!' loudly, brushing away the world and its woes, rubbed a knuckle into each eye, said 'Here's something you won't get in the Free State', and jumped on me as before. In the wrestling match that followed, she kept breaking off to listen. 'Was that him?' she would say, or 'Did you hear a noise?' It made it difficult for me to concentrate, but Belle seemed quite capable of doing the work of two. She was excitable; where other girls, if one was lucky, simmered, she seethed. In a nuclear age, one would think of a meltdown. Out of a blur of clothing and a tangle of limbs, she said: 'I'm all worked up. You'd better get going.' I thought she wanted me to go home, but in her lexicon 'get going' had a different connotation. It was hard to believe, but my faith in the inherent depravity of women was about to be vindicated. The lean years were done with. I was trying to get my trousers off when she froze.

'Christ, he's out of bed!'

It was true: I had heard a floorboard creak. Her bosom, most of it exposed and some of it in my eye, was heaving. She said: 'We can't stop now, it's too late.' She got off the sofa, went to the door and stood with her back tight against it to repel intruders. 'We'll have to do it this way.' She pulled at her skirt, wriggling her hips. I saw a pair of French knickers descending slowly.

Men have been driven wild by sights less heady, but another vision had taken squatters' rights inside my head. I saw her father pitting his poor strength against the door as I ravaged Belle up against it, and dropping dead from the effort. Worse still, I saw him succeed in getting his head into the room, only to succumb from the sight of his daughter and a total stranger bucking like two dinghies in a Force Nine.

I said: 'We can't.'

Actually, it was a question. I needed only to have my feebleness swept mockingly to one side, and the story would have been different. Instead, a light went out in her face. She said: 'No. No, you're right, it's too risky.'

No kettle had ever gone off the boil so quickly. It was as if she had been instantly and magically replaced by a well-behaved twin. I turned my back to allow her to put her clothing in order. She noticed and said: 'Ah, thanks; you're nice. Now you'd better go on home. I have to get him back into bed.'

I gave her my address, kissed her goodbye and walked the two miles or so to the hotel, racing past the Residents' Lounge in case the man from last night should emerge, scissors in hand. It was an hour before Abie came in. He was trembling. His face was white.

I will say for him that he was not one to preface his news with such coy invitations as 'You'll never guess what happened.' Disdaining all preamble, he came straight to the good stuff with 'I think I've killed her.'

'Killed who?'

Of course, it was Clara he meant. He had seen her home; they had sat at the foot of her stairs; he had kissed her. At this, she had gasped, had a violent spasm and threshed uncontrollably about, arching her body in a series of terrifying shudders. Abie, babbling 'Stop, I didn't mean it' – although what it was that he did not mean was unclear – tried in vain to hold her down. At last, when she seemed on the point of levitating, she had collapsed, a corpse, and he had fled. He said with the calmness of a man who saw the hangman's noose swaying gently, inches from his face: 'I'm surprised the police aren't here.' I took care to put the two twin beds between us before I told him that Clara was an epileptic.

A few days later, I received a letter from Belle saying how impolite Abie had been to leave her friend lying sound asleep at the foot of the stairs for her father to trip over in the morning. Later still, one Sunday evening while I was at the pictures, a policeman came to our door. He asked: 'Does Jack Keyes live here?' My father answered yes. The policeman said: 'Well, I have very bad news for him. His old fella is dead.'

He handed my father a telegram that, because the day was a Sunday, had come to the police station. It said: 'Father dead love Belle.' All my own father had to do was look in a mirror to know that he was alive and well, but he was not the better of the experience for a month.

My parents were growing old. For years, they had seemed ageless, then, almost overnight, I saw them as a stranger might. My father's legs had become stiff; he walked with a stick; his clothes were too big. My mother lost some of her old appetite for a grievance; she avoided the east wind. For the first time, I thought of them as mortal. One of my earliest memories is of seeing the funeral of Biddie Byrne, who lived at Number 5 in our lane, and saying as my mother tucked me into the vast summer meadow of a double bed I shared with her: 'Mammy, you and me will never die, sure we won't?' Naturally, and since I was spoiled rotten and denied nothing, she assured me that we would not. It took only a few years to realise that, if there were exceptions, we were not of their number; it was most of a lifetime before I knew with certainty that my mother had been right unbeknownst, that nothing dies.

One day in the future, I was to write a play about my father, who was a simple man. My mother's role in it was by comparison minor, partly because I knew that she was too prickly a person, forever conscious of the world's opinion, to take kindly to being put in a play, and also because I was more than a little in fear of her. She maddens me: whenever I try to write about her, a stranger spills on to the page: querulous, sharp-tongued, slow to praise, her antennae alert for an injustice or an imagined snub. As a boy, I would dread being with her in the presence of old ones, for it was then that she was sure to trot out her invariable and final judgment on ingrates: 'The more you do for them, the less thanks you get, and in the end of it they'd hang you.' It was a long time before I began to understand her, and knew that the hard words and harder looks were a preparation for the day when I would fly the nest. In her mind, the desertion had already begun. My every act of independence was part of it: a tram journey to Dublin on my own; a weekend eight short miles away in Powerscourt camping with the sea scouts (I can still remember the strawberry filling on the sandwich cake that was bought especially for my homecoming), a holiday abroad, a dress dance – all were small acts of defection.

Perhaps the least small was my marriage. One evening, on the prowl for girls, my friend Mick and I dropped into a social club named the France-Ireland. We had known happier hunting grounds; most of the female members were well-brought-up secretaries from various embassies, and the *directeur*, a Monsieur Boisseneau, did not permit close dancing. When Mick attempted vertical copulation after his first ten seconds on the dance floor, Monsieur Boisseneau tapped him on the shoulder. ' 'Ere,' he said, 'we 'ave three rules. We do not discuss releegion, we do not discuss politeecs, and we do not show too much what ees in zee 'art.' 'A dead loss,' Mick said on our way home. As for me, I had met a Belgian girl and, four years later, set off for Liege to be married.

Quite apart from the cost of travel, there was no question of my parents going to the wedding. 'Ah, it's too foreign,' my mother said flatly, deciding for them both. In case foreignness were not reason enough, she blamed my father, saying that he would never get on an aeroplane with his rheumatics. 'What are you talkin' about,' he said, 'or do you know what you're talking about? Amn't I up ladders every day of the week?' To which she said: 'You'd be a nice article to take to a foreign country.'

On the night before I left for Belgium, I thought the least I could do was spend the evening at home, but she would have none of it. 'What do you want to be stuck in the house for? Sure you may as well go to the pictures.' She added with a sniff: 'You'll be gone tomorrow, anyway, and long gone.' And so off I went to the Pavilion to see *The Night My Number Came Up*. I had robbed her of a wedding, and she was too proud to accept crumbs.

I may not have understood such small torments, but there were areas to be instinctively avoided, like a piece of torn skin that is too raw to be touched. Many Irish mothers cherish the hope that their doted-on son will enter the priesthood, but they do so, I suspect, for reasons that have less to do with piety than that another woman may not get her talons into him. When eventually I acquired my Belgian girl friend, the problem arose of how to introduce her to my mother, and I hit upon a method as ingenious as it was craven.

Our drama group was performing Bryan McMahon's play *The Bugle in the Blood* at the Bernadette Hall in Rathmines, and I reserved front-row seats for my parents. I placed my girl friend, Paule, next to my mother, but without telling either who her neighbour was. Instead, I gave my mother a large bag of sweets before setting out for the hall. My entrance came half-way through Act One, and I fetched a glance at the front row. Three sets of jaws were working in unison.

There are worse forms of cowardice, and one of these is to look away when one sees old age and infirmity come upon the Titans of one's childhood. I was guilty of this, not in terms of material neglect, but I turned my back upon my parents' mortality. It was a form of emotional cut-off, a refusal to look at them, and, for close on a year after my mother died, it preyed upon my mind. What nagged at me was nothing as strong as remorse, but rather the feeling that a son could have done better.

One evening, when I was lying in bed between sleep and waking, an experience occurred that I would hesitate to recount if I had not seen it repeated in every detail in a recent BBC television documentary on near-death 'out of body' phenomena. It was not a dream, of that I am certain, but a signal received on a wavelength of the mind. I was in a garden that was a blaze of colour, looking outwards over a white picket fence. My mother appeared on the path outside walking past and stopped at the closed gate. She was wearing a brown jacket and skirt and a hat I had seen in a photograph taken in 1927. She stopped to talk to me. She looked well and was amiable: not so much affectionate as polite. She said I was foolish to worry about her, that it was a waste of time that could be more pleasantly spent. She continued on her way, and my impression was that she had better things to do than stand talking to the likes of me.

I like to think that it was true.

9

So many now-acclaimed geniuses would never have been heard of were it not for me. It was I who first told the world about Dickens, Tolstoy, Maugham and Frank O'Connor. I discovered – on my honour I did – Alfred Hitchcock, Ernst Lubitsch and Jean Renoir, not to mention Georges Feydeau, Sean O'Casey and Kaufman and Hart. Verdi and Puccini were nobodies until I spread their names. They and others were my personal and exclusive discoveries. I would open a book, walk into a picture house, switch on the wireless, and at once I was a missionary, bent on spreading the true Word to the heathen. I knew that no one had yet heard of these gods of mine; otherwise, why were no comets seen, no fires on the hilltops, no bonnets hurtling over windmills? There was a girl in my office named Margaret O'Sullivan; she was from the country, red-haired, ten years older than I and a great reader. One morning, during the tea break, I changed her entire life, as I thought, by telling her of my latest protégé, a French writer named Maupassant. I was babbling about him for a time before I noticed that she was looking at me as if I had just announced my engagement to a Protestant.

'You don't read *him*?' she said.

I said: 'Yes, why not?'

She said, and her voice was as shrill as a playground: 'Don't you know what he died of?'

In Ireland, even today, you can get blind drunk and run down a hobble of old-age pensioners, and there are those who will sympathise and blame not you, but the drink itself: a good man's failing. Let you embezzle, and take the soda bread from the mouths of widows and their children, and, although fingers may wag, you will be privately admired for 'a cute whoor'. If you break a shopkeepers's head and steal his takings, the law may deem it a crime, but only a killjoy will call it a sin. This is not amorality, but rather a matter of elbow room: the loathing of sexuality looms so large in Irish life that all other offences must be shouldered aside to leave space for it to flourish. The difference between Irish Catholics and Christians is that where sex is concerned the former are inclined to invert the precept of the latter: that one should detest the sin while loving the sinner. A few years ago at a press conference, I saw a trim blonde lady across the room and thought her gamesome of eye. I asked my host, a Southerner and an industrialist, who she was.

'Oh, you know,' he said languidly. 'The kind of woman you want to hurt.'

'Pardon?'

He spelt it out for me. 'The kind you want to beat up.'

I said: 'But I don't beat up women. I don't even *want* to beat up women.'

He gave me the amused look of a man who knew all about my perversions in a sound-proofed basement room in Waterloo Road, accompanying it with a nudge that told me not to insult his intelligence. He said: 'Now come *on!*'

His glance alighted on his own wife standing near by. They smiled and airmailed each other a kiss.

If illicit sex were on occasion permitted a toehold – metaphorically speaking, that is – it was confined to the rarified world of the arts and, even there, the demarcation lines were unyielding. A British television director working in Ireland made off with a blonde singer, the wife of a professional man, and thereafter found that work in the Radio Telefis studios was, of a sudden, non-existent. When, rather than starve, the pariahs betook themselves to London, a certain impresario – the doyen of Irish theatre – boasted of his role of getting rid of them. 'We don't want them and their sort here,' he told me, adding a derisive Dublin term I have never been able to track to its source: 'Dirty elders!'

163

Bemused, I reminded him that a prominent Irish play director and an actor's wife had for years been having an affair that was as stormy as it was public. I said: 'How is it that no one ever chased *them* out of the country?'

'Ah,' he said with a smile that forgave my failure to grasp the niceties of such matters, 'but they're our own!'

When Margaret O'Sullivan asked me if I was aware of what Maupassant had died of, it was because she knew, as did all clean-living people, that an immoral man – or woman – could not possibly write a moral book. As a theorem, it stood so transparently to reason that you half-expected to find it in Euclid. At a debate on censorship at the Mansion House, I heard Sean O'Faoláin speak of the shame he had felt before his family and friends when a book of his was banned, making him in the public sight a pornographer. By then, the government list of proscribed books – itself a volume as bulky as Apuleius' *The Golden Ass*, which, after seventeen centuries, had at last been deemed unfit for the Irish to read – was approaching its peak figure of 12,000 titles.

The censors were not, as one might suppose, prodigious readers. All that was necessary to have a book removed from the shops and the public libraries was to send a copy to the Censorship Board with the offending passage marked. This, taken out of context, as in the case of Kate O'Brien's mere reference to lesbianism in *The Land of Spices*, was quite enough. As adolescents, we cherished banned books for their rarity value as much as for their salacity, although I remember vainly ransacking smuggled copies of both Richard Llewellen's *How Green Was My Valley* and L.A.G. Strong's *The Bay* in search of the dirty bits. Strong had a particular influence on me, for in *The Garden* and *Sea Wall* he wrote about Dalkey, the sea front at Sandycove and the Victorian roads I walked every day. One of his characters, the lame and kindly Paddy Kennedy, nicknamed 'the Wingman', was actually known to my father who described him to me as he described nearly everyone else, as a 'queer harp'. Seen through a stranger's eyes, the strand at the White Rock, the rock pools along the front at Scotsman's bay, the sweep of the hill down into Glasthule, and even a tram ride to the pictures ceased to be ordinary and took on a grandeur that was never lost. Upon reading his book of short stories, *Travellers*, I wrote to Strong, young pup that I was, pointing out that his initials – for 'Leonard Alfred George' – spelt *lag*, the Irish word for 'weak'. His response, signing himself 'Weak Strong', was to invite me to tea when he next came to Ireland. I sat facing him for an hour, tongue-tied, and he probably went away thinking that I had been unable to come and had, by default, sent my idiot brother.

I knew two writers by sight: the poet, Patrick Kavanagh, and his arch-enemy, Brendan Behan. Kavanagh haunted Parson's bookshop on Baggot Street Bridge and ceaselessly cleared his throat with the sound of a very old car trying to start and failing. One morning, I came tripping over my feet into the shop, and the doyenne, Miss O'Flaherty, begged me to make less noise. 'Mr Kavanagh,' she whispered, 'is having his breakfast.' I peered behind one of the shelves and was in time to see him draining a Baby Power as fast as it would empty. He put the bottle in his pocket, made a hawking noise that caused the pages of *Ireland's Own* to flutter on its rack, and took out a safety razor. Then, without soap or even water, and to the accompaniment of a rasping noise that made my skin crawl like a snake, he proceeded to rid himself of a two-day beard.

Years later, I sat beside him on a flight from Rome to London and, as the stewardess went past, he called to her: 'Miss, for the love o' Jasus give us a large Paddy.' She either ignored him or failed to hear. His voice rumbled like a bowling ball through the cabin: 'English bitch.' He added, just as loudly, and each syllable was caked with the cow dung of Mucker, County Monaghan: 'British whoo-err!'

In the case of Kavanagh, the man existed almost wholly in his poetry, the finest since Yeats's; his voice and appearance were merely the leftovers. He had the look of a pig-jobber: the arms forever folded high, as if in aloof disdain that he had been offered a runt; he wore thick farmyard boots and a sweat-stained felt hat and had an askew face that seemed to have been squeezed in a vice. For all his harrumph and bluster, he could be faced down and was terrified of Brendan

Behan, who knew with a slum-dweller's instinct who would run from him and who would stand. On hard-up days, when our lunch was a three-ha'penny potato cake eaten out of the fist as we ambled down Dawson Street, Behan was a familiar sight. He was not yet famous as a writer, but had been a Republican and an inmate of both Borstal in England and Mountjoy in Dublin. Such credentials defined him as a 'character', which is usually a Dublinese synonym for a bowsie or gurrier. He was a house painter, and it was said of him that he was decorating a certain pub, working and sampling the stock every weekday during the Holy Hour, and that the task had so far taken him two years. A friend of mine worked in his spare time for the Catholic Truth Society and sold religious booklets from a barrow outside the Pro-Cathedral. Behan came up with the careful belly-forward, head-back walk that told you his feet were tiny.

He asked: *'Tuigin tu Gaelig?'* ('Do you understand Irish?')

My friend proudly answered: *'Tuigim.'* ('I understand.')

Whereupon Behan unleashed the deafening roar of *'Tuigim* me bollix!' and went on his way, a listing galleon in a following sea.

He was unshamable: a show-off with an insatiable hunger for attention. His eyes were everywhere at once: in search of an audience, finding it, gauging its mood, dancing to its tune. Around town, he was known to be a 'decent skin' and 'one of our own'. Either term defined anyone who pronounced 'Jesus' as 'Jayzus', never employed a noun without propping a 'fuckin' ' up against it like timbers shoring up a tenement, got drunk and broke windows, gave half-crowns to children in the street, called old ones 'missis' and told them that they were the 'heart of the rowl', and displayed just enough erudition to hint that it was but the tip of an iceberg which good taste decreed should not be shown in its awesome entirety. All of this may have been innate and genuine to begin with, but once Behan discovered that the quality a Dublinman is most praised for is the absence of affectation, he milked the image for all that it was worth, knowing that anyone who fetched him a bleak look or threw doubt on his rough-hewn goodness would be scorned as a begrudger.

He had a street wit that was deadly. One of the highlights of an annual onset of culture known as *An Tostal* and now happily defunct was an historical pageant held in Croke Park. The climax of this was provided by the actor, Anew McMaster, who, wearing a white beard and dressed as St Patrick, saved Ireland for Christianity by tearing about the field and overturning a number of pagan idols. Behan had managed to scale half-way up one of the pillars of the grandstand and endorsed the proceedings with repeated roars of 'Good oul' God!'

He could be genial, but no Dublin street was wide enough or long enough to be shared with another writer. The city itself was too small, and his fear, even of those who offered him no threat, was so naked as to be endearingly childlike. My own first play had hardly begun to limp through an inglorious three-week run at the Abbey when I ran foul of Behan, who by now was known as the author of *The Quare Fellow*. Every morning on my way to Merrion Street, I called into Parson's bookshop, which was a haunt of his as well as of other writers. As I waited to be served, he would shuffle over and glare murderously from a range of a few inches. It was an undeclared war of attrition, and I fought back by pretending to be unaware of the vast, stubbled face, the pale blue eyes ringed with blood, and the sour smell of last night's pints. I knew it enraged him to be ignored, and yet to address me directly would be to lose face. After a week or so, he took to haranguing the ceiling.

'Is *Esquire* banned in this country?'

No one answered.

More loudly: 'For the love an' honour, is there ne'er a one to answer a civil question?' The ladies who managed Parson's allowed for the waywardness of the artistic soul, but I noticed that Behan did not court banishment by using an obscenity. 'I asked is *Esquire* banned here?'

Miss O'Flaherty simpered: 'Sure, Mr Behan, don't you know it is.' (It was true, for it was in those days notorious for its photographs of women showing not only their legs but also as much as three inches of bare midriff.)

'Is that so?' Behan said, still to the ceiling. 'I hear tell I have a play in it this month. I was paid for it right enough.'

He named what seemed to me an enormous sum. 'Yes, I got the readies, the few shekels, but when a man can't read his own bloomin' play it's a bit of a —'

By then I was clear of the shop and pushing my bicycle at a run over the hump of the canal bridge.

Over the next two or three weeks, buying my morning paper was purgatory. There were, of course, other newsagents along the way, but this was a duel between Behan and me, although whether the battle was territorial, or for a purely moral ascendancy, I had no idea, nor, I think, had he. One day, he would brag that *The Quare Fellow* was due to go on at a place called Stratford East, and where the hell was that? On another, he would ask if anyone had ever heard of fillum producer named Metro or Mayer or something who was trying to take out an option on his play. Then, staring at a point just southwards of my ear, he would say: 'What's an option when it's at home?'

One day, he did not appear. I had a holiday from him for perhaps a week and was beginning to think I was rid of him for good when he came into the shop almost blind from the ravages of a hangover. He had not washed for days; his face was purple, the eyes sunk in his head. There was spittle on his chin. *In extremis*, he spoke to me for the first time. He said: 'Hey, for Christ's sake, what day is it?'

Perhaps I thought he was trying to be funny. Or I may have been dismayed at seeing him come back to torment me. Whatever the reason, I snarled 'Shag off!' and flung out of the shop.

Behan came after me. He stood on the summit of the bridge as I pedalled off, his face a muddy, blood-coloured sunset. He brought into sight a fist that was usually out of sight inside the sleeve of his black overcoat. 'That's lovely,' he bellowed. 'That's exquisite. That's gorgeous fuckin' language.'

The next and last time we spoke was in the Brazen Head eight years later. He had perhaps six months of life left. He was sober. He said: 'You writin' an'thin'?'

I told him what I was working on and asked the same question of him.

He said: 'No. The way it is, I'm off the hard stuff. Once I get off the beer as well, I'll start writin'.'

A few days later, he went to a luncheon where some joker poured a vodka into his tomato juice. It sent him on a tear that lasted six weeks and landed him in Baggot Street Hospital for a month. When he was discharged I saw him on television and had to look away, for by then death was already on his face.

I remember one other literary encounter in Parson's bookshop, and it happened the year I made a stage adaptation of Joyce's *A Portrait*. It caused something of a splash at the 1962 Dublin Theatre Festival, and Frank O'Connor went to see it as guest critic for one of the Sunday papers. His review began: 'I am proud to say that I did not like *Stephen D.*'

The play was no more than a scissors-and-paste affair with nothing of myself in it, and so in spite of O'Connor's eminence his contempt was no worse than a gnat bite. What did annoy me was not that he disliked the play, but that he took pleasure in disliking it. He himself was a Titan. I revered his stories; I had weaned myself on them; but later, as in the case of Patrick Kavanagh, I learned that whenever a writer is renowned for the depth of compassion in his work, usually very little of the stuff remains in the man himself. It was said of O'Connor that he was tetchy, vain, choleric and, like every Irish writer born to woman, disappointed. Still, I had not thought him small.

A few days after the review appeared, I was in Parson's and saw that a new edition of his stories had come out. I was about to buy a copy when Miss O'Flaherty said: 'No, don't take that one. I have a few here that are signed by the author.'

I said, primly: 'No, thank you. I'd prefer an unsigned copy. I admire O'Connor's work, but I don't care much for O'Connor. If you'll permit me to say so, I think he's a miserable, unmannerly bogman.'

She said: 'Oh, Mr Leonard', and looked in dismay, not at me, but over my shoulder. I turned in time to see a bespectacled man with white hair, white moustache and black eyebrows marching out of the shop, his face tight with anger. She again said 'Oh, Mr Leonard', this time softly, as a mother might weep for an apostate son.

Fifteen years earlier, in the late 1940s, O'Connor was only one of the Irish writers whose work was, in part, proscribed. Joyce, O'Faoláin, O'Casey, Kavanagh (who said: 'It's the price of me for writing poetry that a policeman could understand'): these and others were conscripted into what was known as the Legion of the Banned. In 1946, an amateur production of O'Casey's *Juno and the Paycock* was banned by the clerics who ran the Father Mathew drama festival, not because of its politics or the depicted brutalities of slum life, but because Mary Boyle, who is unmarried, is seduced and becomes pregnant. Radio Eireann solved Mary's problem without going to the extreme of banning the play. In O'Casey's text, the following occurs when Juno Boyle must tell her wastrel husband that their daughter is expecting a baby.

MRS BOYLE: It's about Mary.

BOYLE: Well, what about Mary – there's nothing wrong with her, is there?

MRS BOYLE: I'm sorry to say there's a gradle wrong with her.

BOYLE: A gradle wrong with her! *(Peevishly)*: First Johnny and now Mary. It's not consumption, is it?

MRS BOYLE: No, it's not consumption . . . it's worse.

In the radio production, transmitted to perhaps half a million homes all over Ireland, the last two lines were amended to go as follows:

BOYLE: . . . It's not consumption, is it?

MRS BOYLE: Yis.

We did not feel oppressed by the lunacy: it was a game: us outwitting them. Like scavenger birds on a rubbish tip, we rooted in street barrows for books that had slipped through the net. On principle, we took, when we could find them, ragged copies of *Lilliput* and *Men Only* and even *Razzle, Blighty* and *Reveille*, often with their occasions of sin scissored out by the previous owner. Irish authors were not too difficult to locate; usually their books had had a short run for their money before coming under disfavour, and had thereafter gone into hiding, like Jews from the Nazis. More seriously, a wave of post-war fiction was on its way from America; and, as naturally as a sparrow is swooped on by a hawk, copies were stopped by the customs and held, unread and unaccused, until the censors found time to attend to them. In such cases, there were few of us who did not have a friend, smiled upon by the gods, who went on holiday into the great world beyond Dublin Bay and could be persuaded to bear home, trembling as if for his life, Mailer's *The Naked and the Dead*, Robert Penn Warren's *All the King's Men*, James Jones's *From Here to Eternity* and Salinger's *Catcher in the Rye*, which today is not only looked upon with the indulgence shown to a reformed criminal, but is also a prescribed text in secondary schools.

Once a book was found, the new problem arose of how to pay for it. If the worst happened, you could steal it. My belief is that, thanks to the censors, the Dublin of that time became the world's best-read city. Also, there can have been few better towns in which to be broke. I once mentioned to one of my superiors at work that, apart from having three-ha'pence for an evening paper, I had no money. Envy came into his eyes – or, rather, his eye, for the other one was glass.

He said: 'But you have money at home? Or in the bank or the post office?'

I told him: no, not a penny.

He said: 'What's it like? Remind me. I've forgotten.'

I had no answer. Poverty can be described, for it is a presence, open to the senses: it can be touched, seen, even tasted; whereas being broke is its opposite: an absence. The kind we were, we thought that pockets were for hands and hankies.

One Friday, the impossible happened. There was a pay rise, even for temporary clerks, and, because it was retro-active, seventeen pounds fell in one great lump into my fist. It was not simply a windfall, but wealth: blinding and unreal; and, on that pay-day, four of us did the unthinkable and went for dinner to a restaurant, a basement place named The Subway. The waiter asked if we wanted to see the wine list. We stared at each other, at once helpless, then I heard my own voice say: 'Yes, why not?' I chose a bottle of red; it was brought, and the waiter poured a little into my glass. I had never before ordered wine, but I knew what was required. Aware that here

171

was a great 'first' in my life, I was determined to make of it a moment that could be framed. As my companions looked on in awe, I swirled the wine around the glass, pretended to sniff the bouquet (then, as now, I had hardly any sense of smell), and took a delicate sip. No oenophile ever rolled a Château-Lafite Rothschild around his tongue as jadedly as I did, nor with such world-weariness murmured that it would 'do'.

The waiter said: 'Jayzus, sure it won't p'ison yah, annyway.'

No matter; for an hour, we were children in the finery of grown-ups.

Once, outside the Savoy Cinema, I saw a man in top hat and tails stepping out of a taxi with a woman who wore a glittering black dress that was like a second skin, and to me they were not alive at all. When I was six or so and my parents took me to the Picture House on Sunday afternoons, I would look up and down George's Street in hopes that I might catch sight of the lorry arriving with the lions and crocodiles for the weekly serial, *Jan of the Jungle*; and, in the same way, the man and woman might have been film creatures on their way to the screen.

Jammet's restaurant was a door and two half-curtained windows in Nassau Street. During Horse Show week, you went past it, stepping off the kerb as a couple, bowed out by the doorman, moved into your way. They were gentry, up for the show from Kildare, perhaps, or Westmeath. The man, somehow without giving the least suggestion of loudness, wore a jacket you could play draughts on. His bearing told you that he was the kind of person who would say 'shall' instead of 'will' all the time, as we did. He waited while the woman stood drawing on thin, chamois gloves. She spoke to him in a clear voice that neither whispered nor shouted and, you knew, never would. They had not expected you to move out of their way, because they had not seen you. The ability to look without seeing was what made them the Quality, just as stepping out into the street proved that you were not. You never expected or wanted to eat at Jammet's or the Russell or the Red Bank, heaven forbid, but a sore that smarted in a small, back corner of your mind was that neither were you ever likely to be the friend of anyone who did.

There were legends that walked the streets of the same city as we did, but not the same world. A frequent sight was the playwright, Lennox Robinson. I would gape at him, hardly believing that here was the author of *Drama at Inish* and *The Far-off Hills* in the actual flesh – although there was pitifully little of it. He was beanpole thin, and seemed to be wilting. His head towered above any crowd, as if he were a lone Christian crossing the floor of a mosque at prayer-time. He was hectic of cheek, lugubrious of mien. Threading his way through town, he seemed fey and aloof from the vulgar throng, although his pub obituarists were to say that, as a member of the Abbey Theatre board of directors, he had a Florentine gift for intrigue. He went about with a white Cairn terrier named Sylvester. They were a bizarre couple: the dog at the end of its leash put one in mind of a coracle towing a schooner. And, to use 'schooner' in a different sense, Robinson was often the worse for sherry. Once, with Sylvester, he patiently queued for two hours for the Bing Crosby film, *Going My Way*, at the Capitol Cinema while under the impression that he was waiting for the Dalkey tram. On another occasion, he was adjudicating a drama festival some-where down the country, and his own play, *The Whiteheaded Boy*, was one of the offerings. The actors expected praise; instead, when it was over, he came on the stage, looking like a pair of lazy tongs standing on end and about to collapse. In limp desolation, he wailed to the audience: 'Did you see what they did to my beautiful play?'

He was an unlikely chronicler of simple lives. The people of his plays lived in small country towns. In *The Far-off Hills*, everyone wants what he cannot have. The sixteen-year old Pet looks in the mirror and groans: 'I wish to God I had a different class of a nose.' Harold Mahony, who has not smiled since his wife went mad on their honeymoon, thinks he wants to marry Marian; she, as self-deluding as he is, is set on entering a convent. Robinson, the dreamer, the cloud-dweller, fashioned his earthlings with wisdom and affection, as if he lived among them, upstairs from a shop or in a granite house half-way along Church Street, with a picture of Father Maguire on the parlour wall. There is such a picture called for in the setting of *The*

Whiteheaded Boy, and the author in a stage direction confides to us that the priest is 'No relation, but a lovely man.' It might be said of Robinson that, like Thornton Wilder of *Our Town*, he attempted to 'find a value beyond price for the smallest events in daily life'. As I say, I gawked at him on the street. His fame was such that people could not refer by name to Longford Terrace in Monkstown without adding 'where Lennox Robinson lives'. At their best, his plays were flawlessly constructed and, thirty years ago, were performed by every amateur group in the land. Today, he is an antiquity. His name appears here and there in the biographies of others. There is a life-sized portrait of him in the Abbey bar. He sits, hands folded, six feet and some inches of misery. It is difficult to buy a drink without wanting to offer him a sherry.

The time came when I tried my own hand at writing a play. It was a one-act entitled *The Man on Platform Two*, based on the old legend that Parnell did not die in October, 1891, but was spirited out of reach of his enemies. My friend, Brendan Ryan, who managed a snack bar in Dun Laoghaire, played Parnell and we entered the play for a festival at my old stamping ground, the Little Flower Hall in Bray. Father Browne was as yet the incumbent, and afterwards I was rash enough to invite his opinion. He said 'God bless you' to a lady who was passing, then smiled at the church steeple and told it: 'I don't like political plays. I don't like plays with a spleen.' Before I could ask him what he meant, he said 'Ah, Mrs Kinsella, a word in your ear!' and went off to talk to a woman he had espied with an eye that was somewhere in the back of his head. It took a while before I realised that although sixty years had passed, the clergy had not forgiven the adulterer, Parnell.

Later, I attempted a full-length suburban farce called *Nightingale in the Branches*. Lancos performed it. My crony, Mick, played a character I had based on his own father; Róisín was the mother; and Jimmy Keogh ad-libbed and said 'boinng' and 'gedoink' to his heart's content. A few years later, under another title and with only two words ('Yes, Da') of the original dialogue retained, it became Barry Fitzgerald's last film. Meanwhile, our production came and went, and the audiences from work

174

laughed and said wasn't it great, considering. My name was on the showcards; I was at last an author. To my disgust, the world went on turning regardless, and I continued to be stuck tight in the Land Commission like a sheep in a bog hole.

Mr Drumm, who could no longer stand the sight of me, had ordained my banishment to the room behind his, where my immediate superior was a Mr Cramer, a burly man with a cultured accent, a moustache and an Eric Von Stroheim haircut. He could not sit still, but constantly tore around like a demented bull. If he thought he might miss the bus home to Ranelagh at lunchtime, he would bark like a distraught wolfhound, send his table crashing into mine, which in turn rammed me in the stomach, and go charging out, lost in a slipstream of whirling paper. To no one's great surprise but his own, he eventually dropped dead.

Although he did not seem to be well-read, he once told me that he had a library of two thousand books. It was a rare confidence, for in the most kindly way he was a snob. As a mere Staff Officer, Grade II, he had either come down in life or failed to rise in it; but his family were gentlefolk, and he had been brought up to believe that, while all mankind were his equals, he was not of necessity required to treat them as such. We liked him, and thought that his death would be a toss-up between a heart attack and being run over, for he could not see a priest without rushing across the street to pay his respects.

At work, it was understood that on arrival we had ten minutes' grace in which to peruse the morning paper. One day, when Mr Cramer caught me covertly reading it at five past ten, he made such a huffing and puffing about it that I sulked and deliberately did not remind him, as I usually did, when the time came for his lunchtime bus. Suddenly, he jumped up, bellowed 'Blazes Kate, I'm destroyed!' and went tearing out, doors banging into the distance like cannon fire. He missed the bus and returned after lunch, eating Rennies as if they were peanuts. Later, red in the face, he said that Mr Drumm wanted to see me.

'Mr Cramer believes that he has cause to complain of

you,' Mr Drumm said, making a church roof of his fingers. 'He alleges that you are wanting in respect.'

I asked, coldly: 'On what grounds?'

His nostrils twitched as if at an offensive smell. He had not spoken to me in a year. I had disappointed him. Everyone did, sooner or later, but to me, encased with him each morning in the same train compartment, he had made himself vulnerable. He never spoke of his life, but of books, or a rare visit to the cinema, and his wit impaled those of his colleagues, and they were legion, whom he considered to be time-servers or hypocrites. In my case, what happened may have been that I started to avoid him rather than be looked down upon as his toady. At any rate, he decided that his confidences had been betrayed and his good nature – which was virtually non-existent – abused. For all his prickliness, I had been fond of him. Being myself a mumbler, I was besotted with his gift for a phrase and his preciseness of speech. Also, he had a barbed integrity which he kept alive at the cost of letting much else perish: his friendships, peace of mind and, in Merrion Street, cronyism and the rewards for holding one's tongue. His enmity hurt me; I felt ill-used. Now, behind the coldness of his regard, there was the hurt of a cast-off suitor. For a moment – and then it was gone – I felt an urge to throw my arms around the old fool.

He said, echoing me: 'You ask on what grounds?'

Unwisely, I attempted to play him at his own game and say something trenchant and well-formed to the effect that, in the matter of collecting arrears of rent from the tenant farmers of Cork and Galway, I was his and Mr Cramer's to command, but it was not my function to act as the latter's personal nurse and alarm clock. Instead, I made a hames of it, mislaying a verb, marooning a noun on a foreign shore, starting a jerry-built sentence that caved in half-way through when, without warning, nasal catarrh closed upon me like a sea fog. Cruelly, Mr Drumm let me finish or, rather, wind down like an old timepiece clogged with grease. I fell silent; he waited; I snuffled and bubbled, and he waited some more. Then he showed me how it should be done.

'My friend,' he said, making it sound as if he would as soon seek out the companionship of an asp, 'your want of breeding is beyond mortal remedy' – I flushed, taking this to be a jibe at my pedigree or, rather, my lack of one – 'but between us we may yet instil in you the rudiments of good manners.'

What was damnable was that while one part of me wanted to throttle him, another was admiring his knife-clean enunciation and his command of language.

'According to rumour,' he went on, 'you have written a play for the theatre. I am told, and I would imagine it to be true, that among the desirable attributes of a dramatist, indeed of a writer, are humility and compassion. You seem to possess neither.'

He glared at the five or six other occupants of the room, who were happily listening. Their heads ducked out of sight behind the arrears schedules that were propped in front of them on wooden frames. Having disposed of them, Drumm returned to his muttons. I half-expected him to offer me a cigarette and a blindfold.

'As long as Mr Cramer continues to be your superior officer, you will show him courtesy and respect, do you hear me? In particular, you will do or say nothing . . . nothing, do you understand?' – I tensed myself, for here it came – 'to undermine his harmless delusion that he is a gentleman.'

There was a gasp, ecstatic and concerted, from behind the arrears schedules. I was not, after all, Drumm's victim; Mr Cramer was. I had merely been used as a cat's-paw to make him seem a fool and an upstart. By going-home time, the story was all over Collection Branch. By lunch-time next day, it had penetrated to the uttermost parts of the Congested Districts Board in Hume Street and Forestry in Merrion Square, and as Mr Cramer, in a stampede of one, went pounding towards the Ranelagh bus and his home-cooked lunch, there were winks and sniggers of 'Jayzus, did you hear what your man Drumm said about Jacko Cramer?' On the instant, he had a nickname unto death: 'Jacko the Gent.' I wondered why Drumm had done it: perhaps because Mr Cramer was forever putting on airs; more likely for the simpler reason that the Land Commission begot its own kind of pygmy cruelty.

Nobody, the State least of all, cared about us, and so we came not to care about each other. Indifference bred a meanness of spirit, which, in turn, engendered the petty jealousies and feuds, the tale-bearing and begrudgery that in time dragged to earth even those who flew highest. There were some who thought the work all the more tolerable because it required no skill; they did it, skimping if they could, for eight hours a day, slept for another eight, and lived an eight-hour life. At the end of the road, they would tell you, you could not whack the old pension. I wanted more. In the vaguest of ways, I had thought that once I had written a play I would be magically transported to a new existence. Every half-year, I refused to sit for an examination in written and oral Irish which would have led to advancement: I was afraid that a rise in salary might sap my will when the time came to break loose. Now, as the seasons came around again, it seemed that I would end my days, not merely as a civil servant but, thanks to my lunatic optimism, as a rank-and-file clerical officer: the common fate of boozers and losers like Joe McAteer and the chronically unwashed, such as 'the Needler' Maguire.

I had failed, too, in my chosen extra-mural career as a philanderer. As if in obedience to a secret oath taken at the onset of puberty, the women in my life, no matter what their shape and age, perversely declined to bend to my will. Even certified nymphomaniacs would smile at me half-way through our first and, not to put a tooth in it, last evening together and thank me in advance for being the first man in years to have respected their frailty. There is a kind of time limit in such areas, and, having exceeded mine, I gave up and became engaged to marry. As the wedding day approached, I was presented with a travelling bag by my colleagues. Drumm boycotted the ceremony. Pointing his umbrella, as if aching to impale those arriving for the speeches, he disdainfully stalked off to catch the 5.14 to Dalkey. The speakers were Mr Kilfeather, the Assistant Principal of our branch, and Mr Cramer, who had been pressed into service as the reluctant understudy for Drumm.

Kilfeather arrived, limping; it was the souvenir of a mishap

from the previous week. He was an obnoxious man with obnoxious habits, and one of these was to quit his room at 4.45 each
day, walk through the adjoining office that contained perhaps
thirty clerks, and immure himself in the men's lavatory on the
far landing. At precisely 4.57, the chain was pulled, and he would
emerge, ostensibly to return to his room, but actually to see if
anyone in the large office had dared to put his street clothes on
three minutes ahead of time. The ploy would have been less
contemptible had it not been so transparent; but it happened
that a clerk named Oliver Whelehan had a habit as obnoxious
in its way as Kilfeather's. Whenever he used the lavatory, he
would conclude his business by unravelling perhaps fifty feet
of toilet roll and ramming it into the bowl, leaving the thing
unflushable until plumbers came from the Board of Works. No
one knew why; nor, perhaps, did Oliver.

One day, the week before my presentation, Oliver made
his customary use of the lavatory, and, a few minutes after he
had gone, Kilfeather arrived on his daily routine of espionage.
He lowered his trousers and underpants, sat, filled his pipe, lit
it and dropped the match down the front of the toilet bowl. A
few moments later, a loud *whoof!* sound was heard, followed
by a cry of anguish, and a few women clerks who had the
great good fortune to be passing were treated to the sight of
Kilfeather hopping out of the W.C. with his trousers around his
ankles and his pubic hair smoking a tramp steamer outward
bound for Mombasa.

As well as his limp, he had the more permanent affliction
of a speech impediment, which caused him to pause and say
'Ummm' after every four or five words. Today, the audience
writhed as each 'ummm' became longer and more tortured than
its predecessor. I stood, red in the face, aware that a clerk
named Donal Coughlan was conducting a conversation of his
own immediately to my rear. Coughlan was tiny, with ears like
teacup handles. He resembled a gnome. Because of treatment
with cortisone when the drug was still in its experimental stage,
his hair had fallen out and he was almost stone deaf, and, like
many deaf people, he did not so much speak as yell. Kilfeather
battled on, wishing me ummm happiness and hoping that all my

ummm troubles would be little ummm ones. At last, he hit an 'ummm' that seemed endless: the room shivered as if a power plant were operating on the floor below. He paused as if to make a run at whatever he had in mind to say, whereupon, Coughlan roared in his Cork accent: 'Errah, deh trout down dere are very sulky, very sulky altogedder!'

At this, Kilfeather gave up and passed the torch on to Mr Cramer who, quite simply, had nothing to say. He huffed and puffed for a minute, and then inspiration struck.

He said: 'I'm sure we all wish Mr Byrne the very best, and we hope now that he's getting married that he'll settle down to work like the great man he is and give up all this playwriting nonsense.'

A frisson of sheer joy went through the audience. Mr Cramer, unaware that he had said anything out of the way, gave me the travelling bag with the best wishes of my colleagues, said 'Blazes Kate, look at the time!' under his breath and went hurrying out, followed by Kilfeather. At once, there was laughter. Everyone knew where my ambitions lay, and that he had put his foot in it. 'How,' Arthur Nolan said, 'can a man be so bloody insensitive?' 'Old gobshite,' someone else said.

I smiled and affected to share in the joke. Privately, Mr Cramer's gaffe had struck a chord. There was that wooden trunk in my bedroom at home; it was my writing table, and to use it as such I was obliged either to bark my knees or sit with my legs to one side, out of the way. The alternative was the kitchen table downstairs, with my mad aunt Mary maundering on, as if she somehow knew that it made me as crazed as she was. On summer evenings, my mother would tell me that the sun was still splitting the trees and here I was hunched indoors over an old copybook. In the winter, she nagged at me to go to the pictures or to see my friends instead of giving them the go-by. 'And sign's on it,' she would say, 'in the wind-up you'll have no one left who'll throw a word to you, no more than they would to a dog.' Worst of all was when she would tell my father and Mary to be quiet because 'Jack is at his writin' ', and the noise of three people deliberately not making a sound was louder than any thunder. And so I worked upstairs in the front bedroom, and let a summer and an autumn slide by, fashioning that first play of mine, crying at times when words, knowing that I was not their master, jeered at me like cornerboys. When Lancos performed it, my mother was in the audience. Afterwards, I asked, trying not to sound too eager: 'What did you think?'

All she said was: 'Too much oul' talk.'

Somehow, in a way I never understood and never shall, it had angered her: not the play itself, as harmless as it was, but that I had written it. I never again invited her to see a play of mine, not out of pique or in revenge, but to avoid a second slap in the face, as light as the first had been. She, who could take mortal offence at an unintended slight, did not mind in the least. Probably she was relieved.

I had expected too much of that play, pinned too many hopes on it. Like an inmate of the Chateau d'If, his brain softened from the years of solitude, I had convinced myself that by burrowing through a single wall I would at once reach freedom and the outside world instead of, as happened, another part of the prison. Now, while I laughed with the others at Mr Cramer's failure to recognise that he had a potential genius on his hands, a small chill voice whispered that perhaps he was right and it was time I gave up the 'playwriting nonsense'.

10

On the few occasions when I am caught off guard and land myself on a public platform, there is always a smiling lady who raises her hand and asks if I have any advice for young writers. I invariably reply 'No', and for two reasons: first, because the blunt negative always gets a laugh, and secondly because writing is neither profession nor vocation, but an incurable illness. Those who give up are not writers and never were; those who persevere do so not from pluck or determination, but because they cannot help it: they are sick, and advice is an impertinence. When the Abbey Theatre announced a competition for new Irish plays, I forgot all about Mr Cramer's finger-wagging and went to work. This, I knew in my bones, would be the Big One.

It was nothing of the sort. I called it *The Italian Road*. I had been to Italy on holiday and stayed at a resort named Varazze some miles from Genoa. It had the only sandy beach on the Ligurian Riviera, but I never saw it. There was a heat wave, with temperatures in the high nineties, and I spent my days under a sun umbrella trying to make a glass of beer last for an hour. Eventually, I fled northwards to Milan and attempted unsuccessfully to find the cathedral: not one of the streetcars announced *Cathedrale* as its destination; they were all bound for a place named *Duomo*, whatever that was when at home. So I went to a music hall instead and heard an old tenor named Gino Franz sing tearfully in front of a rippling backdrop of Naples and Vesuvius. The audience was rowdy; empty bottles clattered down the aisle. Two utterly inept acrobats came on and were hooted off; the Neapolitan backdrop was again unfurled, hitting the stage with a thump, and Gino Franz reappeared by public demand, quite overcome – as he doubtlessly was at every performance – by the acclamation. The more humility he evinced, the louder were the cries of 'Bravo!', and when he wept the audience stood, cheering. I had the time of my life, applauding and shedding tears of maudlin delight, and from that evening on Italy became not a reality but a myth: a kingdom to be one day regained.

My play was a kind of homage to the ideal. A youth, whose father is for no explained reason a schoolmaster in Ravello – a place in which I have not set foot to this day – lives with his alcoholic mother in a seaside boarding-house outside Dublin. He dreams that his estranged parents will become reconciled and bear him off to Italy and the sun. The action required that the play be set during school holidays; Christmas was too festive, summer too cheerful for the requisite greyness, and so I settled for Easter. When amateurs later performed the play, an eminent critic wrote of its brilliant symbolism, pointing out that the first act took place on Spy Wednesday, the day of betrayal, the second on Good Friday, the time of sacrifice, and the third on Easter Sunday, the day of spiritual rebirth. No one has ever believed that a playwright simply sits down to write a play without a thought entering his head of symbols, metaphors or subtexts, and Irish drama critics were in those days, as they continue to be, a breed of quack psychoanalysts in unswerving pursuit of what O'Casey called 'magnificent meanin's'. Unfortunately for *The Italian Road*, there were no critics moonlighting as play readers for the Abbey, who turned it down flat.

The standard was so abysmal, a letter tactfully informed me, that no prize would be awarded. I was not so much dismayed as stunned, for I had recently been at the first night of the previous year's winner, a play called *John Courtney*, and it was so flat-footedly dull as to send me out of the theatre grinning from ear to ear in the certainty that I had the contest in my pocket. What I had not grasped was that the tastes of the Abbey did not run to a play set in a Dun Laoghaire boarding-house and more concerned with the fate of its characters than with the perennial theme of what was wrong with the country.

The archetypal Abbey play of the 1950s was dominated by the seemingly Promethean figure of the 'Warrior': a doughty one-time guerrilla leader who is now a powerful businessman and county councillor. His integrity has been sapped by avarice; those who oppose him are genially ridden down. He has a kept woman named Margot in the nearby metropolis of Mullingar; she brazenly accompanies him to the Curragh races and smokes in public. He, the playwright is saying, is the New Ireland. His wife is a wretched creature, ignored by all and with nothing to say. This is because she is being saved up for a three-minute speech cunningly positioned at the end of the play and on that account assured of a round of applause. There are two children of the marriage: a daughter who is in love with the local school-master, a young radical; and a son whom the Warrior forces to enter a seminary because of the social cachet of a priest in the family. There is a Machiavellian clergyman: the canon, who, as the local powerbroker, is a crony of the Warrior. And the mandatory comic relief is provided by a peripatetic handyman who believes that a wooden leg is hereditary.

The action has to do with how, for dynastic reasons, the Warrior marries off his daughter to an egregious middle-aged politician. To this end, the canon falsely accuses the girl's lover of interfering with one of his pupils, and an enraged mob – their voices are heard, off – drive him from the town. As counterpoint to this, the son arrives home and tells his father that he has no vocation for the priesthood. The Warrior says 'To think that I, F.X. Mulmartin, have spawned not a son but a weak-kneed, whingeing girl,' and sends him back to the seminary. Before he leaves, the boy says: 'Mother, I can't face it. Speak to me.' This being still Act Two, she says nothing.

The last act is the strongest. The son is led in, now dribbling and hopelessly unhinged by the horrors of ordination, and the daughter, rather than yield her body to a satyr, hangs herself upstairs in her wedding dress. The mother makes her speech, telling the Warrior that she has only stayed with him for the sake of the children, adding pathetically, 'There was a day long gone, Frank, when I had the good thought for you', and leaves the house forever. This coincides with the arrival of a letter from the mistress in Mullingar saying that she is actually an apostate nun and has decided to return to the convent. The final scene has been foreshadowed for an act and a half by the Warrior absent-mindedly rubbing his chest, wincing and muttering: 'The devil take that feed of greasy bacon.' This is known in the world of drama as play construction, and it enables the Warrior to succumb convincingly to a heart attack. He dies alone as sunset turns the room to flame, and a single autumn leaf flutters down outside the window. Slow curtain.

The Italian Road boasted few of these marketable ingredients. Also, it was probably not a very good play, but it was the best I could do. When you are young and a work is rejected, it is as if you were a rider thrown by a horse, and the worst part of it is not simply the bruising, but the convalescence of the spirit before you again seize both courage and reins. I stared at the returned script and the covering letter, which was not even personally typed, but stencilled, and grinned stupidly at my wife in a frail attempt to conceal the shame. We had been married for not much more than a month: it was an indecently short time in which to be found out.

She said: 'Why don't you send the Abbey *Nightingale in the Branches?*'

This was the suburban comedy that had been done by Lancos. Reasoning that I had nothing to lose, I at once gave her cause to regret the suggestion by touching her for eight pounds to have the script retyped – thirty years on, the realisation comes that I never repaid it. When I was on the point of mailing the play, it occurred to me that its having been previously performed by amateurs was bound to lessen the chances – already, to my mind, microscopic – that the Abbey would accept it. I typed a new title page, renaming it *St Luke's Summer*, and then set about disguising myself with a pen name. I thought of *The Italian Road* and of its callow young hero pining for Goethe's *Land wo die Zitronen blühn*. His name was Hughie Leonard, and it seemed to be a kind of poetic justice that, if by some miracle the Abbey did accept the play, I would be forcing him down their throats in one way, if not another.

If I had paused to think, what I needed least in all the world was another name. Legally, I was John Joseph Byrne: at least on my birth certificate my mother's name was given not as Anne Byrne, but as Annie, and she – with, it seemed to me, an unbecoming want of invention in a playwright's one known parent – had not only visited upon me the leaden names of John and Joseph, but also gave me a legacy of twenty years of utter misery by putting the stroke of a pen across the box headed 'Name of Father'. (For a time, I toyed with the idea that my natural father was no less than the dramatist, Denis Johnston, not only out of my admiration for his kind of plays that, uniquely, gave off neither the stench of tenements nor the headier smell of farmyard manure, but also because he had the same contempt for Anglophobic nationalism as I did. When at last I met him, I thought of asking him straight out, but funked it, mainly because in my mind I could see him recoil in horror with a cry of 'Christ, no: anything but that!') My adoptive parents' name was Keyes, and in Dalkey I was known as Jack Keyes and still am. It is as good a name as any other, even if, as I said earlier, there are those who utilise it as a means of keeping me in wherever they like to think my place is. In the Land Commission, I used the name John Keyes Byrne to set it apart from the common or garden John Byrne, which is as indigenous to Counties Dublin and Wicklow as John Smith is to London or Jean Dupois to Paris. Now, to John Joseph Byrne, Jack Keyes and John Keyes Byrne, I was about to add a fourth name and – by way of making a proper olla podrida of the affair and, in more senses than one, a jackass of myself – a fifth. Not only was Hugh Leonard added to the pantheon – and no such person exists, save as a name on a theatre programme or a title page – but also there came into being a Jack Leonard, a kind of half-way house used by those in the writing trade who knew me too well for one name and not well enough for another. The quack psychoanalysts might suggest that I was in search of an identity. I prefer to think, and it may be the same thing, that I did not have a name I cared to lay claim to as my own.

When submitting the play, I gave a false address: that of friends of my wife's parents, a Belgian couple named Ronsquin.

One day, six weeks later, Mme Ronsquin tottered, gasping for breath, up to our front door waving a letter signed by the Abbey's managing director, the ogreish, Ernest Blythe. A contract was enclosed. The Abbey, having turned down the better play, had snapped up the other: my suburban farce that was seven parts Lennox Robinson to three parts Kaufman and Hart. Not only was Mme Ronsquin delighted for me, but so was her husband, a sprightly Walloon who, to my mortification, kissed me on the cheek and, using the *morceau* of English at his command, informed me that 'My whiff and me are very glad.' For several days, such was my rapture that I was in danger of drifting away from earth and over the trees. I was an Abbey playwright, the heir of O'Casey and Synge. The reality, as I discovered when I met Ernest Blythe, was not so glamorous.

Mr Blythe – even years after his death, my awe of him persists to the degree where I must grit my teeth to divest him of the Mr – had at one time been Minister for Finance and caused a sensation by reducing the old-age pensions by a shilling. He made other concessions – free coal, for example – to atone for it, but it never crossed his puritan mind that the old people preferred to put up with chilblains and spend the money as they pleased. I can almost hear him say in his thick Lisburn accent: 'Ach, d'ye see, they'd only squander it on drink.' It was his ruin as a politician, and, like a daughter who has gone to the bad, he was shown the door, told not to darken it again and sent out into the storm, fetching up on the Abbey board of directors. It was not long before he had become its virtual dictator and was treating the theatre with the same high-handedness he had shown to the old-age pensioners.

I first met him in his Dickensian office in the Queen's Theatre, which until recently had been a vaudeville house featuring a group of low comedians who styled themselves The Happy Gang, and a troupe of dancers of uncertain age and forbidding aspect, known as the Queen's Moonbeams. I had, as an adolescent, been privileged to see one of the latter come on as a dancing fireman, drop her hatchet and split her tights as she bent to pick it up. Alas for culture, those delirious days were past; the Abbey had burned down, and the Queen's was the home of the company until a new theatre was built.

My Blythe was a bulky man, made bulkier by a black overcoat two sizes too big, which he wore in the office. He had the round, inscrutable face of a Buddha. As he spoke, his hands were constantly on the move, the stubby fingers combing the air as if, like Irving's Mathias in *The Bells*, he had just espied the wraith of a murdered Jew. The simile is misleading, for I have never met a man less likely to pass the time of night with any ghost. He had hardly invited me to take a chair when, for no apparent reason other than the making of small talk, he launched into a genial reminiscence of the Civil War and told me how six Die-hards had been captured and were held by the Free Staters as hostages.

'Mick Collins wanted us to shoot all six of them,' he said, 'but I told him no. I worked it out mathematically, d'ye see, that we'd achieve the desired effect if we plugged only four. So I had my way. We shot the four of 'em, and I was right.'

He beamed as if he had just finished telling me the story of Goldilocks and the Three Bears. I realised then where his strength lay: he did not give a damn for the opinion of any man on earth. He ran the Abbey as if it were an almshouse and he were the Master. It was by his decree that only fluent Irish speakers could become members of the company. In consequence, perhaps a third of those engaged were accomplished bi-linguists who, as actors, had their work cut out merely to stroll on, enquiring: 'Hurling, anyone?' One of my own plays had a cast of seven characters, of whom six were Dubliners, all members of the same family, and the seventh a Londoner. In the Abbey production, the accents were recognisably: Dublin (two: one tenement, one Rathmines), Mullingar (one), Donegal (one), Waterford (one), and Cork (one). As for the Londoner, the actor could not rise to an accent other than his own, and so I had him say, quite *à propos de bottes*, that he had lived for twenty years in County Cavan. To Mr Blythe one Irish accent was as good as the next, and, in any case, he regarded the performing arts as so much bunkum. The main function of the Abbey, he believed, was to revive the Irish language. Although he did not say so, at least in my hearing, I think he looked upon plays such as mine that were *not* in Irish as necessary evils. Another of his edicts was that actors' names were to be printed in Irish in programmes. When a players' council was at last formed and it was timidly suggested that the choosing of one's own stage name might be construed as a basic human right, Mr Blythe gave an assurance that changes would come, adding under his breath: '. . . as slowly as the sands of the sea.'

In spite of a natural compassion towards my fellow-humans, I have always managed to endure the sufferings of actors with fortitude. Where my own fortunes are concerned, the point at which I sit up and pay attention is when a theatrical producer tells me that any fool can write a play. Mr Blythe not only said this, but sportingly proceeded to edit mine without any reference to me. To my apologetic suggestion that I would be more than willing to make my own cuts, he said, chuckling at such unheard of impudence, 'Ach, will ye go 'way outa that!' and swept me through his office door and into Pearse Street. In the display cases in front of the theatre I saw showcards for the forthcoming production of Behan's *The Quare Fellow*. It was currently having a great success in London, and Mr Blythe had for once broken his own rule by, in this case, actually asking for the stage rights of a play instead of letting the author come to the Abbey, hat – and script – in hand. Only he, however, would and did dare to change the *Fellow* of the title to the more Dublinesque *Fella*.

He had, he told me with honest pleasure, a genius for play titles. He did not like *St Luke's Summer* at all, and I came to dread the almost daily envelopes bearing the Abbey emblem of Queen Maebh trying to hold back an apparently rampant wolfhound, for they were certain to contain Mr Blythe's latest proposals for a sure-fire title. I parried them on one pretext or another: *in extremis*, I would tell him that a particular suggestion was an unwitting quotation from Shakespeare, knowing that, out of an innate loathing for all that was literary and therefore high-falutin, he would at once disown it. At last, he tired me out. He gave me my pick of either *The Big Day* or *Happy Birthday*, and I plumped for a lack-lustre hybrid: *The Big Birthday*.

When he discovered, as he was bound to, that the play

had already been performed by amateurs, there were ructions. I had, he said, exposed him to the sneers of journalistic cornerboys and yahoos. Then the master showman, as he knew himself to be, came to the fore: he issued a press release declaring that the play had been 'wrested from the heart of the amateur movement'. I was forgiven. He even told me that I could now revert to my own name instead of hiding behind an alias. For me, it was too late; the new name had brought me luck, and I was superstitious.

In time, I was introduced to Ria Mooney, who was to direct my play. Mr Blythe knew that plays directed themselves and that any theory to the contrary was 'cod', and so he had given Miss Mooney the sinecure of staging each and every Abbey play. She was a delightful lady, if understandably exhausted, and she was part of history, for in 1926 she had played the prostitute, Rosie Redmond, in *The Plough and the Stars*. She told me of the Abbey riots and how Yeats, assuming to himself the stature of demi-god, had strode on to the stage to chastise the rabblement with 'You have disgraced yourselves again!' What she remembered most vividly, however, was a cadaverous young man who sat in the front row of the dress circle, his sunken eyes burning as he snarled at her: 'Get off! You're a disgrace to your sex.' A few months later, she found herself seated next to him at dinner and recognised him at once. He was Sean MacBride, the future Nobel Prize winner and the most shameless example of poacher-turned-gamekeeper since François-Eugène Vidocq.

When rehearsals started, I was introduced to the cast and thereafter stayed away until I could bear the suspense no longer. Finally, I took a day's leave from the office, cycled to the Queen's Theatre and was propping my bicycle against the kerb when I heard a furious thumping. I looked up and saw Mr Blythe banging on the window of his office. He vanished and reappeared a moment later, flapping down the stairs, his hands outstretched as if uprooting clumps of air.

'Go home to hell outa that,' he shouted. 'They've only been at it a week.'

He all but flung me at my bicycle, which toppled into

Pearse Street. By the time I looked around, he was gone back to his office, probably to mutilate and re-christen some other unfortunate's play. A few years later, I spoke to him for the last time. He wanted to explain why, as a County Antrim Calvinist with not a spark of fantasy in his make-up, he was less than enamoured of a new play of mine.

'I like what's real,' he said. 'I don't like plays with a ghost in 'em.'

I answered him sourly, for I had by then learned impudence: 'Well, that disposes of *Macbeth* and *Hamlet*.'

He smiled, not at the sarcasm, but at my having perpetrated what to his mind was a *non sequitur*. He said: 'Sure how do them two enter into it? The Abbey doesn't do foreign plays.'

As for *The Big Birthday*, it was a shrug of a play: not a failure, not a success. It ran for three weeks; later in the year, it was revived and made into one of those films in which Irish talents cavorted to an Elstree jig, addressed their betters – and they were legion – as 'yer Honour', and were as quaint as thatch. It is amusing that film people who pay for a play will then pay all over again so that it may be turned into a thing that is not that play. No matter, I had what I wanted: I could at last put 'playwright' after my name.

Not long ago, I met a lady named Kitty Carlisle Hart in Providence, Rhode Island. I have always been hopelessly star-struck, and I remembered the Marx Brothers' film, *A Night at the Opera* as a soulful Allan Jones serenaded her with 'Alone (with a sky of romance above)'. Moreover, she had married one of my gods, the playwright, Moss Hart. I told her of my admiration for his autobiography, *Act One*, than which there is no riper or funnier theatrical memoir, and said what a pity it was that he had not lived to write *Act Two*.

She said: 'Oh, I don't know. It would only have been "And then I wrote, and then I wrote . . ." '

I recognised the cliché. It was a staple of 1940s film biographies of popular composers. A midway point was invariably reached where the hero had won through to a plateau of success and there was no more to his story than a bout of marital influenza and its cure. To give the illusion of plot, his voice would be heard on the soundtrack saying 'And then I wrote . . .', whereupon the audience was treated to Betty Grable dancing to 'Hello, Albuquerque, hello', or a glum, cleft-chinned John Payne declaring that 'The worst things in life are free.'

In setting down these words, I took as my brief the part of one's life that is a kind of waiting room. Now, if it is not already too late, let me pay heed to the warning implicit in 'And then I wrote . . .' and go no further than recall the manner in which I at last saw the door of that room creak open. It happened not all at once, but so imperceptibly that it was not clear, even to myself, that I was free to leave.

I am thinking of a July evening. My wife had been in the Rotunda Maternity Hospital overnight, awaiting the birth of our first and, as it transpired, only child. By now, my superior in the Land Commission was a lanky, almost skeletal, Kerryman who invested his spare cash on life insurance and kept the policies in a drawer in his table. I asked him for the afternoon off so that I could go to the Rotunda. He raised a hand, bidding me not to interrupt him. He was staring into the open drawer, his lips moving as he counted the policies. He muttered 'Shag it' under his breath, then looked at me.

He said, singing it: 'Ye what? Ye want to go to deh Rotunda. Go, den. Get deh hell out.'

I had turned to leave when he called me back. 'I bought a new wireless. 'Tis superb.'

'Is it?'

' 'Tis. Do oo know, deh wife Jetta and me, we can hear deh trains on it. True as God. All deh way up Trimlestown Avenue, we can hear deh train leaving Booterstown station.'

As I stood, itching to be off, he gave an impression of a steam train getting under way as heard through his new radio set. There was a slow, rhythmic '*Choo*-choo-choo-choo . . . *choo*-choo-choo-choo' which took forever to pick up speed. When the throttle was at last open, the performance showed no sign of abating, and I listened helplessly as the train thundered through Merrion Gates and towards Sydney Parade. As I was wondering if he intended to go the full distance to Westland

Row, a wag somewhere at my rear gave an uncannily good imitation of a locomotive whistle blowing eerily across a western prairie: '*Whoo-ee-whoo!*' It was so startling that the train faltered momentarily on its journey, allowing me time to flee.

At the Rotunda, the hall porter said there was no news and so I went to the pictures. When I emerged at four thirty, it was raining. Normally, Irish weather is like the Irish character: it is rich in variety, but it lacks stamina: it sticks to nothing for long. This rain was different; it was down for the night. It had come in from the Atlantic, sighing across the Midlands: a soft, seemingly inoffensive drizzle that soaks through clothes, flesh and soul until you know it is there for life. I tried to shelter in doorways; it followed me. I went into Mooney's and there discovered that I had exactly a shilling in my pocket, twopence of which was earmarked for my bus fare home. The cheapest drink to be had was a glass of plain porter for tenpence-ha'penny, and I, the by now twice-produced Abbey playwright, was that vital halfpenny short. I could have ordered a lemonade or tomato juice, but whereas one can nurse a glass of porter or stout indefinitely, a soft drink is, for no reason this side of the paranormal, unnurseable.

Whenever I see Dublin in my mind, the day is July 11th, 1957. The sky, implacable, walks on stilts of rain; no grey stone could be as cheerlessly grey as the blank Tuscan face of the Rotunda; the rain had turned the dirt of the streets to shining grease. A plan formed in my head, and I went to stand at the junction of Parnell Street and Gardiner Street. It was still the age of the bicycle, and the cyclists came in their hundreds, like Apaches in a western, only not with war whoops, but silently, except for the jangle of a bell and the hiss of tyres on the wet. They rode huddled in rainproof capes, great waves of civil servants from across the Liffey: Northsiders who seemed to be treading air on their way to a warm room and tea. I knew – at least, I hoped – that somewhere in their number would be my workmate and best friend, Gerry Colgan. After perhaps twenty minutes and against the odds, I spotted him and jumped out into the tangle, calling and waving before the lights could change. I begged him to lend me a shilling; even that wretched ha'penny would do.

I still see the bicycles whirring past and the drop of rain that declined to part company with the end of his nose as he confessed that his earthly fortune was a shilling less than mine. He would, however, go home, borrow money from his mother and return within the hour.

In the event, it was two hours, and by then I had paid four fruitless visits to the front hall of the Rotunda. There are not many aspects of human misery that a hospital porter does not encounter in his lifetime, but I doubt if a more sodden and pitiable sight than I was ever trailed pools of rainwater on the marble floor. When Gerry at last turned up, he was clutching a half-crown which we bore like the Holy Grail into Mooney's. Augmented by my own pittance, it was enough to pay for two pints of 'plain' which by a miracle of husbandry we eked out for three hours. The vigil should, if life had had the good taste to imitate the movies, have ended touchingly with the cry of a newborn and a joyous dance in the rain. Instead, and still childless, I went splashing off towards the last No. 52 bus. My daughter arrived at 2.40 a.m. and made her parents the butt of derisive jokes by being born on July 12th, known as Orangeman's Day.

One of the more familiar scenes in popular fiction is when the hero gazes upon the pink, wrinkled face of his first-born, who is usually a son, and vows – let the mountains crumble and the seas run dry – to lay the world at his offspring's feet. Thus fired, he sweeps all before him and becomes either a great man (*My Son, My Son!*) or a ruthlessly corrupt one (*Edward, My Son*). I made no such fine promise; on the contrary, I ballsed up what could have been a poignant moment when I showed my new daughter to Gerry when, a day later, he came with flowers and grapes, and getting my statistics in reverse, said: 'Look at her! She's six hours old and weighs only thirty-six pounds.'

What finally pushed me through the door of my private waiting room was not fatherhood, joyful as it was, but those hours spent walking, aware that the rainwater had become warm in my shoes: the slow, soaked trudge around Parnell Square, or down O'Connell Street to the river and back; the vigil in a dripping doorway across from Parnell himself, bronze and unpitying under his awning of Galway granite. The image is perhaps romantic; the reality was defeat. I had stayed in the civil service to help support my parents – at least that was what I told myself – who, now that I was no longer at home, were getting on insultingly well without me. I had remained in it for another two years because – and again it was what I told myself – a married man had at least one other to provide for. At least in part, it had been cowardice, done to buy safety – 'Made for life!' my mother had crowed. Instead, and on the night my daughter was born, I had not in my pocket the price of a glass of porter. If there were such a thing as a diploma in failure, it was mine. I stood face to face with it as the Student of Prague faced his *alter ego*. In thirteen years, my pay in the Land Commission had risen to just over eight pounds a week. I could hardly have been worse off without it.

Not very long afterwards, Granada Television bought my play, *A Leap in the Dark*. For reasons that one could only describe kind-heartedly as eccentric, they arranged a repertory production in Oldham to ascertain that it was suitable for television, and I was invited to assist with the rehearsals. They would telephone later and let me know the dates. I looked at my annual leave docket; every day and half day had been used up. I found a minute sheet and wrote out my resignation. I was amazed at how simple it was. A child could have done it; there was no skill involved. I gave it to our typist, said 'Any old time will do', and saw her add it to her pile. About an hour later, I heard her scream. When she brought the typescript to me, her eyes were twin bird's eggs. I put the paper, unsigned, in a drawer of my desk and sat back. I had never felt so content. All afternoon, people went out of my way to walk past where I was sitting. They did not speak; I might as well have been the scene of a crime. A few days later, the expected telephone call came. Faces rose into the light; everyone knew it was for me, for the caller asked for Leonard, not Byrne. I said, just loud enough to be overheard: 'Yes, I'll fly to Manchester on Sunday', hung up and took the resignation from my desk. I signed it and my heart sang with every step as I bore it the length of the room to my superior, who was again counting his insurance policies.

He had heard rumours; he said: 'Are oo off, den?' Three days· later, an acknowledgment came from Establishment Branch. I have it still.

> '. . . You will be paid to 23rd September inclusive, but as your leave allowance to 23rd instant is 10½ days and as you have taken 21 days' leave to date, a deduction in respect of 10½ days' excess annual leave will be made from the balance of salary due to you.'

It did not say goodbye.

This time there was no valedictory speech. Someone – Arthur Nolan, I think – came over on my last day and, almost apologetically, gave me a small leather cigarette box that could not have cost more than a pound. Only a few people shook hands; I did not think less of them, but I was surprised, for their silence revealed what I had not suspected: that they felt as trapped as I had done. At four thirty, I spared their blushes by walking out of the room, papers in my hand as if I were going to Records Branch or the strong room, but instead went home and stayed there for all time. It took perhaps three years before I could wake up of a morning without the beginnings of a cold sweat because the dream was over and today was the day I must go back.

Not long ago, I bumped into a man, a civil servant nearing retirement, who sang the praises of a play I had written. In Dublin, one learns to winnow goodwill from the occasional gambit: the pawn given in return for an attack. When I thanked him, he segued into a bleak smile and said: 'And I liked that television thing you wrote. That was great.'

Another pawn gone. 'Thank you.'

His smile was now in need of a crutch. 'Oh, aye,' he said. 'You gave it to us hot and heavy. Yes, you made a good thing out of that.'

I could all but hear the jingling of the pieces of silver – all thirty of them – in my pocket. When I did not respond, but waited for more, he added: 'And out of us.' I nodded and made to go, leaving the field to him, but he caught at my arm.

'But you outsmarted yourself the day you quit the service.

196

Yes, you did, and do you know why?' I waited, while he made a meal of it. 'I'll tell you why.' Then, triumphantly: 'Because you could have been an Assistant Principal by now!'

He hurried off in the best of good humour, leaving me bested, worsted and unpensionable.

On the Sunday after I left the Land Commission, I caught my flight for Manchester. I had flown only a few times before and hated it. The Fokker-Friendship aircraft looked frail enough to disintegrate in mid-flight; what was worse, I was seated next to an elderly Dublin woman, dressed entirely in black. Her lips moved as we taxied towards the runway, and rosary beads were entwined in her fingers. I wondered if she had had a premonition. We took off, and she prayed all the way over the Irish Sea to Anglesey, her eyes closed, the beads clicking through her fingers, milestones to heaven.

It was the calmest of evenings, with the sun smirking behind us, as if it shone only on Ireland. The Isle of Man was visible to the north. I drank a whisky, ordered another and began to think that today might not after all be my last. My life outside the waiting room – my real life that is – was starting. A fat grin had begun to spread when a slip of paper was passed back to me. In those pre-jet days, there was time for the captain to issue a flight report giving such details as air speed, altitude, time of arrival. I glanced through it; at the bottom, next to 'Weather at destination' was written 'Fair'. It suited me at that moment to enjoy a bit of symbolism, seeing as it was in my favour. The fatness of my grin had become almost obese as I gave the paper to the woman in black. She opened her eyes, blinked at me, blinked at the slip, and took a pair of spectacles, mended with string, from her handbag. I went back to my daydream. After a moment, she put a hand on my sleeve. I looked and saw that it was raw and calloused; it had been a hard life; now she was on her way to stay with a son or daughter who had married and settled in Manchester or beyond: it was her first time in an aeroplane. In Dublin, you would call her an old one. She held the flight report in front of my face, then let go of my sleeve to point to the bottom line that said 'Weather at destination'. The entwined rosary beads dangled into my lap.

Symbolism can cut both ways. There was doom in her eyes as she said piteously: 'Oh, my Jayzus, only "fair".'

FOR THE BEST IN PAPERBACKS, LOOK FOR THE

In every corner of the world, on every subject under the sun, Penguin represents quality and variety – the very best in publishing today.

For complete information about books available from Penguin – including Puffins, Penguin Classics and Arkana – and how to order them, write to us at the appropriate address below. Please note that for copyright reasons the selection of books varies from country to country.

In the United Kingdom: Please write to *Dept E.P., Penguin Books Ltd, Harmondsworth, Middlesex, UB7 0DA.*

If you have any difficulty in obtaining a title, please send your order with the correct money, plus ten per cent for postage and packaging, to *PO Box No 11, West Drayton, Middlesex*

In the United States: Please write to *Dept BA, Penguin, 299 Murray Hill Parkway, East Rutherford, New Jersey 07073*

In Canada: Please write to *Penguin Books Canada Ltd, 2801 John Street, Markham, Ontario L3R 1B4*

In Australia: Please write to the *Marketing Department, Penguin Books Australia Ltd, P.O. Box 257, Ringwood, Victoria 3134*

In New Zealand: Please write to the *Marketing Department, Penguin Books (NZ) Ltd, Private Bag, Takapuna, Auckland 9*

In India: Please write to *Penguin Overseas Ltd, 706 Eros Apartments, 56 Nehru Place, New Delhi, 110019*

In the Netherlands: Please write to *Penguin Books Nederland B.V., Postbus 195, NL–1380AD Weesp*

In West Germany: Please write to *Penguin Books Ltd, Friedrichstrasse 10–12, D–6000 Frankfurt/Main 1*

In Spain: Please write to *Longman Penguin España, Calle San Nicolas 15, E–28013 Madrid*

In Italy: Please write to *Penguin Italia s.r.l., Via Como 4, I-20096 Pioltello (Milano)*

In France: Please write to *Penguin Books Ltd, 39 Rue de Montmorency, F-75003 Paris*

In Japan: Please write to *Longman Penguin Japan Co Ltd, Yamaguchi Building, 2–12–9 Kanda Jimbocho, Chiyoda-Ku, Tokyo 101*

FOR THE BEST IN PAPERBACKS, LOOK FOR THE 🐧

BIOGRAPHY AND AUTOBIOGRAPHY IN PENGUIN

Just for William   Nicholas Woolley and Sue Clayton

Originating as a film for the award-winning BBC2 documentary series *Forty Minutes*, *Just for William* is the story of William Clayton, diagnosed with leukaemia at the age of nine – and the story of a family who refused to give up hope in the battle against one of the deadliest diseases of all.

The Secret Lives of Trebitsch Lincoln   Bernard Wasserstein

Trebitsch Lincoln was Member of Parliament, international spy, right-wing revolutionary, Buddhist monk – and this century's most extra-ordinary conman. 'An utterly improbable story … a biographical scoop' – *Guardian*

Tolstoy   A. N. Wilson

'One of the best biographies of our century' – Leon Edel. 'All his skills as a writer, his fire as a critic, his insight as a novelist and his experience of life have come together in this subject' – Peter Levi in the *Independent*

Fox on the Run   Graeme Fowler

The intimate diary of a dramatic eighteen months, in which Fowler became the first Englishman to score a double century in India – before being cast down by injury and forced to come to terms with loss of form. 'One of the finest cricket books this year' – *Yorkshire Post*. Winner of the first Observer/Running Late Sports Book Award.

Backcloth   Dirk Bogarde

The final volume of Dirk Bogarde's autobiography is not about his acting years but about Dirk Bogarde the man and the people and events that have shaped his life and character. All are remembered with affection, nostalgia and characteristic perception and eloquence.

Jackdaw Cake   Norman Lewis

From Carmarthen to Cuba, from Enfield to Algeria, Norman Lewis brilliantly recounts his transformation from stammering schoolboy to the man Auberon Waugh called 'the greatest travel writer alive, if not the greatest since Marco Polo'.

Home Before Night

A delightful evocation of his Dublin childhood in the thirties and forties, Hugh Leonard's autobiography is like an Irish *Cider With Rosie* – crammed with people and conversations, rich in poetry, full of love, laughter and rare pleasures.

'Entrancing . . . the playwright author's gift of language and apparently total recall makes his account of growing up in the thirties and forties absolutely irresistible' – *Sunday Telegraph*

'Impossible to put down . . . a brilliant, multi-faceted gem' – *Hibernia*

'An unqualified delight . . . [he has] a marvellous eye for character, the ability to weave show-stopping funny stories into larger narrative and to recreate the past with the sensuous immediacy of childhood' – Irving Wardle in *Books and Bookmen*